ISBN 978-1-334-29794-6
PIBN 10708777

For support please visit www.forgottenbooks.com

English
Français
Deutsche
Italiano
Español
Português

www.forgottenbooks.com

Mythology Photography **Fiction**
Fishing Christianity **Art** Cooking
Essays Buddhism Freemasonry
Medicine **Biology** Music **Ancient
Egypt** Evolution Carpentry Physics
Dance Geology **Mathematics** Fitness
Shakespeare **Folklore** Yoga Marketing
Confidence Immortality Biographies
Poetry **Psychology** Witchcraft
Electronics Chemistry History **Law**
Accounting **Philosophy** Anthropology
Alchemy Drama Quantum Mechanics
Atheism Sexual Health **Ancient History**
Entrepreneurship Languages Sport
Paleontology Needlework Islam
Metaphysics Investment Archaeology
Parenting Statistics Criminology
Motivational

"You see, for a while he was the biggest man in the country. He never got to be President, but he was the biggest man. There were thousands that trusted in him right next to God Almighty, and they told stories about him and all the things that belonged to him that were like the stories of Patriarchs and such. They said, when he stood up to speak, stars and stripes came right out in the sky, and once he spoke against a river and made it sink into the ground. They said, when he walked the woods with his fishing rod, Killall, the trout would jump out of the streams right into his pockets, for they knew it was no use putting up a fight against him; and, when he argued a case, he could turn on the harps of the blessed and the shaking of the earth underground. . . . A man with a mouth like a mastiff, a brow like a mountain and eyes like burning anthracite—that was Dan'l Webster in his prime."[1]

—*Stephen Vincent Benét*

[1] From: *Selected Works of Stephen Vincent Benét,* p. 32. Rinehart & Company. Copyright, 1936, by Stephen Vincent Benét.

DANIEL WEBSTER
and the
SALEM MURDER

HOWARD A. BRADLEY
Late Professor of Speech
DARTMOUTH COLLEGE

JAMES A. WINANS
Professor Emeritus of Public Speaking
DARTMOUTH COLLEGE

ARTCRAFT PRESS
COLUMBIA, MISSOURI
1956

Table of Contents

Introduction

This is the story of a famous murder, "murder most foul, as in the best it is," and of the trials of John Francis Knapp and of Joseph Jenkins Knapp. It is also the story of the part Daniel Webster played in those trials. His summation in one of those trials is thought by some to be the greatest ever delivered in America.

It is not our purpose to glorify Daniel Webster, but to present a more complete analysis of the case than has yet been published. In 1891 William H. Moody, who later became a Justice of the Supreme Court of the United States, said that "a much better report of an exceedingly interesting trial and one where the law settled is of almost daily application, might be prepared." We have brought to light a sizable body of material that has been undisturbed for many years in newspapers, pamphlets, letters, diaries and official records.

Edmund Pearson found in the affair all the elements of the perfect melodrama, "resurrecting in the early years of the nineteenth century the apparatus of the eighteenth century romance, and at the same time anticipating a favorite device of the modern detective story — the murdered millionaire alone in his house. Pearson added, "There was hardly one omission of scene, of cast, or of stage property. There was the morbidly respectable and extremely horrified community of Salem; there was a dark conspiracy, involving hired desperadoes and the black sheep of two good families;— there was a whitehaired and blameless old gentleman — a man of wealth — asleep in his bedchamber; there were dirks and doubloons; and there were lurking figures of men in 'camblet' cloaks. There was even talk of a cave in the woods, where a gang of 'harlots, gamblers and sharpers' used to gather. . . . What a romantic place was my native County of Essex a century ago."[1]

A historian of Salem tells us that the murder and the trials made a greater impression on the social history of the town than the witchcraft trials, which just passed along in the day's work. The trials probably filled more newspaper space than any trials of a

[1] *Murder at Smutty Nose and Other Murders*, p. 250. Charles Scribner's Sons, New York.

similar nature up to that time. The streets of Salem, Boston, and even New York, were flooded with broadsides that told the story of the crime, usually in very bad verse that was not at all restrained by the facts of the case. There were about a dozen pamphlets, all purporting to give the evidence produced in court, and they sold in tremendous quantities. One pamphlet which told the "life of the celebrated murderer," was so popular that it was reprinted fifteen years later. Another told amazing tales of the "wild achievements and romantic voyages" of John Francis Knapp, including his visit to Napoleon on St. Helena, although Frank was only ten years old when Napoleon died. The murder was the topic of innumerable sermons. Even today its story is occasionally re-told in magazine articles or in the pages of Sunday supplements, while the strictly legal aspects of the case are discussed in modern works on evidence.

Technically, Webster's function in these trials was simply to assist Attorney General Perez Morton and Solicitor General Daniel Davis; but it is probable that he actually controlled the management of the prosecution. Both Morton and Davis were well along in years. At the moment, Webster was undoubtedly the "first citizen" of Massachusetts. He had, only a few months before, delivered his "Reply to Hayne" in the United States Senate; and he was also one of the outstanding lawyers of the country.

Since Daniel Webster is the central figure in this volume we would stress the fact that we have on our hands not only a series of trials, but also a "trial of a trial." Webster has been much praised, but also much condemned for his conduct of the case. Some hold that he went too far beyond the rules of the law, that he sometimes stretched his evidence to the breaking point and that at times he shouted down the opposition instead of answering its arguments. William L. Moody wrote to a friend in 1891: "The conviction was really beyond and against the evidence and was an example of judicial murder." But equally good authorities declare that he was justified in using every means to secure the conviction of guilty men.

No verbatim report of the testimony of witnesses or the arguments of counsel in these trials was ever made. There were many reporters present, some from Salem and the surrounding towns, a number from Boston, and at least one, the enterprising James Gordon Bennett, from New York. In addition to the newspaper reports, there are at least five reports of Knapp's first trial and four reports of his second trial in pamphlet form. A number of pamphlets dealing with the trials of Joseph Knapp and George Crowninshield were also printed. Then, of course, there is the official report of the cases argued and determined in the Supreme Judicial Court of Massachusetts. We have compared these sources with care, and have drawn from all of them in constructing our own version of the testimony of witnesses.

We have seen in the Clerk of Court's office in Salem many of the original papers and original exhibits that were used by the prosecution, including summonses, letters, authorizations, and affidavits, as well as official charts showing locations of buildings in the vicinity of Captain White's house with measurements of distances carefully marked, the two confessions of one of the prisoners, and the nine handwritten indictments that landed six men in jail, indictments that ranged from larceny to murder.

The unusually rich resources of the Essex Institute at Salem have provided us with a variety of unpublished materials such as letters to the prisoners, letters about the prisoners, letters about the trials, and some letters that were exchanged between the lawyers of the defense and their friends; we have seen the minutes of the "committee of vigilance" and the notebooks in which Dexter, Rantoul and others jotted down extracts from the testimony of witnesses, with lists of questions obviously prepared for use in examination and cross-examination. The Institute's extensive collection of biographical and genealogical data, its accumulation of paintings and photographs, and its excellent files of local newspapers have all been helpful in bringing back to life these trials of more than a hundred years ago. We also found Frank Knapp's own copy of the published evidence that was given in his trials, and read the pungent observations that he had written on the margins. And, after some extended and amusing negotiations, we were privileged to see, and even to touch, the two-foot club with which the murder was committed.

After some years certain members of the Institute's board were convinced that we were not planning a sensational work that might prove more embarrassing to some people in Salem than books and articles already published, or at least, that some one might do far worse, we were given permission to print any materials in their library. And for this leave we express our thanks.

We have found an abundance of valuable material regarding Daniel Webster and the trials (as well as a very extensive collection of pamphlets that were issued at the time of the trial) in the archives of Baker Library at Dartmouth College.

The Knapp-White case is one of the few murder trials in which Webster had a part, and one of very few cases in which he appeared on the side of the prosecution. It is one of the very few jury trials in which his summation argument is preserved in anything even approaching adequate form. It is the only one in which the arguments of his opponents are reported at length. Finally, it is the only case that we know of in which it is possible to piece together from a variety of sources a reasonably complete narrative of the testimony as it was presented in court.

We regret that the limitations of space do not permit us to present more of this material than we do, but we give the more significant parts.

In preparing this volume, we have, of course, been aided by many friends and we have drawn on the facilities of many libraries. It would be cumbersome and difficult to list all of our indebtednesses, but we gratefully acknowledge them nevertheless. At least two libraries must be mentioned — the Baker Library at Dartmouth College and the Library of the Essex Institute. Our colleagues in the Department of Speech at Dartmouth College have helped us in numerous ways, and we are glad to express our gratitude to them. Finally, we are under a signal debt to Raymond S. Wilkins, Justice of the Supreme Judicial Court of Massachusetts, and to Elwin L. Page, former Justice of the Supreme Court of New Hampshire. They have offered many valuable suggestions and have kept us from making a number of errors; but they are not in the least responsible for any errors that may have crept into the finished volume.

◈

Much of this introduction was written by Mr. Bradley, but I must add a footnote. He died in 1950. We put in much work together during several years, but he did more than I. He did his full share in analyzing the evidence and the writing of this book; but his great work was in searching through pamphlets, biographies, diaries, letters and newspapers, and in talking with many who knew much or little about the case. He came to know the Salem of 1830 better than all but a few of its natives. He found much material unknown to, or ignored by, the biographers of Webster. If research is a prime element in scholarship, then in this work Bradley was a scholar. I am sorry I cannot publish a book long enough to include many more of his discoveries.

J. A. Winans

CHAPTER 1

THREE FAMILIES
IN THE TRAGEDY

THE PICTURE OF Captain Joseph White can be seen in his former home, now a part of the Essex Institute. The young lady who will escort you through the house will tell you she knows nothing about him and never heard of his murder.

In 1830 Captain White was eighty-two years old, but still vigorous. He had wealth and influence. His wealth came from the sea, and especially during the years that followed the Revolution when resourceful men opened new and daring routes of commerce. In the process they brought to Salem unmeasured wealth and made her one of the commercial crossroads of the world, even a rival of Boston.

After Captain White retired from the sea sometime before 1800, he still sent vessels over the oceans and he also took a large part in Salem's business. But while high praise is bestowed upon him, the pastor of his church, Dr. Bentley, had in 1788 denounced him for engaging in the slave trade; and Bentley wrote in his diary that the owner of the Felicity "confesses he has no reluctance in selling any part of the human race."

At the time of his death Captain White lived in the stately mansion at 128 Essex Street. This house was designed by Samuel McIntyre and is now one of the show places of the city. The Captain's wife was dead and he had no children. Mrs. Mary Beckford, his niece, was his housekeeper. The household also included Lydia Kimball, the maid-of-all-work, and Benjamin White, probably a distant relative, who did odd jobs about the place.

Stephen White, a nephew of the Captain, lived near by. He was a member of the upper house of the Massachusetts legislature. He had married a sister of Salem's outstanding legal light, Justice Joseph Story.

The daughter of Mrs. Beckford, Mary White Beckford, a charming and beautiful girl, had lived in the old man's home for a number of years, and he became very fond of her. But, unfortunately for everyone, young love entered the picture and destroyed the happy relationship.

Captain Joseph Jenkins Knapp, Jr., who was employed on one of Captain White's vessels, fell in love with Mary. When it was noised about that they wished to marry, White became enraged because he thought Knapp was a fortune hunter. He told the pair that if they married, he would not only discharge Knapp but would cut Mary out of his will. They were married in 1827 and White carried out his threat. In 1830 Joe and Mary were living on the farm White had presented to Mrs. Beckford at Wenham.

The Knapps were well thought of in Salem. Captain Joseph Knapp, Sr., was a shipmaster and a merchant. He and Captain White were frequently associated in business transactions. Knapp and his family lived for many years on the south side of Essex Street, not far east from the home of Captain White.

Three of his sons figure in this story — Joseph, Nathaniel Phippen, and John Francis. Joe was born in 1805, Nathaniel the following year, and John in 1810. Nathaniel was usually called by his middle name, Phippen, and John Francis was nearly always known as Frank.

Joe went to sea in his teens, and by the time he was twenty was registered as Master of the *Governor Winslow*, a small brig that his father owned. The next year he was listed as Master of a 240 ton ship, *Caroline*, that belonged to the Whites. The records of the East-India Marine Society of Salem show that he was admitted to membership in that organization in 1825, and membership was limited to those "who have actually navigated the seas beyond the Cape of Good Hope or Cape Horn, as masters on supercargoes of vessels belonging to Salem." He seems to have been a rather uninteresting fellow, but he was a skillful dancer, and perhaps that was why Captain White's grandniece found him attractive.

When Frank was sixteen or seventeen years old he got acquainted with George and Dick Crowninshield. It is said that they induced Frank to steal three hundred dollars from his father so that the three of them could take a trip to New York. The money did not last long, and the trio, under the expert guidance of Dick, turned to petty thievery. They arrived in New York in May, 1827, and it was three months before they were arrested and sent to jail.

After their release, they separated. George got a berth on a ship that sailed for New Orleans, and it was on that voyage that he

THE PINGREE HOUSE
Salem, Massachusetts

Built in 1804. Samuel McIntire, Architect.

The Pingree House was built in 1804 for Capt. John Gardner. In 1811, he sold the house to his brother-in-law, Nathaniel West, who in 1814 sold it to Joseph White. In the year 1834, the estate of Joseph White sold the house to David Pingree.

became acquainted with John Palmer. Dick headed for the south, and it is said that he became engaged to the daughter of a wealthy planter in Charleston, "to whom he had appealed as the nephew of a former Secretary of the Navy." The engagement was abruptly broken, however, when information regarding Dick was obtained from friends in Salem. Frank returned to his home and the story of his misdeeds was glossed over and a place was found for him on a Salem ship. In January of 1830 he left the sea and remained unemployed for several months. During this period, his friendship was renewed with the two Crowninshields, who had also returned to their home.

Captain Knapp's son Phippen was of a different sort. He had not gone to sea. He went to Harvard instead, where he was graduated in 1826. At the time of White's death, he had just been admitted to the bar of Essex County. A classmate at Harvard said that he was a universal favorite there. He was apparently not an outstanding student, but he was frank, honest and dependable. His moral character, said his classmates, was exemplary.

The Crowninshields were a prominent and wealthy family of Salem. Two of Richard's uncles were nominated as Secretary of the Navy, though one did not serve. But Richard Crowninshield, Sr., was not an outstanding member of the family. He married a girl from Ireland who was a maid in a New York hotel. In 1804 their third child was born and he was christened Richard. George was born two years later.

Mrs. Crowninshield was an extraordinary woman, with a lively temper and a venomous tongue. The family became the subject of constant gossip in the community. Dr. Bentley wrote in his diary, "The tales of this family exhibit something yet unknown in this part of the country, for want of domestic economy, education of children, management of affairs and conduct among their servants and neighbors."

Tradition has it that one of Richard's early exploits was to set fire to the school house because he disliked the teacher. In 1820 he was sent to Bradford Academy. In 1822 Dick and three of his cousins from Salem enrolled in the American Literary, Scientific and Military Academy in Norwich, Vermont, just across the river from Dartmouth College. His father wanted Dick to go to Harvard, but he never got there. Some time later he and George opened a machine shop in Danvers (now in Peabody) where the family lived.

CHAPTER 2

THE MURDER AND
THE COMMITTEE OF VIGILANCE

O what a horrid tale to sound,
  In this our land to tell,
That Joseph White, of Salem town,
  By ruffian hands he fell!
Perhaps for money or for gain,
  This wicked deed was done,
But if for either, great the pain
  This monster must be in.

— From a broadside of 1830

ON THE MORNING of the seventh of April, 1830, Benjamin White found Captain White murdered in his bed. Benjamin will tell the story in his testimony.

The news of the murder spread through the town with amazing speed and overpowering effect. The day after the funeral, hand-bills were circulated announcing that a public meeting would be held that night in the Town Hall for the purpose of devising plans for the detection of the assassin. The meeting was attended by more than two thousand citizens. The Reverend Henry Colman, who played an important role in the later developments of the case, made an address that "was listened to with almost breathless anxiety."

At this meeting a committee of vigilance was formed consisting of twenty-seven men "with power to search every house and interrogate every individual touching the murder." Nightly sessions of the committee were held in the counting house of Stephen White, oaths of secrecy were administered, and one thousand dollars, with the promise of more, was given to the committee by Stephen for expenses. It seems that the entire investigation was handled by amateurs, for we find no reference anywhere to the employment of detectives, and only incidental mention of the efforts of sheriffs and other officers to solve the crime.

Excitement mounted steadily as days passed and no arrests were made. Many were in constant fear lest the murderer strike again. Carpenters and smiths were kept busy fixing bolts to doors and fastenings to windows. Some people provided themselves with cutlasses, firearms, and watchdogs.

It seemed that plunder was not the object of the crime, for although the house contained many valuable things and a considerable amount of money that could have been carried off easily, nothing was touched. And it was hard to believe that revenge was the motive since, according to the newspapers at least, "the victim was universally respected and beloved."

The excitement spread to surrounding towns, and Oliver Wendell Holmes, then a student at Harvard, wrote to Phineas Barnes on May 8th:

Nothing is going on but murder and robbery; we have to look in our closets and under our beds, and strut about with sword-canes and pistols. . . . Poor old Mr. White was "stabbed in the dark" and since that the very air has been redolent of assassination. The women have exhausted their intellect in epithets and exclamations, the newspapers have declared it atrocious, and worst of all the little poets have been pelting the "villain or villains" with verses.

Ten days after the murder, Justice Joseph Story, of the United States Supreme Court (whose two sisters had married relatives of Captain White), wrote to his friend Daniel Webster:

. . . But an entire new direction was given to my thoughts by the horrible murder of Old Capt'n White at Salem — You are aware that he died childless & that his principal heirs are Mr. Stephen White & my Sisters children — It is altogether the most mysterious & dreadful affair that I ever heard of — "Truth is stranger than fiction" has been often said — I never knew any case, which so completely illustrated the truth of the remark as this. Not the slightest trace has as yet been found by which to detect the assassins, (for I am satisfied there was more than one) and we are yet in a darkness rendered still darker by the utter defeat of every conjecture — I have been obliged to go to Salem several times, & every thing there seems in inextricable confusion.

Mr. White left a Will — He has given many legacies to his relatives; but the bulk of his fortune goes to Mr. Stephen White, who will get from 150 to 200 thousand dollars — Three of my nieces will receive about 25,000 each.[1]

---

[1] *Letters to Daniel Webster*, edited by C. H. Van Tyne.

In spite of this discouraging state of affairs, certain bits of information, not known to the public, were being assembled by the committee of vigilance.[2] On the morning the murder was discovered, two friends of the White family visited the Charleston prison to find out whether any of the recently discharged prisoners might come under suspicion. They learned from Joseph Fisher (a convict from Salem who was still in prison) that when he had been a prisoner in the Salem jail three years before, he and a cellmate named Hatch had planned to steal an iron chest from the bedroom of Captain White and thereby "make their damned eternal fortune." The chest was supposed to be full of gold. Fisher said that after he and Hatch had been discharged, they overheard a conversation on the same subject at the Lafayette Coffee House in Salem. One of the men in this conversation was named Palmer, another Richard Crowninshield, Jr.

A little more than a week after the murder, Stephen White received a letter from the jailer at New Bedford who said that a prisoner, who called himself Joseph S. Hall, claimed he could tell something about the murder. Hall turned out to be Hatch, and his story supported Fisher's. Hatch said that after he had been released from the Charleston prison in February, he and a friend named Quiner had frequented certain gambling rooms in Salem, one of which was operated by John Pendergrass and another by Richard Crowninshield, Jr. At these establishments they had heard Richard Crowninshield, George Crowninshield, and a man called Selman talk about stealing White's iron chest. Quiner, who was back in jail again, verified Hatch's story. When Pendergrass was called before the committee of vigilance, he said that a young man by the name of Chase also took part in the conversation.

The committee learned, too, that at various times between a quarter before nine in the evening of April 6 and about four o'clock the next morning, several unidentified persons were seen on the streets close to White's house. The most detailed information came from a young bank cashier, John A. Southwick, and a middle-

[2] Many of the details of the committee's activities may be found in a rare pamphlet, "*Appendix, A Brief Sketch of the Proceedings of the Committee of Vigilance, &.*" The only copy we have seen belongs to the Essex Institute. It is not complete, containing only eight pages. The Institute also owns the two notebooks that were used for recording the minutes of each of the committee's meetings.

aged mariner, Captain Daniel Bray, Jr. These two men said they saw suspicious looking persons in Brown Street near the back of White's house between half-past ten and eleven o'clock.

Although the committee of vigilance worked untiringly, the Salem *Gazette* reported two weeks after the murder, "In every instance in which suspicion has been excited as to any individual, investigation has made it manifest that there was no foundation for the belief of guilt."

Other evidences of lawlessness appeared. The driver of a baggage wagon was attacked at night on the outskirts of Salem. On the twenty-seventh of April Joe and Frank were attacked, they reported, while on their way from Salem to Wenham. The *Essex Gazette* reported their story and added that the Knapp boys "are well known in this town, and their respectability and veracity are not questioned by any of our citizens."

Apparently the committee of vigilance felt that something had to be done even though there was not much to go on. On the second day of May, Richard Crowninshield, Jr., George Crowninshield, Benjamin Selman, and Daniel Chase were arrested for the murder of White. The grand jury met at Ipswich the following day, and Hatch repeated the stories he had previously told. A number of other persons were called, and on the fifth of May the grand jury returned bills in which Richard was charged with having struck the blow that killed White and the others were charged with being present, aiding and abetting the murderer.

All that the committee could present to the jury was evidence that at one time or another these men had been present when there was talk about stealing Captain White's chest. George Crowninshield, Selman and Chase were in Salem on the fatal night; but there was no evidence that Richard Crowninshield was in Salem that night. It is safe to say that when the indictment was found there was no evidence that clearly involved any of the four men in the murder.

The *Marblehead Register* said, "The grand jury were informed that a tremendous 'Mass of Evidence' was in the hands of this notable committee, abundantly sufficient to find a bill, try, convict, hang, draw and quarter these individuals; and from what we have been able to learn, on this ground a bill was found by a majority of one. But the Newburyport *Herald* declared "that the efforts of the committee in Salem can hardly be overpraised."

A LETTER FROM MAINE

On the fourteenth of May, nine days after the grand jury completed its findings against the Crowninshields, Selman and Chase, Captain Joseph J. Knapp, Sr., received a letter from Belfast, Maine. It bore the address, "Joseph Knapp, Merchant, Salem." The letter contained threats of exposure unless Knapp sent the writer three hundred and fifty dollars by the twenty-second of the month. It was signed, "Charles Grant, Jun., of Prospect, Maine." It said, among other things, "It is useless for me to enter into a discussion of facts which must inevitably harrow up your soul — no — I will merely tell you that I am acquainted with your brother Franklin, and also the business that he was transacting for you on the 2d of April last; and that I think you was very extravagant in giving one thousand dollars to the person that would execute the business for you — but you know best about that, you see that such things will leak out."

Captain Knapp did not know anyone by the name of Charles Grant. He showed the letter to his son Phippen, but it meant nothing to him. The next day Captain Knapp and Phippen drove to Wenham to show the letter to Joe and Frank. Joe remarked that it simply contained "a devilish lot of trash" and advised his father to turn it over to the committee of vigilance, which he did on his return to Salem.

In a few days, two more letters were turned over to the committee. One had been received by the chairman, Dr. Gideon Barstow, and like the letter to Knapp, was signed "Grant." The writer asserted that he and Stephen White had committed the murder and that Stephen had promised him five thousand dollars that had not been paid. The other letter had come to Stephen himself and was signed "N. Claxton, 4th." It contained the warning that unless five thousand dollars, or a part of it, was sent before the next day, Stephen would suffer "painful consequences."

The committee thought the letter that Knapp had given them was worth investigating. Accordingly they sent an anonymous message to Grant, General Delivery, Prospect, Maine, and enclosed fifty dollars with the promise that more would be sent later. At the same time they sent an attorney, Joseph G. Waters, to Prospect to watch for Grant when he called for the letter. Grant proved to be John C. R. Palmer. Waters wrote to the committee,

"He is about twenty-three years of age, has insinuating manners, and possesses an acute mind. I cannot but feel an interest in him, and sincerely hope that he will be able to convince all of his innocence."

Young Palmer was very reluctant, however, to give Waters any information until both he and his father were assured that he would be in no danger of prosecution if he gave evidence for the State. He then told his story, and was at once arrested and brought to Salem in chains. Because of his statement Joe and Frank Knapp were at once arrested.

CHAPTER 3

THE KNAPPS HAVE
TWO VISITORS

ON THE TWENTY-EIGHTH of May, the Knapps were brought before Justice Savage for examination; and shortly after they were returned to their cells Joe had a visitor, the Reverend Henry Colman, minister of the Independent Congregational Church in Barton Square. Mr. Colman visited Joe three times that day.

We shall hear much of Mr. Colman. He was a graduate of Dartmouth College, and was forty-five years old. He had a commanding presence. He was tall and well proportioned, and his full eyes and his intellectual brow marked him as more than ordinary. He had been a friend of Captain White and was on intimate terms with Stephen White. They had joined his church. Joseph Knapp, Jr., and his wife were also members. Colman had performed their marriage ceremony, and he said he felt for Mary "the affection of a father." His friends said he had great kindness of heart, but they also admitted that he had a violent temper that frequently got out of control.

However that may be, as a result of his visits to Joe's cell and his visit later to Frank's, he became the star witness for the prosecution. Franklin Dexter, leading defense lawyer, said: "Whatever the government cannot otherwise prove, Mr. Colman swears the prisoner has confessed, and nothing more."

Colman promised Joe that if he would put his confession in writing and testify for the government, he would not be prosecuted for the crime.

While this was going on Phippen appeared. When he learned of Colman's promise he declared that it would be unfair for Joe to accept immunity unless Frank was willing. But when Colman and Phippen went to Frank's cell to find out whether he was willing to have Joe make a confession, become a witness for the government, and then go scot free, they did not realize how important their visit was to be. Later each man contradicted the other and himself as well.

Immediately after the two men left the cell of Frank, Colman hurried to the committee of vigilance, and after long discussion it was agreed that he should go to the attorney general and secure the proper authorization. He reached the attorney general at Dorchester sometime after midnight and obtained from him a document which authorized Mr. Colman to assure one of those charged with the murder that he would be "made a witness at the trial, and that his so being made a witness will be a pledge of the Government never to be prosecuted for that offence; but it will be understood, that this authority is not to operate in favour of Richard Crowningshield, [*sic*] against whom sufficient evidence already appears."

In the morning Mr. Colman hurried back to Salem. There he made it his first business to go with two witnesses to the Howard Street meeting house where he found a club in a rathole under the steps. Who told him where to look for that club was a question hotly disputed in the days that followed.

That important detail out of the way, Colman came to the climax of his strenuous two days in his dual role of "friend of the family" and agent of the committee. He had promised Phippen that he would not go to jail to receive the confession until Phippen had returned from a trip to Boston to seek counsel for his brothers. But even with a relay of horses, Phippen was unable to reach Salem in time to satisfy the excited Mr. Colman. When he did arrive, Colman refused to admit him to Joe's cell, but promised that later he would read him the nine page confession that Joe was about to sign. But before reading the confession to Phippen, Colman went to members of the committee, and they did not think it proper for Phippen to know what had been confessed, although they did permit an extensive summary of the confession to appear in the next issue of the local papers.[1] This publication, strongly condemned by two judges, greatly increased the difficulties of the defense.

The excitement caused by Joe's confession was intense, not only in Salem but in all the surrounding community. Everyone assumed that the mystery was now completely solved, and that the prisoners would be speedily convicted.

---

[1] The confession can be found in the account of Joe's trial, Chapter XI.

CHAPTER 4

"THERE IS NO REFUGE FROM CONFESSION BUT IN SUICIDE"

IN THE EARLY DAYS of Dick Crowninshield's imprisonment he had been unusually calm and self-possessed. He spent much of his time in reading, in visiting with friends who called at his cell, and occasionally in trying his hand at verses not worse than lines you can read in the papers today. He also read books on mathematics and mechanics.

One day about the middle of June, Franklin Dexter, of Boston, who had been retained as chief counsel for the Knapps, came to the jail to visit his clients. As Dexter was leaving, Dick called him to his cell. We do not know exactly what was said during that conversation, but we are told[1] that Dick asked for an explanation of the law concerning principals and accessories, and that Dexter told him that if no principal should be convicted no accessory could be brought to trial. "You," Dexter may have said, "will be indicted as a principal; and while I do not know all the evidence the government can bring forward, I believe that George, Frank, Joe, Selman and Chase will be indicted as accessories." Then Dick may have asked, "If I am not convicted, then George and the others cannot be tried?" "That does not quite follow," Dexter would have replied. "The government would then try to convict one of the others as principal in the second degree, probably Frank Knapp. I do not believe they could do it."

At two o'clock in the afternoon of June — the jailer went to Dick's cell, but Dick did not respond. He had tied together two silk handkerchiefs, fastened one end of this silken rope around his neck, stepped upon a chair, tied the loose end securely to the grating of his cell window, and hanged himself. When found, his feet were touch-

---

[1] Robert S. Rantoul says in *Personal Recollections*, written in 1916, that he learned from the son-in-law of Rufus Choate that Dick did ask Dexter this question on one of Dexter's visits to the jail. Robert S. Rantoul was the son of the youthful attorney who assisted the defense at the trial.

ing the floor, "from which his knees were not more than a foot distant, it being necessary for him to bend his limbs considerably in order to produce strangulation."

Dick's suicide was interpreted by most as conclusive proof of his guilt. Anyone who suggested that an innocent man might take his own life under such circumstances, even to assure his brother's safety, was thought very foolish indeed.

CHAPTER 5

CHIEF JUSTICE PARKER EXPLAINS THE LAW TO THE GRAND JURY

ON JUNE 5 the legislature passed an act requiring that a special term of the Supreme Judicial Court be held at Salem on July 10. The act specified that the attorney general, the solicitor general, and at least three of the justices should attend the session.

When the court met, all four of the justices were present, Chief Justice Isaac Parker and Associate Justices Samuel Putnam, Samuel Sumner Wilde, and Marcus Morton.

From the address of Chief Justice Parker to the grand jury we take a few passages. He deplored the unusual publicity that had been given to all the facts connected with the investigation and expressed the fear that it would have a tendency to impede the course of justice.

He explained that the law exacts the death penalty of any person who shall commit the crime of wilful murder, or shall be present, aiding and abetting in the commission of such a crime, or not being present, shall have been accessory thereto before the fact by counselling, hiring, or otherwise procuring the same to be done.

It is not required that the abettor shall be actually upon the spot when the murder is committed, or even in sight of the more immediate perpetrator, or of the victim, to make him a principal. If he be at a distance, co-operating in the act, watching to prevent relief, or to give alarm, or to assist his confederate in escape, having knowledge of the purpose and object of the assassin — this, in the eye of the law, is being present, aiding and abetting, so as to make him a principal [in the second degree] in the murder.

One who is denominated by the statute an accessory before the fact is not only in every case absent from the scene of crime, but is not an immediate participator in it. He had previously, perhaps days or months before, hired, counselled, or procured the deed to be done, but he had no immediate agency in the deed. His crime is deemed by the law to be as great as his who strikes the blow. . . .

There is at the common law a difference, and it is supposed to exist also under our statute, in regard to the form and time of trial, between those who are called principals and those who are called accessories before the fact, it being held that unless there be a conviction of a principal there can be no trial of the accessory. This difference, if it exists, is a relic of the unwise refinement of ancient times.[1]

The proceedings of a grand jury are secret, but information leaked out that Joe Knapp had refused to testify as a witness for the state. Joe's refusal stunned the prosecution. They had counted heavily on his testimony because it seemed to be the only convincing and at the same time clearly admissible evidence they possessed regarding three essential contentions: that a conspiracy existed between the Knapps and Crowninshields, that one of the conspirators struck the blow, and that Frank was in Brown Street at the time.

The fact that Joe's written confession was in the hands of the prosecution did not remove the difficulty in the case against Frank, because the law held, then as now, that one man cannot confess away the life or liberty of another unless he does so in open court where the accused has the right to confront the adverse witness and have his testimony subjected to cross-examination.

Now the prosecution would have to rely on the hope that Mr. Colman would be allowed to testify to the confession that he claimed Frank made to him in the interview of May 28. But there was a strong probability that the court would not admit this testimony, on the ground that the confession was not voluntary.

Of course the essentials of Joe's confession were familiar to everyone because the committee of vigilance had permitted them to be summarized in the newspapers.

When the court convened on Friday, July 23, Chief Justice Parker remarked that there seemed to be an intention of publishing in the newspapers the proceedings of the court from day to day. Such publication, he said, must necessarily be imperfect and perhaps mischievous. There may be no objection to publishing the state of the case as it advances, but there must be no publication of the evidence before the trials are concluded.

The grand jury came into court with the bills they had found,

---

[1] Justice Parker is here questioning his own ruling made ten years before in Commonwealth v. Phillips, 1 Pickering 425. The Massachusett's legislature changed the rule in 1831. The court held to the old rule in the Knapp cases.

and three of the prisoners, J. F. Knapp, J. J. Knapp, Jr., and George Crowninshield, were placed at the bar. The clerk then read an indictment (written in the elaborate legal phraseology of the day) that charged: (1) that J. F. Knapp himself murdered White with a bludgeon and that George and Joseph were accessories before the fact, (2) that J. F. Knapp murdered White with a dirk and that George and Joseph were accessories before the fact, (3) that Richard Crowninshield and J. F. Knapp made an assault upon White, that Richard murdered him with a bludgeon and that J. F. Knapp was present, aiding and abetting, that Richard killed himself so that he could not be further proceeded against, and that George and Joseph were accessories before the fact. Nothing was said in this indictment about Richard using a dirk.

The prisoners pleaded *not guilty* to this indictment.

Attorney General Perez Morton and Solicitor General Daniel Davis appeared for the government.

At the request of the Knapps, Franklin Dexter and William Howard Gardiner were assigned as their counsel.[2] Samuel Hoar, eminent attorney from Concord, was assigned as counsel for George Crowninshield, with Ebenezer Shillaber and John Walsh, both of Salem.

The grand jury had not found any new indictment against Chase or Selman, and both were discharged on motion of their counsel, Mr. Lemuel Shaw; after, as the *Marblehead Register* said, these "innocent individuals suffered all the ignominy and deprivation of three month's imprisonment through the unwarrantable organization and officiousness of a self-constituted body called 'Committee of Vigilance.' "

It was the wish of the other prisoners that they be tried separately.

---

[2] Franklin Dexter, brilliant son of Samuel Dexter, was thirty-seven years old. He came into prominence in 1828 when he acted for the defence in the trial of Theodore Lyman for a criminal libel upon Daniel Webster. Mr. Gardiner was thirty-three years old. Both these men were from Boston and both were graduates of Harvard University.

CHAPTER 6

DEATH OF A LEARNED JUDGE—
ENTER DANIEL WEBSTER

WHEN THE COURT MET on Tuesday, July 27, for the trial of Frank Knapp, Leverett Saltonstall, President of the Essex Bar, announced the death of Chief Justice Parker; and the court, after the reading of resolutions in token of respect, adjourned for one week.

There can be no doubt that the friends of the prosecution were glad to have trial delayed. There was a growing feeling that not only additional evidence was needed, but that new legal talent was needed to assist the officers of the government. Minds turned to Daniel Webster, but would he serve? The only detailed account we find of the way in which he was induced to take a hand in the trials is in Harriet Martineau's *Retrospect of Western Travel*. While her information was secondhand and not accurate in every detail, it was undoubtedly gained from those who were very familiar with the facts.

"A citizen of Salem, a friend of mine, was deputed to carry the request. . . . Mr. Webster was at his farm by the seashore. Thither, in tremendous weather, my friend followed him. Mr. Webster was playing checkers with his boy. . . . My friend was first dried and refreshed, and then lost no time in mentioning 'business.' Mr. Webster writhed at the word, saying that he came hither to get out of hearing of it. He next declared that his undertaking anything more was entirely out of the question, and pointed, in evidence, to his swollen bags of briefs lying in a corner. However, upon a little further explanation and meditation, he agreed to the request with the same good grace with which he afterward went to his task. He made himself master of all that my friend could communicate, and before daybreak was off through the woods, in the unabated storm no doubt meditating his speech by the way.

"He needed all the assistance that could be given him, of course; and my friend constituted himself as Mr. Websters' fetcher and carrier of facts. . . . At the appointed hour, Mr. Webster was completely ready."

It seems that Webster was in Salem not later than July 30th. It is interesting to speculate on the course of events had Chief Justice Parker lived and the trial had not been delayed. It is almost certain that Webster would not have been brought into the case, for the first trial at least; and we believe that by the time the reader has concluded this volume, he will agree with us that without Webster's help none of the prisoners would have been convicted. There is a strong probability, too, that one important witness, Benjamin Leighton, whom the prosecution had discarded, would not, except for Webster, have been re-examined.

CHAPTER 7

THE FIRST TRIAL OF JOHN FRANCIS KNAPP

(Tuesday, August 3 to Friday August 13)

ON THE OUTSIDE BALCONY of the courthouse George Washington is said to have received the homage of the multitude; but it is doubtful if even the Father of his Country drew a larger crowd than did the trials of the Knapps forty-eight years later. Hours before the trial began refreshment stands were erected, heavy chains were strung around the square so that horse-drawn traffic could not enter, and tanbark was spread to deaden sound.

The courtroom was too small for the crowd that tried to enter. James Gordon Bennett reported that crowds came "rushing against the railings like the tide boiling up the rocks of Nahant." The people even jammed the jury box and the benches of the court. There was such "fierceness, levity, rudeness and roughness that the front of the gallery cracked again."

A little before the justices arrived Webster appeared in the rear of the courtroom. Bennett said he looked well and comfortable, but that the defense attorneys did not make much of an impression. "In the hands of such a man as Webster, a dozen of them are a mere mouthful."

J. F. KNAPP.   J. J. KNAPP, Jr.   GEO. CROWNINSHIELD.

Justices Putnam, Morton and Wilde presided.

When the prisoners were placed at the bar, the reporter of the *New Hampshire Sentinel* of Keene wrote: "J. Francis Knapp sprang forward first with a quick and vigorous motion, more like a bound than a step. J. Jenkins Knapp followed rather languidly, and Crowninshield came last with a quiet easy air; and thus stood before me three young men, well and rather genteely dressed, and of fair presence."

The prosecuting attorneys entered a nolle prosequi on the indictments on which the prisoners had previously been arraigned, and read a new indictment to them. The change from the last indictment to which they pleaded was that the fourth and fifth paragraphs charged that Richard Crowninshield murdered White with a bludgeon *and a dirk.*

To this indictment Frank Knapp pleaded *not guilty.* The court ruled that since Joseph Knapp and George Crowninshield were indicted only as accessories, they were not obliged to plead until a principal had been convicted.

The attorney general moved that The Honorable Daniel Webster be permitted to take part in the case on behalf of the government. The defense counsel made no objection. Justice Putnam said the court was happy to have so distinguished a gentleman take part in the trial.

After nineteen peremptory challenges and eleven for cause, a jury was impaneled and sworn. The indictment was then read to the jury, and the attorney general addressed the jury. We shall give very little of his statement.

THE ATTORNEY GENERAL'S OPENING ADDRESS

On his authority Mr. Colman had received the voluntary confession of Joseph Knapp, Jr., but when Knapp was called to testify before the grand jury, he had refused on the advice of his counsel. "But as the inquiry before the grand jury may not be considered as calling him as a witness upon the trial, I shall in the course of the examination of evidence again call him as a witness, and if he again refuses to testify, everyone will acknowledge that the pledge of the government will be completely redeemed, and his promised protection will be forfeited."

The attorney general proceeded on the assumption that the actual murder had been committed by Richard. He said the government did not expect to prove that the prisoner at the bar actually gave

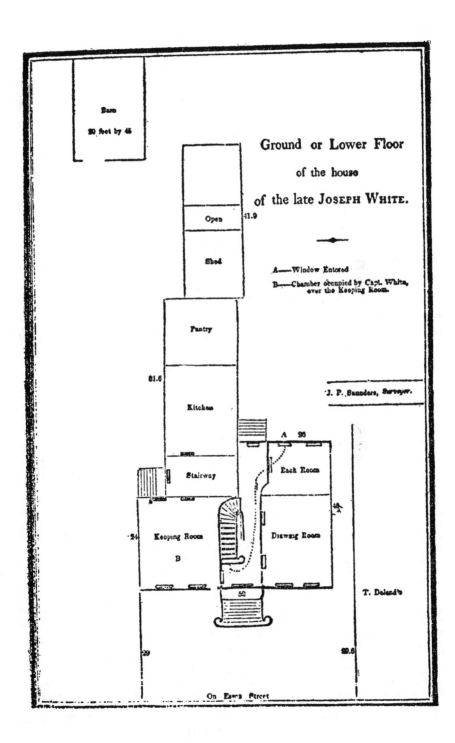

Ground or Lower Floor

of the house

of the late Joseph White.

A——Window Entored
B——Chamber occupied by Capt. White,
over the Keeping Room.

J. P. Saunders, Surveyor.

the blow or the stabs that caused the death of White—"for he who, it appears, did the deed . . . has gone and hanged himself."

But, he continued, "It is altogether immaterial whether the prisoner at the bar actually gave the mortal blows, provided he was present, aiding and abetting the person who inflicted them. It was not necessary for the abettor to *do* anything, provided he was *ready* to do it. . . . The government are first bound to prove the corpus delicti, that is, that the deceased Mr. White came to his death by the hand of external violence. We shall then prove that the death was effected by a wicked conspiracy and combination of individuals, of which the prisoner at the bar was one . . . , and to this point we shall offer Joseph Jenkins Knapp, Jr. But if we cannot prove this vile conspiracy and combination to murder the deceased by the disclosure of this accomplice in the crime, by the blessing of God, we will prove it by other testimony in the case. And if, in the opinion of the court, we shall be able to show that such a conspiracy existed, another principle of law will be relied on: that when a conspiracy to do an unlawful act is proved, the acts of any one of the conspirators, done in effecting the object of their combination, may be given in evidence against any other of the conspirators."

The attorney general then called the first witness for the prosecution of John Francis Knapp.

CAPTAIN WHITE WAS MURDERED—THE CORPUS DELICTI

Benjamin White[1]

Q. (The attorney general) Were you employed in the family of Mr. White? A. I was, sir.

---

[1] We believe that most readers of this book will wish to scrutinize the evidence in order to see how the case worked out and to be able to judge, as they read the closing speeches, whether a given argument has a sound basis of testimony back of it, or whether the evidence is distorted or overvalued. Many have deemed Webster's speech unanswerable, and among the many were teachers of public speaking, including the writers of this book, before we studied the evidence. A summary of the evidence will not satisfy the critical reader. No summary we have found is satisfactory, and we doubt if we could make a better one. Some of the evidence was summarized in the original reports and we have summarized more, and we have cut out some minor details; but to go further would defeat the purpose of the book, which is to give a clear picture of the case "without prejudice." Some who have read our manuscript find difficulty in following out the evidence. We have put in headings and notes that may help. It would be possible to read the speeches first and turn back to the testimony, using the list of witnesses at the back of the book; but we do not advise this course. At any rate, no one can understand these trials, or get much pleasure from reading the book, without knowing the evidence, with its quirks and turns, and noting the struggles between lawyers and witnesses and between lawyer and lawyer. If one wishes merely to read the speech of the godlike Daniel, he can turn to other books, with their notes of praise.

RESIDENCE OF HON. TIMOTHY PICKERING, OFF LARCH ROW, WENHAM, DURING THE EARLY PART
OF THE 19th CENTURY.

From a photograph taken in 1897.

The house on Mrs. Beckford's farm in Wenham which had been the estate of Hon. Timothy Pickering until his death in 1829.
Leighton testified that the conversation he overheard took place near the wall that is barely discernible at the extreme right.

Q. State to the court and jury what you know about the murder of Captain White. A. On Wednesday morning, the seventh of April about six o'clock, I came down into the kitchen and, on opening the shutters of the eastern window, saw the back window of the northeastern room open and a plank put up to the window. . . . I then went up the back stairway to Mr. White's chamber and saw that the door from his room to the front hallway was open, and that he was murdered. . . . He was cold. . . .

Q. Did you see any blood? A. I think I did see some blood on the side of the bed or on his flannel.

On the afternoon before the murder I was at the farm in Beverly with Mr. White.

Q. (Webster) Who lived in the house besides Captain White? A. Mrs. Beckford, myself, and Miss Kimball lived in the house. Mrs. Beckford is a middle-aged lady.

Captain White's chamber was over the southwest parlor, the keeping room. The house faces south on Essex Street. It is three stories high. . . . Mr. White's chamber has four windows, two southern, one western, and one northern looking into the yard.

The prosecution then called *John P. Saunders* [a member of the committee of vigilance], a surveyor, who swore that the plans of Captain White's house and premises were correct.

White then continued his testimony.

Mrs. Beckford was at Wenham on the night of the murder. She went away about twelve o'clock that day.

Mr. White went to bed about twenty minutes before ten. He was eighty-two years old. . . . It was his custom to sleep immediately after retiring for three of four hours, and then to lie awake. . . . The head of his bed was against the eastern wall of the chamber, near the door which opened into the front hall.

Mrs. Beckford's furniture was in the back parlor, which was entered and was used by no person but herself.

In Captain White's chamber there were shutters to all the windows and blinds to the front and western windows. I did not notice the state of the windows that morning, but the blinds were open. . . .

J. J. Knapp, Jr., was in habit of coming to the house often. He was at the house several times within a month before the murder. [Compare this with his statement when he was recalled.]

There is an avenue[2] and two doors on the west end of the house, and to get at the opened window, one must pass along that end, through the avenue, through a garden gate, around the buildings and up to the garden to it.

There is a shutter at my east window, but not at the west.

Frank Knapp never went there till after the murder, when he watched with the body.

When I went to bed the weather was overcast.

Cross-examination. Q. (Dexter) Do you recollect that some person was expected to see Mr. White that evening. A. I don't know.

Frank Knapp assisted at the funeral.

There was nothing missing after the murder.

Re-direct examination. Q. (Webster) How late did you see J. J. Knapp? A. I had seen Joseph Knapp there within two or three weeks previous to the murder. He usually came when Mr. White was not at home, about four o'clock in the afternoon. He had free access to all the rooms when the family were out.

On the insistence of Mr. Dexter all who expected to testify were excluded from the courtroom.

Lydia Kimball

She swore that she was a domestic in the home of Captain White at the time of the murder and had been for sixteen years. . . . She agreed substantially with Benjamin. . . . Her own room, over Mr. White's had all the shutters open except on the west side. "In Captain White's room all the shutters were open except one-half of the one nearest his bed. . . I could generally tell when he was awake, if I myself was so, by a kind of cough or hem which he had when awake, which was usually in the latter part of the night." She did not hear him on the night of the murder. It was not his custom to leave a light burning in his chamber. No one called at the house after one o'clock on April 6.

Dr. Samuel Johnson[3]

I was called about six o'clock to Captain White's. I . . . found him lying on his right side . . . and diagonally to the bed. There was a mark of considerable violence on his left temple. I told Mr. Stephen White that an inquest should be called.

---

[2] The word "avenue" was applied to lanes, alleys, or any outside passageway not rising to the dignity of the street. We shall find one of the witnesses calling a farm lane an "avenue."

[3] For forty years he was one of the most prominent physicians in Salem.

In the presence of the coroner's jury, the shirt was stripped off and the body exposed. We found five stabs in the region of the heart, three in front of the left pap and five others still farther back, as though the arm had been lifted up and the instrument struck underneath it. I examined a number of the stabs with a probe and found that it would penetrate from one to three inches. It was my belief at the time that either the wound on the head or the stabs would have caused death.

The instrument which gave the blow on the head was probably some smooth instrument that would give a heavy blow without breaking the skin, and the instrument used in giving the wounds in the side was probably a dirk.

On the second examination we found thirteen stabs. There was no appearance of a struggle.

Cross-examination. The inquest was holden about an hour after I went to the house. The second examination took place thirty-six hours after death.

There was no appearance of more than one weapon having been used in giving the stabs. The front wounds gaped more than the others and were three-quarters of an inch wide.

The body was nearly but not quite cold. The human body retains its heat for some time if covered up. Mr. White was an old man, but he was rather fleshy. The blow on the head, by checking circulation, probably prevented the loss of blood.

From all the circumstances, my first opinion was that it had been done three or four hours. There was, however, nothing to prevent it having been done six or eight hours. My first impression was that he had lost more blood than we afterwards found he had.[4]

THE CONSPIRACY

At this point the attorney general said that he had proved that the murder was committed. He would prove next that there was a combination to commit the murder. For that purpose his first witness would be Joseph J. Knapp, Jr.

---

[4] The time of the murder was a question of great importance. Notice that Dr. Johnson only admits the possibility of a time earlier than two or three o'clock. It is notable that the government did not choose to ask the witness his opinion as to the time of the murder.

Joseph J. Knapp, Jr.

When asked if he was willing to be sworn, the witness answered in the negative by shaking his head.[5]

The attorney general asked Joseph Knapp the reason for his refusal, but Dexter objected. The court said that the witness was not obliged to state his reasons.

THE COURT: The government say they have pledged themselves not to proceed against him if he would testify; he does not testify, and now that pledge is recalled.

DEXTER: It was stated by the attorney general in his opening that Knapp would refuse to testify in pursuance of advice of counsel. I feel it my duty to state distinctly that I have never given such advice.

GARDINER: And I have never given such advice.

DEXTER: The only other counsel, Mr. Rantoul, who had access to him, is ready to make the same statement.

Benjamin Leighton

Q. (The attorney general) Have you ever heard a conversation between Joseph Knapp, Jr., and John Francis Knapp? A. I have.

Q. (Webster) Where do you live? A. I have lived with Mr. Davis at Wenham, at the house where Mrs. Beckford and Joseph J. Knapp, Jr.'s family live, since the sixth of October last. Joe Knapp's family came there to live a few days after I went. [John Davis was a son-in-law of Mrs. Beckford and apparently manager of her farm.]

About a week before Captain White was murdered, I went down to the lower end of the avenue, got over the wall, and sat down by the side of the gate that is across the avenue to take a little nooning.

I sat a few minutes and then heard men talking on the other side of the wall. Without rising so as to be seen, I looked round through the slats of the gate and saw the two Knapps coming down the avenue. When they came near the gate, Joseph said, "When did you see Dick?" Frank said, "I saw him this morning." Joseph said, "When is he going to kill the old man?" Frank answered, "I don't know." Joseph said, "If he does not kill him soon, I will not pay him." Then they turned back and I did not hear any more.

This was about two o'clock in the afternoon. . . . It was Friday

---

[5] It is hardly too much to say that by that shake of the head Joseph Knapp broke his neck.

before Captain White was murdered, I think. It was within the week previous to the murder.

I shall be eighteen years old the thirtieth of next December. I am under no mistake about the conversation. I am sure of the persons; they were not more than three or four feet from me. Joseph J. Knapp, Jr., has lived in the house where I lived and John Francis Knapp came to the house frequently. I never told anyone that I had heard any such conversation.

Q. (The attorney general) Did you ever see Richard Crownin-shield, Jr., there? A. Not that I know of. I did not know him.

Frank Knapp came up to Wenham one evening after the murder in a chaise about nine o'clock; I do not know the day. It was about a fortnight or three weeks after the murder and two or three weeks before he came there to live. I believe Mrs. Beckford was living there then. There was a gentleman in the chaise at the door; I did not know him, but he was a tall, slim man, not so thick as Frank Knapp.

I went to the door when the chaise drove up. Joseph Knapp met Frank at the inner door, and they went into the room together and shut the door. They were together an hour, I should think. Nobody was in the room with them.

Cross-examination. I did not go before the grand jury. I don't know what the grand jury is.

I did not say anything to Mr. Davis about the conversation I had heard. I have been called upon to tell what I know about it by Mr. Waters and another gentleman I did not know. They sent for me to come to Mr. Waters' office. I told them I could not recollect at that time I had ever told anything about it. I did not tell them I knew nothing about it. I was in his office in the forenoon and afternoon.

I knew they [the Knapps] could not see me get over the wall because I have tried since. I tried because if they did see me and knew I heard them, I was afraid they would kill me.

I saw Mr. Waters a week ago last Thursday.[6] They asked me if I recollected telling Mr. Starrett anything. I told them I did not. . . . Mr. Starrett was there. . . . They told me I must recollect it; they would make me recollect it when I came to court. They bothered and frightened me and I could not remember.

[6] The twenty-second of July, two days after the grand jury began its hearings.

Q. (Dexter) On your oath, did you not tell them that you did not know anything about it? A. I believe I didn't.

Mr. Starrett told Mr. Waters I had told him something. I told Mr. Waters I did not recollect it; but if he would come up the next day I would tell him all that I knew. I thought then of the conversation between the Knapps; but I told them I could not recollect it, because I didn't calculate to say anything about it.

I told Mr. Starrett because I spoke before I thought. I saw Mr. Waters again last Saturday[7] at Lummus's tavern in Wenham. He came down there with Mr. Choate and Mr. Treadwell. I told them I had been down to Salem but could not recollect then; I was in a strange place and frightened. Then I recollected what I had told Starrett, and told them the same story I have told today.

They did not tell me they had a warrant against me. Mr. Davis afterwards told me they said they would carry me off if I did not tell all I knew. They did not threaten me.

The day I heard the conversation between the Knapps, they walked to within three or four feet of the wall, which was four feet high. I heard nothing else that I could understand. They stood by the wall two or three minutes and then went back. It was after they stopped that I heard what I have testified. I did not tell the conversation to anybody before the murder. I could not think, till after the murder, what it was about. Then I supposed the Knapps must be the murderers.

I did not mention this conversation before the murder, because I did not think of it.

Re-direct examination. On the day after the murder I went to Starrett's shop and he said, "What is the news about the murder?" I said, "They think I don't know anything about it, but I know a little more than they think I do." I spoke before I thought.

Frank used to be around me with his dirk, and pricked me with it. He did this more than once, and other persons saw it. Thomas Hart saw it.

The first time I told the conversation was to Hart, and it was not long ago. I next told it to Mr. Waters.

Re-cross-examination. Starrett did not ask me what I knew. He did not ask me what I had overheard.

---

[7] July 31, the day after Webster entered the case, nine days after the first interview, and four days after the date first set for the trial.

I am afraid now, if the Knapps get clear, they will kill me.

DEXTER: So you don't mean they shall.

Wednesday, August 4, 1830

When Mr. Colman was called to testify, he asked the court to explain the nature of the oath tendered him. He said that he was bound to tell the truth, the whole truth, and if the government stopped him in the course of his testimony, he would not have told the whole truth.

The court directed Mr. Colman to proceed, and expressed the belief that he knew the nature of an oath, and that he would use it in all purity.

Henry Colman

Q. (The attorney general) What do you know relative to the confession by J. F. Knapp? A. I had no personal acquaintance with the prisoner, not having known him even by sight until the twenty-eighth of May when he was examined before Justice Savage.

On the afternoon of that day I went to his cell with his brother, Phippen Knapp, at Phippen's request. When we went in, Phippen said, "Well, Frank, Joseph has determined to make a confession and we want your consent." I am not able to give the reply of the prisoner in his precise words, but the effect was that he thought it hard, or not fair, that Joseph should have the advantage of making a confession, since the thing was done for his benefit or advantage. I now give his words as nearly as I can recollect them. He said, "I told Joseph when he proposed it that it was a silly business and would only get us into difficulty." Phippen, as I supposed, to reconcile Frank to Joseph's confessing, told him that if Joseph was convicted there would be no chance for him (Joseph), but if he (Frank) was convicted he might have some chance for procuring a pardon. Phippen then appealed to me and asked if I did not think so. I told him I did not know; I was unwilling to hold out any improper encouragement.

DEXTER: We object to any continuation of this confession. It is now in evidence that Phippen, with a view to reconcile Frank to Joseph's confessing, told him that if he were convicted, he might have a chance of pardon. This was a direct inducement to a confession.

The court said they would hear counsel for the government.

After arguments by Webster, Gardiner, and Dexter, the court, with Justice Putnam dissenting, ruled that anything said by the prisoner, after what Phippen said to him regarding the hope of pardon, was not admissible.

Mr. Colman recalled. Webster asked the witness whether anything further transpired *before* the remark of Phippen Knapp to the prisoner and the appeal to the witness to confirm it. Mr. Colman replied that Phippen made the statement several times, and that the appeal to him was made towards the conclusion of the interview.

Dexter submitted that this was improper. The witness had been requested to state the conversation in the order in which it occurred, and had professed to relate it in that order. Could he now postpone to the close of the interview the appeal to himself?

The court ruled that he could not state any conversations of Frank's subsequent to the remark of Phippen.

Mr. Colman said that nothing further took place before the remark made by Phippen Knapp.

Q. (The court) Tell all that was said about encouragement. A. Mr. Phippen Knapp said to Francis that if Joseph was convicted there would be no chance for him; but if Francis was convicted after the confessions of Joseph as State's witness, Francis would stand a chance for a pardon. This was early in the interview. Francis then asked me to use my influence or interest for him. I told him that I could promise nothing, but I wished him well and I thought his youth would be in his favor. It was just at the close of the interview that Phippen appealed to me. Phippen had told Francis more than once in the course of the conversation that there might be a hope of pardon.

Q. (Webster) Was there any encouragement of any kind or degree to induce Frank to confess any fact within his own knowledge? A. There was none, neither promise nor pledge — nothing more than has been stated.

Q. (The attorney general) Did not Francis tell you where to find a certain weapon? A. —.

DEXTER: You must not state it. What Frank said is not evidence.

After some argument, Mr. Colman continued:

Soon after this interview I found the club under the north steps of the church in Howard Street. I went there on the twenty-ninth of May, about one o'clock, with Dr. Barstow and Mr. Fettyplace [two members of the committee of vigilance].

The witness produced a heavy club about two feet long which had been neatly turned in a lathe. In the large end of the club a considerable quantity of lead was fitted.

Q. (Webster) What induced you to look there? A. I was told it was there.

Q. Who told you it was there?

Dexter objected. It was intended to criminate the prisoner by his confession of his knowledge that the club was there. This was using a fact to bring in a confession improperly obtained.

The court, however, ruled that it was competent for the government to prove that the instrument was found by the witness in consequence of information from the prisoner.

Mr. Colman said he was told by the prisoner at the bar.

The defense did not cross-examine the witness.

Mr. WEBSTER: We now propose to prove by the next witness that the murder was the result of a conspiracy in which the two Knapps and the two Crowninshields were engaged.

John C. R. Palmer

Q. (The attorney general) Do you know the prisoner at the bar? A. I do.

Q. Did you know Richard and George Crowninshield? A. Yes, I have been at their house in Danvers.

I have seen the prisoner at Crowninshield's in Danvers. The first time he came on the afternoon of the second of April, about two o'clock, with a young man named Allen. They came on two white horses. I saw the prisoner in company with George Crowninshield. I did not see them in the house; I saw them from the window of the chamber. They walked away together. I did not see them again until after four; Richard was with Allen. Allen and Frank then went away. George and Richard immediately came into the chamber where I was.

Q. (Webster) Was there anything said there about the murder of Captain White by both George and Richard Crowninshield? A. Yes.

Q. Did you hear any such proposition from George in Richard's presence? A. George, in the presence of Richard, proposed to me to take part in this murder.

Q. What object was proposed by that murder? A. The object of the murder was something that Frank Knapp had told them. I can't tell without telling what Frank said.

Q. What motive had you? A. I was to have one-third of the money George Crowninshield received.

Q. What sum was that to be? A. One thousand dollars.

Q. Who, according to the contract, was to pay? A. Joseph J. Knapp, Jr.

Q. Was any method of murder proposed? A. Richard said it would be easy to meet him that night and overturn his carriage, for George said he had gone to his farm in Beverly.

Q. What benefit was Joseph to get out of his death? A. To have a will destroyed.

Q. What reason had you to meddle with it? A. George said that I was in want and that this would be a good time to supply that want. They said the housekeeper would be absent from home at the time he would be murdered.

Q. Did Francis come to the Crowninshield's house again? A. Francis came again on that same day about seven o'clock in the evening in a chaise and alone. He stayed then over half an hour. Richard went away with him in the same chaise. I did not see Frank afterwards till this time. Richard came home about twelve o'clock that night.

Q. When did you leave the Crowninshield's house? A. Next afternoon, Saturday.

Q. When did you next see the Crowninshields? A. At night at their home on the ninth of April last. I stayed there a short time. . . . On the evening of the twenty-seventh I saw the Crowninshields again at their house about ten o'clock. I stayed till the twenty-ninth. Richard gave me four five-franc pieces; I asked him to let me have it and promised to return it.

I then went to Lowell, then to Boston, then to Roxbury, then to Belfast. While at Belfast I wrote a letter to Joseph Knapp.

A letter was shown to Palmer which, he said, was the one that he wrote.

DEXTER: I object to reading the letter.

THE COURT: Its bearing upon the prisoner should appear.

WEBSTER: The government expect to show that in consequence of the discovery of this letter, Frank Knapp endeavored to divert public attention by causing two other letters to be written. To this end we shall call Mr. Allen.

Dexter said he objected to Allen also, because all his evidence related to acts done subsequent to the consummation of the conspiracy.

JUSTICE PUTNAM: Everything done to conceal the murder was a part of the conspiracy. The criminals would naturally endeavor to throw suspicion upon other persons. The court rules, however, that the connection of Palmer's letter with the conspiracy should be proved before the letter itself is introduced.

William H. Allen

Q. (Webster) Have you ever seen these letters before? A. Yes, I put these letters into the Salem post office on Sunday afternoon, May 16, between five and six o'clock, at the request of J. J. Knapp, Jr. He gave them to me and said that his brother Phippen and his father came up to Wenham the day before and brought an anonymous letter from a fellow down East, which contained a "devilish lot of trash," such as, "I know your plans, and your brother's, and will expose you if you don't send me money." He said that they had a good laugh upon it, and that he requested his father to give it to the committee of vigilance. "What I want to see you for is to have you put these letters into the post office in order to nip this silly affair in the bud."

The content of the three letters which Mr. Webster now read to the jury has been sufficiently set forth in our approach to the trials.

Palmer, cross-examination. On the night of the murder I was at Babb's, the Halfway House in Lynn. I was there from seven in the evening till nine in the morning. I first came to Salem three years ago. I went to Danvers to see the Crowninshields on an invitation from George.

Q. (Gardiner) Where did you reside in the meantime? A. Don't recollect very well.

Gardiner made an extended attempt to impeach the credibility of the witness by frequent references to his imprisonment at Thomaston, Maine, for robbery. The court overruled Webster's objections. Had the robbery taken place in Massachusetts Palmer would not have been a competent witness in a Massachusetts court.

Q. (Gardiner) [The question refers to Palmer's visit to the Crowninshields before the murder.] Where did you stay at Danvers? A. I lived with the Crowninshields in their room, apart from the rest of the family.

Q. Did the family know you were there? A. I don't know.

Q. Where were you when you first gave testimony in this case? A. In jail.

Q. Did you come to Salem of your own accord? A. I did not; I was in the custody of an officer.

Q. On what process? A. I don't know. I have never been able to find out why I was confined.

Q. Who did you see? A. Half a dozen people, Mr. Colman, Mr. White, Mr. Waters, and my father.

Webster objected to the course of the examination, and Dexter replied that he expected to show that the witness had been harshly used, that he had been brought from Belfast in irons, placed in close confinement in a condemned cell, that he was not allowed to see any person except such as belonged to the committee of vigilance, that when his father called he was at first refused. The court ordered the examination to be continued.

I was chained during the journey to Salem.

Q. To whom did you first disclose your knowledge in Salem? A. To the committee of vigilance.

Q. Were you compelled to do it? A. I was not.

Q. Have you been told that you were in danger of going to state prison if you did not confess? A. I have not.

Q. Were you threatened with a prosecution? A. No, sir.

Q. Have you ever heard of certain flannels supposed to have been stolen in Danvers? I have read of them in the papers.[8]

Q. Have you heard it intimated than on certain conditions you would not be prosecuted for stealing flannels? A. No, sir. There has been an offer that if I would come forward I should have protection from the government for this murder. I have repeatedly refused their protection. I meant to meet the charge.

Q. Did you not know that when you entered court this morning you were discharged from your imprisonment? A. I supposed I should be. They had no claim to hold me.

Q. Under what name did you pass while you remained at Babb's Halfway House? A. I went by the name of George Crowninshield.

Q. What induced you to give that name? A. I owed Mr. Babb something and he requested a name.

_____

[8] On March 1 a bale of flannels was stolen from the building of Mr. Sutton, of Danvers, while Palmer was at the Crowninshields. It was found under a quantity of hay in the Crowninshield barn on June 13, two days before the suicide of Richard.

Q. Did you leave any pledge with Mr. Babb? A. I left a silk handkerchief.

Q. Do you know that a large reward has been offered for the discovery of the assassin? A. I do.

Q. When did you learn of it? A. On the ninth of April.

Q. Have you taken any measures to secure that reward? A. I have not been actuated by that.

Q. Do you expect any reward in consequence of your share in bringing this matter to light? A. No, sir.

Q. What was your object in writing to Joseph Knapp? A. I wished to know whether he had a hand in the murder.

Q. Why? A. I wished to make it public.

Q. Why? You had a motive? A. I didn't think it ought to be concealed.

Q. You knew there was a committee of vigilance; why did you not inform them? A. I wished to advise with someone else, my father.

Q. Had you any other desire than to bring out the perpetrator of this horrid murder? A. I can't say that was all; perhaps I thought I should have some part of the reward.

Q. Have you now any expectation of getting the reward? A. I have not.

Q. Why did you not tell before the murder of the conversation at Danvers? A. I thought the scheme was not true. They said they were joking.

The witness related further that while he was in prison, his father came to his door and the jailer told them not to talk about the murder.

Re-direct examination. Q. (Webster) Have you ever complained of ill treatment? A. No. No one that I wanted to see has been refused. I have refused any pledge from the government of indemnification or protection.

Allen, recalled.

On the second of April, Frank Knapp and myself stopped at Dustin's Hotel in Danvers; Frank proposed to rest at the Crowninshields. We had two white horses. We first met Dick. I wanted to see the factory, and Richard went with me over to it. I left Frank and George at the house. . . .

Cross-examination. Went to Danvers between two and three

o'clock. Frank did not request to be left alone with George. We were separated half to three-quarters of an hour.

Re-direct examination. Q. (Webster) What was the dress of Francis? A. His usual dress — dark frock coat, velvet collar, glazed cap, camblet cloak with nothing unusual about it. Glazed caps and camblet cloaks were common dress.

William Osborne

I keep a livery stable in Salem. Francis Knapp has been accustomed to hire horses from me. The charges on my books against him since April 1 are as follows:

April 1, horse and gig to Lynn Mineral Springs.

April 2, saddle horse to Dustin's in Danvers. William H. Allen had a saddle horse the same afternoon. Francis Knapp had a chaise the same day in the evening. I find the charge of horse and gig to Spring altered, the word "Spring" is erased and "ride" substituted. I think the alteration was made by Francis Knapp; it is in his handwriting.

April 3, saddle horse to Wheeler's, which is about half a mile from Dustin's, and the same distance from Crowninshields. I do not recollect the time of day. The last charge on that day is a saddle horse to Francis Knapp to Wheeler's.

April 5, saddle horse to Wenham.

April 6, horse and gig to —. This is my own handwriting. I do not know where he went; no price is put down; have never ascertained where he went.

April 19, horse and gig to Wenham, and over Frank's name I find the name of J. J. Knapp.

April 23, horse and gig to Wenham.

April 24, horse and gig to Wenham. This is the last charge on the book that day; there are eleven previous charges.

April 25, one-half horse and gig.

April 27, horse and gig to Wenham.

Cross-examination. I make charges when horses are given out. Don't know where they go. I leave a blank till I ascertain. Always considered Francis Knapp honorable and allowed him to make any alterations in charges to him. He rides considerable; don't know as more so in April than beforehand. March 30, horse and gig to Wenham. March 29, half of the charge of horse and gig to Spring. March 28, quarter of charge of carryall. Not often hired horses in the evening, but did in afternoons. Can't tell much about the time of day by my method of charging. The father of the prisoner failed on the sixth of April. No charge to prisoner from that time to April 19.

Thomas Hart

I live with Mrs. Beckford at Wenham and am hired to work on the farm. I went there on the ninth of last April and was hired by Captain Joseph Knapp. I know John Francis Knapp. Mrs. Beckford came there to live about the fifteenth of April, and Frank Knapp about the twenty-eighth.

One Saturday evening, about the twenty-fifth of April, Frank came there. He came about seven o'clock.

Joseph Knapp went out with him to the chaise and remained a quarter of an hour. I think I heard the voice of a third person in the chaise. They then came into the house and went into a room by themselves and stayed about ten minutes.

The chaise came a little after seven and stayed a little more than half an hour.

Joseph, on the Tuesday after this Saturday, gave me some five-franc pieces to buy meal with.

Frank Knapp has worn a dagger, and I have seen him several times prick Benjamin Leighton with it while out in the field. One night after we had gone to bed, Frank came up and pricked Ben through the bedclothes. Ben asked him not to, and he said, "Lay still, you will not feel it after a little time." This was after the murder.

Ezra Lummus

I live in Wenham and keep a public house there, about a quarter of a mile below where Mrs. Beckford lives. I saw Dick Crownin-shield at my house for the first time in the latter part of March. He and a young man, I didn't know who, came to my house on that day; they left their chaise, went away and were gone some time. The man with Dick Crowninshield had on dark clothes and a glazed cap, I think.

Ten days or a fortnight after the murder, on Saturday, I believe, Dick Crowninshield came again with a person whom I did not know. They paid their bill with a five-franc piece. I did not notice them particularly as there was a good deal of running in and out of the bar. I can't describe the man who was with Dick, but he was about my height and rather stout, stouter than Frank Knapp, I think.

Mrs. Ezra Lummus

Mrs. Lummus testified that about the twenty-fourth or twenty-fifth of April some persons were at the inn and passed a five-franc piece. She did not know either of the men. One had on a dark dress, but she did not know how the other was dressed.

Captain Josiah Dewing

I came home from sea last spring and brought three or four thousand five-franc pieces. About five hundred were for Joseph Knapp, Jr. So far as I know, all but his went into the bank as a deposit. The distribution of them was about the twenty-first of April last, and I have the receipt for his portion. J. J. Knapp, Jr., was the ship's husband [one who has care of a ship while it is in port].

Several witnesses were called to prove that George Crowninshield paid out three five-franc pieces on May 1, the day before he and his brother were arrested. *Daniel Marston*, who kept a victualing cellar, swore that these pieces were not a common currency — not as common as silver dollars; but *George Smith*, clerk in a grocery, said he frequently received them. *Joseph Shatswell* testified that he took in about one five-franc piece for each three silver dollars.

Stephen C. Phillips, a member of the committee of vigilance, was then called to the stand to testify to the report that the two Knapp brothers had given to the committee of a robbery said to have been attempted upon them at Wenham. Dexter objected to any statement of any robbery. He said that it was a crime totally distinct from the present trial. Webster argued that the pretended robbery was in furtherance of the design of the conspiracy. The court ruled that any evidence having a reasonable tendency to show that the prisoner wished to divert public attention from himself would be admissible.

Thursday, August 5

Webster said that since the last adjournment, the counsel for the government had considered the position in which the case now stood, and in which it was likely to be placed in consequence of the rule excluding the testimony of Mr. Colman as to certain confessions; and the counsel had instructed him to say that when they had concluded the examination of their other witnesses, he should move the court to hear argument again, and more at large, upon that point.

Stephen C. Phillips[9] recalled

I have known Joseph Knapp some years but have never known Frank until recently. On Tuesday, the twenty-seventh of April, it was stated in town that the Knapps had said they had been attacked at Wenham. This created considerable excitement and they requested the committee of vigilance to make inquiry. I took minutes of their statements.

Mr. Phillips read the minutes. It seemed that the Knapps repelled a furious attack by three men, two of whom resembled the men seen in Brown Street on the night of the murder.

Nehemiah Brown

I am keeper of the Salem jail. On the fifteenth of June, a little before two o'clock in the afternoon, I called at Richard's room and had no answer. I looked over the top of his door and saw him hanging at the grate. He was hanging by two handkerchiefs. Took him down and called in physicians.

Warwick Palfrey

He said in his cross-examination that he published an article respecting the finding of flannels in the Crowninshield's barn. He thought the publication was three or four days before Richard's death.

John McGlue

On the night before the murder I saw Richard Crowninshield, Jr., standing opposite Captain White's house. He was not doing anything. I was going up along on the south side of Essex Street. He had his head turned up so as to look toward the coffee house or that way. I think he was standing a little farther west than the house of Captain White.

It was about half-past eight in the evening. He walked up with me ar far as the post office [in the East India Marine Building].

Cross-examination. The Lafayette Coffee House is west of Captain White's house, a short distance. Richard Crowninshield, Jr., was opposite the upper end of the house. I did not see him more than a minute or so. He might have been there an hour for all I know. This was Monday night.

---

[9] Mr. Phillips (1801-1857) was a graduate of Harvard College, a member of the Massachusetts Legislature, and later a member of Congress. He was a prominent and successful merchant.

A group of witnesses testified that they saw George Crowninshield in Salem on the evening of April 6, going about town. *Richard
Burnham* saw him with two companions, one of whom looked like
Daniel Chase, on Essex Street at about eight o'clock. Shortly
before nine *Joseph Anthony* saw George and Chase with a third,
whom he did not know, going from Essex Street into Central Street.
Thomas W. Taylor, at about a quarter after nine, saw George with
an unrecognized person pass down Newbury Street toward Williams
Street. *Benjamin Newhall* saw George, between half-past nine and
ten o'clock, pass down Williams Street with another person. Newhall knew Frank Knapp well, but he did not recognize George's
companion.

FRANK KNAPP'S PRESENCE AT THE MURDER

Stephen Mirick

I live directly opposite to the corner of Mrs. Andrew's yard, on
the north side of Brown Street, the last house in Brown Street
before you go into Newbury Street. [Mrs. Andrew's house was
in the position of the H in the chart. North of it was an open yard.]

About fifteen minutes before nine, on the evening of the sixth of
April, I saw a man standing at a post directly opposite my shop,
on the opposite side of the street. I had a fairly good view of him;
I did not know him. He remained there, apparently waiting for
someone, and this led me to be more particular in noticing him.
He stood there till the bell rang for nine, changing his situation
a little. When anyone came down Brown Street, he went into
Newbury Street and then turned so as to meet him at the corner;
and if anyone came down Newbury Street, he went into Brown
Street and turned to meet him in the same manner. From this
post he could see up Newbury and Brown Streets, about as far up
one street as the other. . . . He remained there till twenty or thirty
minutes after nine. I did not see him go away, and he was there
when I shut up my shop and went home. He had on a frock coat
which came round him very tight, was very full at the top and bottom; it was of a dark color. I can't say what he had on his head.

Q. (Webster) Have you seen any person since that you supposed
to be the same person? A. I did not see the man's face. I did not
see the defendant till I saw him before the grand jury.

Q. Have you seen that person since? A. I have.

Q. Where have you seen that person, and what name did he

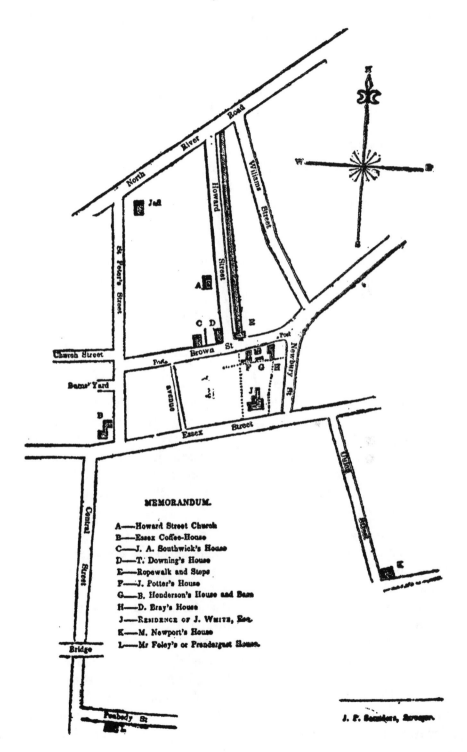

MEMORANDUM.

A——Howard Street Church
B——Essex Coffee-House
C——J. A. Southwick's House
D——T. Downing's House
E——Ropewalk and Steps
F——J. Potter's House
G——B. Henderson's House and Barn
H——D. Bray's House
J——RESIDENCE OF J. WHITE, ESQ.
K——M. Newport's House
L——Mr Foley's or Prendergast House.

bear? A. I think I saw him when he was brought up before the grand jury, and when he was brought up once or twice since. I think it was Francis Knapp. I can't swear positively, but I believe it was he.

Q. (The court) Was this belief derived from personal observation or from what you heard from others? A. From both, that is, from my observation at the time and from the description of the person seen that evening.

Q. From your observation alone, do you say it was Frank Knapp? A. No. I should not. I can't say positively from my own observation, but the size and height of the man I saw correspond very nearly to the prisoner.

WEBSTER: Would it be proper to ask what the circumstances were that induced the witness to believe they were the same?

Dexter objected. He said that nothing could be evidence but the personal knowledge of the witness.

THE COURT: His belief arises from two sources; what he had from others is not evidence.

Peter E. Webster

He testified that his place of business was near the Knapp home, and that he knew Frank well. On the evening of April 6, he went to the post office, and then proceeded homeward, passing through Howard Street sometime between nine-twenty and ten o'clock. He overtook two men walking slowly, arm in arm, in the middle of the street. Both wore glazed caps and camlet cloaks. He passed within six feet of one of the men whom he took to be Frank Knapp; he did not notice the other man.

Cross-examination. The witness only judged that it was Frank by his air and manner. Neither man spoke to the other. He sometimes spoke to Frank and sometimes did not. He did not know either of the Crowninshield brothers.

The night was cloudy and a little damp, and the witness was certain that it was the sixth of April. He took notice of the men because there were seldom visitors in that part of the town so late at night. He thought that the man was Frank before the Knapps were arrested, and mentioned it to Mr. Foster; but whether before or after the arrest he was not sure. He could not say positively that it was Frank because he did not see his face. The men walked slowly as if waiting for someone.

Five-franc pieces were not very common, but he usually took in some every week.

John A. Southwick

I am cashier of the American Bank. I live in Brown Street, next house but two to the westward above the ropewalk [a long building fronting on Brown Street and running back along the east side of Howard Street]. Downing's house makes the corner of Howard Street.

On the evening of the murder, I left my father's house in Essex Street about half-past ten to go home. As I passed the ropewalk, I saw a young man sitting there; as I passed him he dropped his head. I stopped at Downing's door, then walked back — I think that time — then returned to Downing's house, and then to my own. He dropped his head every time I passed him. I felt sure it was Mr. Knapp. I passed him three times on the steps. He had a brown camlet cloak and glazed cap. I was brought up alongside of him, within a few houses of him, from his boyhood. When I passed the third time, I went into my house; my wife was up. One time when I went in, I spoke to her.

This same person was in my mind all evening after I saw him. I came out of my house and walked to the corner of Downing's house, looking for this person down Howard Street, when Captain Bray came up. He asked what I was out there so late for. I told him I had seen a person on the ropewalk steps, and about there, that looked suspicious, or whom I thought suspicious. He said he had seen one also. Pointing up to old Mrs. Shepard's house, he said, "There he is now, on the opposite side of the street farther up." I looked and saw the person standing there.

He came down by us without apparently taking notice of us and went to the post nearly opposite Captain Bray's door and leaned over the post.

While he was at the post we went in at the west end of Bray's house at the end door. We went up the backstairs into his front chamber. When we went in only half of one shutter was open. I stood back and Bray watched. In a short time he said, "Another one has come up. Now they have passed along to the west side of the house." On looking out of the west window we saw one of the persons running across the street. He ran around the ropewalk corner. The other went down toward the Common; I thought he went round the corner.

Then Mr. Bray and I came out, and went down Howard Street, up around Williams Street, and back home. . . . Mentioned to my wife what I had seen; I told her I had seen a person that I supposed was Frank Knapp. . . . I do not recollect the dress of the person leaning on the post.

Cross-examination. The time when I first saw this person was about half-past ten. I know because I knew at what time I left my father's house and it was a two or three minutes walk.

The man upon the steps was two or three feet off when I was nearest to him. I did not speak to him because I had nothing to say to him, and he hid his face. Perhaps I should not speak to him three-quarters of the time when I met him. He rather evaded speaking. I don't know that I saw his face. His dress was a camlet cloak and cap; I can swear to it. I judged it was Frank Knapp from the general appearance of the man. He was not wrapped up, for I could see that he sat cross-legged. It was a cloudy night but the moon was at the full. It did not rain then; it was misty at times.

I did not see the man on the steps get up and go away, but it is on my mind that it was the same man I saw at the post. I have no doubt he had on a glazed cap; I swear positively that I did not see any fur about the cap.

I went out the second time from suspicions expressed in the house when I told what I had seen. I have not known that Howard Street is a place of assignations for the last six months. I cannot say what I suspected him of.

I can't say whether the man Captain Bray pointed out to me had a cloak and cap. I thought it was the same I had seen on the steps, because I had seen no other in the street. I had the same suspicions about the man who walked down the street that I had of the man on the steps.

Q. (Gardiner) Did you not say upon your oath before Justice Savage that you only knew the person from his dress? A. I said I judged him from his general appearance; and though my observation was slight, I was always of opinion that it was J. F. Knapp.

I cannot describe the dress of the person who came up and joined the man standing at the post when we were in Captain Bray's chamber. The post was within seven feet of Bray's door, six or eight feet to the east of the window. I saw two men, but can't swear to the dress of either.

I don't recollect that I have told any person that I could not tell who the person was on the steps. I never said the man on the steps was William Peirce, but I compared him to William Peirce in size and appearance.

I cannot tell how the man running across the street was dressed. I knew it was one of the same persons, because they appeared to be watching and engaged in the same business. We were looking out of the window five or six minutes.

I never said either of those persons was Crowninshield or Selman or Chase.

I was at Ipswich before the grand jury. I did not state to them that I supposed the person that I saw on the steps was Frank Knapp; I said nothing about him. I was sworn to tell the whole truth. I did not say that it was Selman or that it was not; I said I thought that it looked some like Selman.

Captain Daniel Bray, Jr.

I live in Brown Street and in the lowest house on the south side.

On the evening of the sixth of April, I was passing down Brown Street from St. Peter Street, and when I passed the fourth house I saw a man dressed in a dark frock coat, dark pantaloons, and a shining cap standing at a post. The frock was very full at the bottom. I was on the north side of the street and he was on the south. As I passed on, I saw another man looking or peeping down Howard Street, who I found was Mr. John Southwick. He said that when he went into his house, a man of very suspicious appearance was sitting on the ropewalk steps. I turned round and observed, "There stands the man now." I could see him very plainly up towards Shepard's house, it was so light.

I walked on with him close to the ropewalk, and stood so as to get out of the wind, when the man who stood at the post passed along on the south side and took his station at the post at the northeast corner of my house, next to the bounds between my house and that of Mrs. Andrews. I asked Southwick to go with me into my house to see what he was about. We passed about twenty feet from him, and entered my west door. We went up into my chamber, because the sliding shutters in the room below were closed, and we could not unclose them without noise.

I looked out of the window and, by pressing my face against the glass, I could see the man at the post and never lost sight of him while he stood there, which was five or six minutes, when another man came up from the eastward, in the middle of the road and not far from the sidewalk. I saw him when he was 150 to 200 feet off. From my window I could see down Brown Street and the Common, so the man must have come through Newbury Street or we could have seen him sooner.

The man that came from the east had on light clothes. He then ran as hard as he could down Howard Street. The other at the same time started off in the opposite direction, and was out of sight towards the east.

I have known the prisoner since he was a boy—knew him years ago. I have seen him in prison and at the bar. I can't tell whether he was one of those I saw that night. Size and appearance agree very well.

I had heard the clock strike ten, and should think it was thirty or forty minutes after when I met Southwick, but did not take much notice until after the murder.

Webster said it would be remembered that Benjamin White, the first witness, stated that all the occupied sleeping rooms of Mr. White's house had windows on the north or west sides or both. The government wished to prove that the corner near which this man was, was a very convenient spot for observing Mr. White's house and perceiving when the lights seen through those windows were extinguished.[10]

Bray. After the murder I went up on Downing's steps and could see all the north and west windows of White's house. I could see a light in the chamber where he slept, the windows of the room over that, those of the room on the same floor over the kitchen, and those of the room over this. These cannot now be seen because of the leaves on the trees.

Cross-examination. The steps of Downing's house is the only place where I looked. The windows could not be seen from the ropewalk steps, or from Shepard's post, or from the post near my house, or while walking under the fence on the south side.

Southwick did not then tell me that it was Frank Knapp, but he has told me since, I believe after the arrest; but I cannot recollect. I did not then hear Southwick say that the man looked like William Peirce.

---

[10] It will be interesting to see whether Webster ever succeeds in placing the man in any spot from which these windows could be seen.

Captain Bray's house as it looks today. The post at which the person stood was near that of the electric light post visible at the left of the picture.

Joseph Burns

I was born in old Spain; have lived here about twenty-five years. My place of business is in St. Peter Street. I keep horses to let. My place of business is near the head of Brown Street. I know Francis Knapp and had a conversation with him in the stable after the murder and after the committee of vigilance was appointed.

It was just after the Wenham robbery. He came into the stable and asked me if anybody was in the stable besides me. I told him no. We went upstairs. Then he asked me if I knew anything about Captain White's murder. I told him no; I wished to the Lord I should, because I would make it known pretty quick. He said the committee had heard that I was out on the night of the murder till about ten o'clock, and he said, "If you saw anybody, any friend, out that night in the street, don't you let the committee know it, for they will try to pump something out of you." He said his brother Joseph was a friend of mine and set a good deal by me, that they had got a good deal of money, and that he himself too was a friend of mine. I then said that I knew all the members of the committee, and if they wanted me anytime, I was ready to answer them to anything. Then I asked Knapp what he thought of the Crowninshields who were in jail. Mr. Knapp said they were as innocent as he and I. I asked him, "Who did it then?" He said, "Captain Stephen White must be the one." I said, "Don't you tell me such a thing as that. I know Captain White and have known him ever since he was eighteen or nineteen years old." Then he put his hand under his waistcoat where he had a dirk and showed me the handle. I said, "Damn you, I don't care for you nor twenty dirks." Then he said that he was a friend to me, and had come to give me this information so that I need not get into difficulty.

I know Joseph Knapp, Jr. He used to come to my stable to hire and put up horses. Francis was there on the week before the murder. He sometimes wore a cap and sometimes a hat; he usually left one of them there. He also wore a cloak or surtout, and likewise left one or the other of these.

Nathaniel Kinsman

I reside in Brown Street. A few days after the murder I could see the window of Captain White's chamber from the southeast corner of Mr. Downing's house. I could see the north window of Captain White's sleeping chamber and that of the chamber above. As far west as the next house to Mr. Downing's (which is the one in which I reside and is eighteen to twenty paces farther up) I could still see the window. East of the southwest corner of Mr. Downing's house, I could not see it.

There is a passageway from Essex Street to Brown Street. It is not public. There are two passageways with a gate to each which you must open. It would be nearer to go from the ropewalk steps to Captain White's house by Newbury Street than through either of these.

In *cross-examination,* Mr. Kinsman said that he could see the windows very plainly without getting up on the steps of Downing's house.

Philip Chase, who with Dr. Barstow and Mr. Treadwell constituted the sub-committee of the committee of vigilance, testified that "it was rather more than halfway across Howard Street that I first saw [Captain White's] window."

Mary Jane Weller

I know George Crowninshield. On the evening of April 6, between ten and eleven o'clock, he came to my house. I heard the clock strike eleven after he came in. That morning I went out for water and met James Stearns who told me of the murder. I then went to the door and knocked; George got up and opened it. I went in and told George and Mary Basset. He appeared to be alarmed, and Mary was alarmed. I wanted to go down to Captain White's to see the body and asked Mary to go. George was unwilling to have her go; he said there was a reason for it. He told me that morning not to say anything about his dirk. He said that if there was a scrape in Salem it was always laid to the Crowninshields. He stayed there all day and did not go away until evening. The dirk was about as long as a case knife. It had an ivory or bone handle.

Cross-examination. Q. (Dexter) What sort of weather was it the next day? A. You know as well as I do. You needn't think for to make me afraid with your silly questions. I ain't going to have any fun played on me.

Owing to the loose manners and impertinence of this witness, the court asked Dexter if he thought it expedient to examine her. Dexter said he did not desire it, and the witness responded, "I am glad of it."

Benjamin White was recalled. He testified that the last time Joseph Knapp, Jr., was at Captain White's house was the Sunday before the murder. Mrs. Knapp was also there; Captain White was not at home.[10a]

Jonathan Very

I live with Mr. Osborne and have care of his stables. On the afternoon before the murder Frank Knapp had me bring the horse Nipcat and a chaise to him behind the courthouse. I do not know why. I never carried a chaise to him before.

FRIDAY, AUGUST 6

John Treadwell, cashier of the Merchants Bank, testified that five-franc pieces did not circulate freely.

Cross-examination. I am one of the committee of vigilance. I was authorized by Stephen White to state that certain expenses would be paid.

Mr. Dexter said it was proper for the defendant's counsel to state that they should be obliged to introduce some testimony that they would gladly have left out. They would like to state also that they had the utmost respect for Mr. Stephen White.

Webster said that it was proper to reply to so formal an allusion to Mr. White. The whole character, conduct and motives of Mr. White were open, and they were ready to meet any charges that could be brought.

Mr. Gardiner said, "We do not threaten." Webster retorted, "Then I defy."

Palmer recalled. He told about a visit to Dick and George Crowninshield on the evening of the ninth of April. Dick said people thought they had some hand in the murder, and they meant to leave home. George said he melted down his dirk the day after the murder because there was a committee appointed to search the houses. But they said they had no hand in the murder.

David Starrett testified that he kept a store in Wenham. He saw Frank Knapp at the store on the afternoon before the murder.

[10a] Compare this Ben's earlier testimony.

ANOTHER ARGUMENT ON COLMAN'S TESTIMONY

Mr. Webster moved for a re-hearing on the admissibility of that part of Colman's testimony which had been excluded. The government had not had the slightest expectation that it would be excluded. The question of admissibility had arisen suddenly and had been decided without sufficient argument. . . . He contended further that if Mr. Colman's testimony was admitted and it was later found to be improper and unlawful, the verdict could be set aside and no harm could come to the prisoner. But if, in consequence of excluding the testimony, the prisoner was acquitted, the government could not move a new trial even if it was found that the testimony should not have been excluded. "The whole band of conspirators, with their confessions of the murder spread over the whole world, would be at large with perfect impunity."

Dexter replied briefly to Webster's argument set down just above: "This was incorrect because a full court is present, from which there is no appeal. . . . No bill of exceptions could be filed. The point settled now was settled once and forever."[11]

After some deliberation, Justice Putnam said the court were clearly of opinion that it would be proper to hear argument upon the question. It might, at least, produce unanimity in the opinion of the court.

The whole argument turned upon this question: Did Frank consent to Joe's making a confession? This was argued for many hours. Justices Morton and Wilde ruled that the prisoner's confession should be excluded. His consent was given under the influence of what Phippen said to him. The consent amounted to a confession and would be strong evidence against him. It was not a voluntary confession. . Further, said Justice Wilde, "his subsequent confessions ought to be excluded also. The rule is that when a confession has been improperly obtained, all subsequent confessions are inadmissible." Justice Putnam dissented, but reluctantly ruled that "the opinion of the court is that the confessions of the prisoner are rejected."[12]

[11] 16 Pickering 155, in which the Knapp case is cited. It seems to have been at this point that Dexter made a thrust at Webster: Webster had argued *vox* —he would not say *et praeterea nihil* [voice and nothing else], but he would add *felix audacia* [good nerve]. Webster replied that he hoped that was not true. He viewed the subject gravely, and he assured the counsel on the other side that he was not in the insane hospital yet.

[12] We omit most of the argument; first, because the reports are not very good, and, secondly, because, as it turned out, this decision had no effect upon the trial.

WEBSTER SHIFTS HIS GROUND

After this decision Webster stated that the court had misapprehended the views of the government. The government never proposed to offer the assent of Francis Knapp as evidence; they had never put it in the case. . . . The government knew that he did not assent. They now moved the court to call the witness and ask him the direct question concerning this confession; and they also proposed, if the court would admit it, to prove that Frank Knapp never did consent that Joseph should confess.

Dexter protested. The government knew this evidence was in their power, they kept it back. They preferred trying the old plan once more. They found that it would not do and they have now taken this new point. It seems to be a measure of severity which no prisoner ever before experienced in a court of justice.

"If the witness is now called, I will not say that his testimony will be changed, but he understands the position of the cause; he knows the importance of the evidence he is to give, and he is under the strongest inducement which could possibly influence an honest man to vary his testimony.[13]

Justice Wilde said he regretted that the question now proposed had not been asked of the witness before, because it would have saved much labor, discussion and time. The court went wholly upon the ground that an assent had been given by Francis, and the influence producing that assent whereby these confessions had been rejected. But if no such assent had been given, the public were not to be deprived of the use of such testimony through the negligence or inadvertence of the counsel for the government. If the prisoner had answered yes upon the question of assent, his testimony or confession could not have been received. If he had declined to assent, most clearly it could be used, and was not liable to the objection urged by his counsel.

---

[13] Dexter could have pointed out that although Webster had argued that it made no difference whether Frank had consented to Joe's confessing, he had always implied that consent had been given. A glance through his argument will reveal such statements as these: "By consenting that Joe might confess, Frank was saying, 'If Joe wants it more than I do, let him take the advantage.'" "It cannot be brought within any rule of law that the assent of Frank to Joe's confessing was a confession for himself." "But even if Frank's consent could be interpreted as a confession . . . it could not be used to exclude Mr. Colman's testimony." When Dexter said he understood Webster to have argued that the consent might come in because it was in itself no confession, the court said that Dexter was right.

Colman, recalled. Q. (Justice Wilde) *Did the prisoner refuse to assent to the arrangement made, as proposed by Phippen Knapp, that Joseph Knapp confess?* A. *There was neither assent nor refusal.*

Dexter argued that the prisoner's assent must be implied if there was no direct refusal; but the court could not say the prisoner did assent, and therefore the evidence ought to be admitted.[14]

Q. (Webster) At the conversation in the prisoner's cell, which you mentioned before, was anything said by Frank Knapp as to the time of night on which the murder was committed, and if so, what? A. I had been informed that the murder took place early in the evening; I was incredulous and asked the prisoner at what time it took place. His answer was between ten and eleven o'clock. I had been incredulous on the ground of there being but one person in the house, and asked the prisoner about that. He told me that Richard Crowninshield alone was in the house. I asked him if he was at home that night. He said he went home afterwards.

THE COURT: After what? A. The court must draw that inference. I asked him in regard to the weapon and the place of its being concealed, which I have testified before. He told me that it was under the steps of the Branch Meeting House, and under the flight nearest the burying ground. I asked him what had become of the dagger or daggers. He replied that it, or they, had been worked up at the factory.

Cross-examination. Q. Where did you go from to Frank's cell? A. From Joseph's cell at the request of Phippen.

Q. Was Phippen in Joseph's cell with you? A. No, sir. He knocked at the door and I admitted him after I had finished my interview with Joseph.

Q. Was the prisoner told that Joseph had disclosed everything or that he was about to? A. Neither; he was told that Joseph had decided to make confession.

Q. Did you know where the club was before you went into Frank's cell? A. I knew it was under the steps, but not under which steps.

[14] In reporting this portion of the trial, the *New Hampshire Patriot and State Gazette* observed, "The 'godlike' has already forced the Supreme Court of Massachusetts to take back and revoke one solemn decision; and under him there can be little doubt the culprits will be convicted and condemned. . . . Let it no longer be considered that the case of an individual depends upon right and justice, but upon whom he has engaged for counsel, and upon the magnitude of the fee paid to some pretended giant of the law."

Q. Have you stated all the prisoner said in that conversation? A. I have not. After the jailer had told us that it was time to go away, Phippen said, "If Joe is convicted there is no chance for him, but if you are convicted there is some chance for a pardon. Don't you think so, Mr. Colman?" Frank said, "I suppose you will use your influence to get me a pardon?" I told him I could promise him nothing; I wished him well, and hoped that his youth would be in his favor. The jailer had then called us again. *I said, "Mr. Knapp, this is your deliberate consent, is it?" He said, "I don't see that it's left for me to choose. I must consent."* We then left the prison.

Q. Did you not tell Stephen White that Frank told you where the club was? A. I have no recollection of mentioning it to anybody until I found it.

Q. What was your object in going to Frank's cell? A. To gratify Mr. Phippen Knapp, whose conduct was an example of filial and fraternal affection.

The witness stated that Joseph and Stephen White were his parishioners and intimate friends. J. J. Knapp, Jr., was also a parishioner. Mr. Colman had married Joseph and Mary, and he felt for Mary the affection of a father. Frank was not a parishioner.

This closed the evidence on the part of the government.

WILLIAM HOWARD GARDINER OPENS FOR THE DEFENSE

Mr. Gardiner's speech can be pieced together from various sources; but it is not needed for an understanding of the defense. Here we give only excerpts.

Gentlemen of the jury:

I agree with the attorney general that this murder is most atrocious, but you are not to let the enormity of the crime and the general alarm that it has excited prevent a full and free exercise of your judgment. The feeling of vengeance has gone through the whole community, and excitement has found its way into this hall of justice. Nevertheless, you must always remember that the presumption should be for, rather than against, the prisoner, particularly in view of the peculiar circumstances in which he is placed. John Francis Knapp is a young man, about nineteen years old, brought up in the bosom of a peaceful community, and now for the first time is placed at the bar of his country to be tried for his life.

The whole community has been in a state of the greatest excitement. . . . Large rewards have been offered by the state, the town, and the family of the deceased for the detection of the murderers, and a most extraordinary tribunal has been formed under the name of a committee of vigilance, consisting of twenty-seven persons selected from the most respectable portion of the community.

But that is not all. The counsel for the prisoner is now opposed by the committee of vigilance, opposed by a private prosecutor, Mr. Stephen White, opposed by public opinion, opposed by the whole bar of Essex, and opposed by the learned officers of government. But the whole bar of Essex, both of these experienced officers, together with the committee of vigilance to back them, is not enough; more strength is necessary. The most distinguished orator of our time, the high representative of the rights of Massachusetts in the Senate of the United States, with his green and fresh-gained laurels wreathed upon his brow, comes here to aid the host already pressing down the hope and life of the prisoner, to overpower the jury with his eloquence and to "nullify" the prisoner's defense. So determined seems to be the community to establish the guilt of the persons accused, that it is almost hazardous to appear in their defense. The cry of the people is for blood. . . . If public opinion is to outweigh public justice, and a man is to be executed by acclamation, the French Revolution and the tragedy of Notre Dame are not far distant.

Newspaper hearsay or any other kind of testimony, except that which is sworn to within these walls, is worse than idle. . . . A verdict thus founded would be a verdict on suspicion, and *a thousand suspicions do not amount to one proof.* The fact of guilt must be proved . . . in this house and nowhere else, on the sanctity of an oath, and by the personal knowledge of the witnesses.

How many persons have been suspected of this murder — aye, and believed to be guilty? How many false hypotheses have been stated? How many persons falsely accused? The servant has been suspected, and many facts found to justify the suspicion. Mrs. Beckford has been accused of unfastening the window. Joseph Beckford, Benjamin Selman, Daniel Chase, and even Stephen White — the private prosecutor for whom it seemed the murder was committed because he received the greatest benefit . . . all have been examined, and some have been imprisoned until it was found that no accusation could be sustained by the conjectural testimony upon which they had been suspected.

And now, prison birds who have just flown from their cage are brought into court to fasten the crime on the prisoner at the bar. Mr. Palmer, the principal witness, was once charged with this crime and was long imprisoned for the offense; and lately he has been discharged without any reason assigned and made a felonious witness to swear away the life of the prisoner.

The Constitution that governs us is not altogether form; it is substance; and it deems everyone innocent until he is proved guilty. The evidence brought against the prisoner must be conclusive. The government is bound to prove, beyond all doubt, that the prisoner is guilty in the manner and form in which they have charged him. ... The government is bound to prove clearly that the prisoner was present, aiding, abetting, and assisting at the time of the murder, so as to make him — if guilty at all — a principal in the second degree.

The government wishes the jury to infer that an original conspiracy was formed, and that Richard and George Crowninshield, together with Joseph and the prisoner, were parties to it, that the murder was committed by some of them, that the weapon was found and that it was the same weapon with which the murder was committed, and that the defendant went to the place for the avowed purpose of committing the murder. They also show a combination of a great number of facts, but all of them avail nothing unless they bring you irresistibly to the conclusion that the prisoner gave the blow, or was present, aiding and abetting the murderer.[15]

The government have attempted to prove by means of two witnesses that a conspiracy existed. They have claimed that a conversation between the two Knapps was heard by Leighton, and a conversation between the two Crowninshields by Palmer. The evidence of the plan and motive rests altogether upon Palmer. If you discredit the testimony of these two witnesses, the conspiracy falls to the ground. The defense intends to show that these witnesses are not entitled to credit. Palmer is all but an incompetent witness. The law says that if a man is convicted of an infamous crime, he shall not be allowed to raise his voice in a court of justice. But Palmer was convicted just across the line from Massachusetts, and his evidence cannot be excluded. The jury will consider, however, what credit is due him.

[15] Gardiner's statement of the law is not sound, here and in other places.

Their whole evidence, if it proves anything against the prisoner, shows that he was an accessory before the fact.

Evidence is brought to show that a part of those engaged in the conspiracy were seen on that night, at about that time, near the place where the murder was committed. Witnesses are called, after the lapse of a long time, to say that the persons they saw were the individuals implicated. After suspicion is directed against the defendants — after they are told that these are the persons — the witnesses remember that they saw them within about a week. The whole tendency of the evidence, if true, is to prove that the prisoner was an accessory before the fact. . . .

Nothing is more dangerous and nothing is more liable to error than testimony regarding the identity of persons. Identification in this case depends upon the testimony of a number of persons. Mr. Mirick saw a person at a post whom he did not know but who was about the same size as the prisoner. It is safe to say that there are three hundred persons of the same size in this courtroom right now; the prisoner's stature is common and not at all remarkable. Peter E. Webster saw two persons going down Howard Street away from the murder; he saw no face, he saw nothing but a camblet cloak, from which the jury are asked to infer that one was the prisoner. Mr. Southwick is the only person who swears positively that he saw the prisoner, yet he saw no face; he saw a man in a cloak whom he supposed to be the prisoner. The evidence will show that it was probably not the prisoner.

If, however, you believe that the prisoner was the man seen by these witnesses, you are forced to the conclusion that he was not the man who struck the blow. The question then is, Was John Francis Knapp *constructively* present? Even of he was in Brown Street, he was not present except by a mere fiction of law. To make a man constructively present, he must be in a capacity to render assistance, and must be there for that purpose, and must actually assist.

The defense proposes to introduce evidence to show that the man seen in Brown Street was not the prisoner at the bar, that he was in a different place during the evening, and that Brown Street was not a place in which aid and assistance could be given to the murderer.

Monday, August 9

Evidence for the Defense[16]

John P. Saunders

The witness explained the map he had made of the territory near Captain White's house. He said the distance from Brown Street to Essex Street through White's garden was about 295 feet.

Captain Daniel Bray

I have stated that when I first saw the second man, he was in the middle of the street. I have not examined to see which way he could have come from. I have not examined to see if I could see a man coming round the corner. If he had come from the north side of the arched gate of the Common, I could have seen where he came from, but not if he came from the south side. There are two gates or turnstiles on each side of the arch. I could not have seen him coming round the corner if he kept close to the fence. I don't think I saw him the moment he might have been in sight. I could have seen him fifteen feet farther south than I did. There are several paths across the Common leading to both sides of the arch. I first saw this man 150 to 200 feet off. I could not tell whether he came round the corner or across the Common.

Cross-examination. From where I was I could see anyone come out either side the arched gate. If the man had come round the corner on the sidewalk, I could not have seen him until he was within four or five feet of the other man at the post. I don't think I saw him when he first came in sight. The post is ten or fifteen feet from the northwest corner of the house.[17]

Joseph Burns

Frank Knapp's dirk had a plated handle which looked like silver. I am not certain whether or not it had a guard; it had a crosspiece on the handle. It was not drawn. I don't know how long the handle was. I will tell what I know and will not tell what I don't know.

In cross-examination the witness said, "When I thinks, I don't know."

---

[16] In 1830 an accused person was not permitted to testify in his own defense.
[17] This passage is obscure. In his earlier testimony Bray said that the post was "at the northeast corner of my house, next to the bounds between my house and that of Mrs. Andrews." Bray's sense of distance was not good since he places the second man anywhere from 100 to 200 feet away when first seen.

William H. Allen

I have known Frank Knapp from childhood and have been intimate with him. The dirk exhibited is the same that Frank had. Mr. Newhall made it for him or sold it to him. I never saw Frank with any other.

Benjamin Leighton

Frank's dirk had a gilt handle with a little jog to prevent its going into the scabbard. The one exhibited looks like it.

Dudley S. Newhall

The witness was a jeweler. He identified the dirk exhibited as the one he had sold to Frank Knapp the day before the Wenham robbery.

William P. Peircel

My usual dress at the time of the murder was similar to the prisoner's. It was a plaid cloak and a black glazed cap. This was a common dress; almost all the young men wore glazed caps. Before the murder it was not usual to wear dirks. Since that time many use sword canes, but I don't know as to dirks.

Two tailors, *Asa Wiggin* and *Israel Ward,* swore that camlet cloaks were much worn the preceding winter. Mr. Ward said that in January he had made Frank Knapp "a frock coat of olive or dark brown color, single breasted, snug about the body and quite full in the skirts."

Stephen Osborne, a hatter, testified that within the last year he had sold 200 glazed and leather caps, but that only two or three dozen of them had a star on the top and were trimmed with fur like the one exhibited in court. The witness said that this cap was like the one that he had sold the prisoner. [Compare this with Southwick's testimony.]

Gardiner requested that John Palmer be brought into court. He then read copies of two warrants against Palmer. On the first of these warrants Palmer had been arrested and committed for further examination upon the same charges that were made against the prisoner. By the second warrant he was committed by the magistrate to answer to the same charge at the present term of this court.

Gardiner also presented a copy of the records of the court of common pleas, held at Belfast, at which J. C. R. Palmer, Jr., and James

Premble were convicted of breaking open the store of Liberty D.
Wetherbee at Belmont, Maine, and sentenced to two years hard
labor in the State prison.

William Babb

I keep a house of entertainment, called the Halfway House, on
the Salem turnpike between Salem and Boston.

I know Palmer but I have not seen him from the time he was at
my house until last Friday. I am not certain when he was at my
house; my impression is that he came there on the ninth of April
and went away on the morning of the tenth. I recollect the time
because I was discharging a man, George Green, who was signing
a receipt when Palmer asked for his bill. I heard of the murder on
the seventh. Palmer never slept there at any other time, unless he
got into the house unknown to me. My impression is that it was
after the murder that he slept there. I am not positive that I had
heard of the murder before. I know that it was the ninth because
I had a man, George Green, who took too much, and I turned him
away, and he signed a receipt the next morning. Palmer came out
while he was signing and asked for his bill and said he had no
money. It was at that time, I think, and the receipt is dated
the tenth.

Q. Where is Green now? A. I believe he's kivered up in the earth,
and I presume he's dead.

Palmer called himself George Crowninshield and left with me a
plaid silk handkerchief marked with that name; and offered me a
note for sixty-one and one-half cents, signed George Crowninshield.
He said that he would be along in a day or two and pay the bill. I
said, "You don't resemble the family. I know Richard very well,
but you may be a younger brother." He said it might be the case.
I don't know what became of the note.

Cross-examination. The receipt I left at my house. I saw it last
Friday. I can't swear that the receipt was dated the tenth, and if it
were, I can't swear that this was right. But I am positive that it
reads the tenth. The time of day was 7:00 or 8:00 P. M. when
Palmer came there; and it was after seven in the morning, after
the usual time of going to work, that he went away. I can't fix the
time any nearer. He went to the east.

Thomas P. Vose, a commissary of the State prison at Thomaston,
identified Palmer as a former prisoner at the State prison.

James W. Webster

I live in Belfast, Maine. I have known Palmer these eight years. As to his general reputation for truth, I don't think he has any at all. I have always heard a bad character of him. I have heard perhaps a hundred people say that he would not be believed at all in any case in which he was interested. His general character is not good.

Mr. Southwick was recalled to the courtroom to hear the testimony of the next witness.

Ebenezer Shillaber

I have had a conversation with Mr. Southwick respecting the man in Brown Street. I inquired of him, after the arrest of the Knapps, about the men he saw in Brown Street. He told me he recollected seeing a young man there; that he went into Bray's house with him and that after having got there they saw another join the first. Mr. Southwick said that he could not see so well as Bray could. He said that he thought that the man who came from Newbury Street was taller than the man who was in Brown Street.

I don't recollect whether Mr. Southwick gave me any description of the person whom he saw in Brown Street. I asked him whether, for all he knew, the person who came from Newbury Street might not have been Francis Knapp, and the person in Brown Street Richard Crowninshield. He said he could not tell, but for aught he knew, it might be so.

Cross-examination. I was counsel for Richard and George Crowninshield when I made the inquiry.

Gardiner said he should now endeavor to show where George Crowninshield was at the time he was supposed to be engaged in the murder. He recapitulated to the jury the evidence of the government relative to this point.[18]

John Needham

I saw George Crowninshield in South Fields on the night of the murder. The first time was about seven o'clock at the news room at Pendergrass's.

---

[18] The defense gives George an alibi to show that he was not in Salem that night as an accomplice, but as one engaged in his ordinary pursuits and in collecting a debt. We omit most of the evidence, but include Needham's testimony because it exhibits Webster as a humorous cross-examiner. It must be admitted, however, that his humor often reminds one of the old rhyme—
>The sportive ox and festive cow
>Hilarious hop from bow to bow.

Richard Crowninshield paid the rent for that room. Chase and a young man introduced to me as Colonel Selman came in; in a few minutes George came in. They stayed there about half or three-quarters of an hour and they all went away together. I saw them there again between nine and ten o'clock. George was there all the time except about ten minutes that I was out. Joseph Burns, William Austin, and John Osborn were also there and stayed some time. George, Austin, Osborn, and myself came away together. I said that I was going home the nearest way, and George said, "I'm going to Mary's and will go with you." When I got to the gate of our house at the corner of High and Summer Streets, we parted. This was before eleven, because I went to bed immediately and soon after heard the clock strike eleven.

Cross-examination. Q. (Webster) What had you to read at this news room; you took many modern periodicals I suppose? A. Yes sir, we had some papers from Alabama and one from Cincinnati and the *Truth Teller* from New York.

Q. What contribution did the subscribers make for the privilege of reading these periodicals? A. We never paid anything.

Q. How were these works paid for? A. Richard Crowninshield furnished them.

Q. Did you ever play at any games in that news room? A. Sometimes just for diversion we played a game of all fours.

Q. Did you play any other games? A. No sir. We couldn't play at loo, for we had no blue beans.

Q. Then you played all fours just for diversion, and would have played loo if you had had some blue beans? Anything else? A. No sir.

Q. Who kept that room? A. I don't know, sir.

Q. Now, did you not keep that room yourself? A. No sir.

Q. What did you do there? A. I made a fire and filled the lamps and cleaned up the room.

Q. You took care of the room then; that is what I call keeping it. Who paid you? A. Richard Crowninshield.

Q. What did he give you? A. He satisfied me.

Q. What did he give you to satisfy you? A. When he thought I wanted anything, he gave me a little change.

Q. When did Richard hire this room for the amusement of his friends? A. I suppose it was the first of February; the quarter was out on the first of May.

Q. Why did he give up the room? A. After he was suspected of being concerned in this murder, he said he told David Foley, the owner, that he wouldn't have anything to do with the room if the sheriffs were coming over to ransack it and turn everything upside down.

Q. Did you ever see such a diversion there as props? A. Why — I shouldn't be willing, unless it's the judge's request, I shouldn't like to answer that question.

Q. Well, sir, as you see no impropriety in it, and as the judges do not, please answer my question. A. There is a game called props.

Q. Now sir, was not this a gambling house and nothing else? A. No sir.

Q. What do you call a gambling house? A. I call a gambling house a cheating house.

Q. Then you always played fair at this house? A. We didn't bet high enough to gamble, only fourpence halfpenny or something like that.

Q. Was there not liquor kept in this news room? A. Sometimes.

Several other witnesses were called to confirm certain details of Needham's direct testimony.

Matthew Newport swore that George Crowninshield, Daniel Chase, and Benjamin Selman came to his victualling cellar between eight and nine to inquire for John McGlue.

Colonel Benjamin Selman

I came from Marblehead to see Clark Reed about six o'clock on the night of the murder. Chase came with me, and since I could not find Mr. Reed, Chase proposed going to see George who owed him some money. We went to Danvers, and George said he wanted to see Mr. McGlue to get some money. George went with us in a chaise. We stopped at the tavern opposite Dustin's in Danvers, and then came to Salem.

Mr. Selman described his evening in Salem. He had seen George often until they parted at 10:15.

Nathaniel Phippen Knapp

I went to the prison with Mr. Colman. After having been in Joseph's cell I went to my brother Frank's. In the entry between the two Mr. Colman said, "Mr. Knapp, I wish you not to disturb the club. I will get a gentleman for a witness and go and get it myself, for my own security."

I assured my brother and said, Mr. Colman says he has been assured by the committee that they have evidence amply sufficient to convict your brother and yourself. Pamler has applied for a pardon on condition of being a witness, and that promise has been dispatched to him from the officers of the government; the messenger will pass through town this evening in the mail stage, and if one of you does not confess before the mail passes through it will be too late. I told Frank that if either would confess, the committee would stop that message and apply for a pardon in favor of him or Joe, whichever it might be. I told him also that the sub-committee had severally assured my father that Palmer knew every circumstance connected with the transaction, and that the only chance to save his sons was to induce them to confess.

I then asked Mr. Colman if what I had related as coming from him was not true. He said yes, and then went on to state to Frank, "I have seen your brother and have made these assurances and offered him a pardon in case he would be willing to confess. I also assured him that if he committed anything to me in confidence, it never should be revealed unless he should choose to become a witness. I am authorized by the committee to offer this pardon to either of you."

I then said, "Mr. Colman thinks that Joseph had better confess, for if you should be convicted after his confession, you would have a greater chance of pardon than he would." I asked Mr. Colman if he did not think so. He said, "Yes, undoubtedly. Your youth will be very much in your favor; your case will excite great sympathy, especially if it should appear that you were persuaded to what you did by your elder brother. But I don't insist on the preference; I leave that for you to settle between you."

My brother hesitated. Mr. Colman said, "You know the conditions; if you stand a trial you will both inevitably be condemned. If either of you chooses to confess, he will save himself. If Joseph confesses and you should be convicted, you will have a good chance of pardon; but if Joseph should be convicted on your confession, his chance would not be so good. At all events, your chance will be much greater than if you stand trial and are convicted upon Palmer's testimony." He turned to Frank, saying he had but a few moments to choose. My brother said, "I have nothing to confess;

it is a hard case, but if it be as you say, Joseph may confess if he pleases. I shall stand trial."

I recollect nothing more that passed.

Q. (Gardiner) Was there anything said about the club in Frank Knapp's cell? A. Nothing.

Q. Before entering the cell, you stated Mr. Colman requested you not to remove the club? A. I did.

Q. Had Mr. Colman been to the cell of Joseph more than once that day? A. He told me that he had, two or three times.

Q. Was anything said in the conversation about the time the murder was committed? A. Nothing.

Q. Do you remember at what time Mr. Colman stated to you that he had learned something from Joseph? A. Between his second and third visits.

Q. Did he go at the request of yourself or your family? A. No sir, it was against our wishes.

Q. After Mr. Colman came out of the cell, what did he say? A. He said he was going to see the committee. At another interview about eight o'clock, he told me that he was going to Boston with Mr. Treadwell to see the attorney general.

Q. When did you next see Mr. Colman? A. The next morning on the road to Boston, this side of the Halfway House, about ten o'clock.

Q. What took place? A. He told me he had seen the attorney general and showed me a promise of pardon, or a nolle prosequi, in case confession should be made. . . . I told him I could not go back to Salem with him, but wished that he would not go to see Joseph without me. He said he would wait till I returned.

He then said, "I am not sure whether I got the story of the club from Joseph or Frank, but I believe from Joseph." I told him that he did not get it from Frank, for he said nothing about it. He then said he did not know but he had been misunderstood about this by Mr. Stephen White, and begged me to take a note to Mr. White to correct it. I took the note and rode to Boston. I went to the Senate chamber but did not see Mr. White. I was hurried and I returned and gave the note, I think, to Mr. Colman.[19]

---

[19] Mr. Colman later admitted that he wrote this note. His memory of the interviews with Frank and Joe should have been better on the day after they took place than in August, yet he swears at the trial that Frank told him where to find the club.

I arrived in town at three o'clock, I should think, and went to Joseph's cell and asked admission of Mr. Colman who was in the cell. He refused, and said I could not come in. Mr. Brown, the jailer stood at the door. He allowed me to ask him a question, but would not admit me. Mr. Colman said, "You cannot come in now for I have not finished my business," or words to that effect. He said he would meet me at my office as soon as he had finished.

He came to my office about five o'clock on Saturday, bringing with him a paper. I asked him to show me what he had in the paper. He said he could not except in the presence of witnesses. . . . He said he would be at Mr. Barstow's and he would send for me.

In a little while Mr. Barstow's son came for me and I went. I found Mr. Colman there with Mr. Barstow, Mr. Merrill, and Mr. Saltonstall. Mr. Colman then said he could not show it to me, for the committee thought it not proper that I should see it. . . .

I met him again on Monday morning in his chaise in Central Street. He stopped and beckoned to me and said, "You may make yourself easy on the subject I mentioned on the road to Boston; I have seen Mr. White and have not been misunderstood."

The next conversation was at my office, three or four weeks subsequently, as much as a week after the death of Richard Crowninshield. He said, "I have called, Mr. Knapp, to refresh my recollection about the interview I had with your brothers. I may be called as a witness, and I wish to state the truth accurately." He alluded to the club. He said, "You may remember your brother Frank spoke of the club," and I denied that Frank had said anything about it. Mr. Colman said, "Well, you will probably be a witness and have an opportunity to give your account of it." He was somewhat excited. The conversation was stopped when Mr. Dexter opened the door. Mr. Dexter endeavored to reason with him. Mr. Colman said he had been contradicted. He said he surely did not get it from Joseph, and he would go and ask him. Mr. Dexter told him he was excited and offered to go with him. Mr. Colman said he would get witnesses and call for Mr. Dexter, which he did.

Q. About what time did your father fail? A. The assignment was dated on the seventh.

Q. Do you know whether your brother rode more at one time than another. A. He rode less after the failure. I cautioned him about it in consequence of the failure. . . .

The witness was shown a cap and a dirk. He said, My brother

wore a glazed cap like this in every particular. I remember the dirk. I never saw my brother have any other.

Q. Where were you on the sixth of April? A. I was up all night preparing my father's assignment. I went home at one. I left my own office after nine with my father and went to Mr. Waters' house, where I stayed till a few minutes before ten, whence I went with Mr. Waters to his office in Washington Street, where we stayed but a few minutes. From there we came down Essex Street to go to Mr. Waters' house, stopping at our house on the way for an umbrella. It rained when we left Mr. Waters' office and when I got to the house. . . . I stayed at Mr. Waters' till one o'clock. I then went home and found my father had himself just come in.

I saw nothing of the prisoner during the night. I saw him at about eight in the morning of the seventh of April. His usual hour of retiring was ten o'clock; he was the most regular person in the family in this respect.

My father's house is in Essex Street a few rods below Newbury Street. On my way from Mr. Waters' house to his office, Mr. Waters and I passed by Mr. White's house and observed a light in his chamber. I think I called Mr. Waters' attention to it.

Cross-examination.[20] Q. (Webster) Where were you on the night of the sixth of April when you heard the clock strike ten? A. Near the wharves by Derby Street.

Q. Where did you go from the prisoner's cell with Mr. Colman? A. I went from Joseph' cell.

Q. How did you and he meet at Joseph's cell? A. We went together to make the statements which the committee had made to Mr. Colman, or to treat of that business.[21]

Q. What was that business? A. Concerning Joseph making a confession.

Q. What day was it? A. It was Friday afternoon. I had not been to the cell of either brother before.

Q. Did you and Mr. Colman both go into Joseph's cell? A. We did.

Q. What was done there? A. A conversation was had about confessing.

[20] "Notwithstanding the torture of the situation in which he was placed, he gave his evidence with great self-possession."—James Gordon Bennett.
[21] Mr. Colman testified that Phippen came later.

Q. Did Joseph agree to confess? A. The witness said he did not recollect whether Joseph had agreed to confess.

Q. You say you went to treat of that business; can't you recollect whether that treaty terminated one way or the other? A. I can't recollect. It was not positively agreed.

Q. Was it partially agreed? A. It was agreed on certain conditions.

Q. What were they? A. (After a long pause) They were that he should have the preference.

Q. Was it agreed that he should have the preference? A. No sir.

Q. What was his having the preference to depend upon? A. If his brother chose that he should have that preference.

Q. If his brother did not choose, what then? A. I don't know.

Q. Do you mean that it was understood that he should not be State's witness unless Frank consented? A. Mr. Colman told him that unless one confessed, both would be condemned.

Q. Did it depend upon Frank's consent? A. I understood it so.

Q. At whose instance had you gone to Joseph's cell? A. At my own.

Q. Did you ask Mr. Colman to go with you? A. He said he should go and I asked him to let me go with him.

Webster read to the witness the statements he had just made and asked if he wished to alter them.

Q. You went to Frank's cell then under this understanding, that Joseph was not to be State's witness unless Frank consented? A. Yes sir.

Q. Did you go to the prison with Mr. Colman? A. I did.

Q. Do you remember whether you met him at the prison? A. I can't recollect where I met him. I went into the prison with him.

Q. Where was it your purpose to go when you left Joseph's cell? A. To Frank's cell.

Q. Where was it Mr. Colman's purpose to go? A. I presume he intended to go out of the prison.

Q. At whose request did he go with you to Frank's cell? A. As I went in, I thought he desired to enter and I asked him if he would go in.

Q. For what purpose did you go from Joseph's to Frank's? A. To see if he had any objection to taking a trial and suffering his brother to accept the offer of Mr. Colman.

Q. When and where were you to meet Mr. Colman to report Frank's answer? A. I recollect no appointment.

Q. What were you to do if Frank assented? A. I don't know that I was to do anything.

Q. How was Mr. Colman to find it out? A. I do not know.

Q. And yet you swear that you went there to ascertain the fact? A. I went to learn what Frank had to say.

Q. What were you to do when you had learned whether Frank consented or not? A. I don't recollect.

Q. You knew that Mr. Colman was going to the attorney general when he was informed of that fact; how was he to be informed?[22] A. No answer.

Q. Did you know before you left Joseph's cell that Mr. Colman proposed to go to the attorney general that night? A. I don't remember whether he mentioned it before he went to Frank's cell.

Q. How long was it after you left Joseph's cell before you got to Frank's? A. Very few minutes.

Q. What conversation passed between you and Mr. Colman in those two or three minutes? A. About the club.

Q. Had you been in Joe's cell all the time with Mr. Colman? A. I had.

Q. You heard all the conversation, did you? A. Yes sir.

Q. How long were you there? A. I cannot recollect, ten or fifteen minutes perhaps.

Q. Did you hear it agreed at this interview that Joe should be State's evidence? A. That was the time when he agreed on the conditions I have mentioned. I considered it agreed.

Q. What made you consider it agreed? A. He asked me to go and see Frank about it.

Q. Did you hear it agreed that Joe should turn State's witness? A. There was such an understanding.

Q. You say this understanding was to depend on Frank's subsequent consent, do you? A. I do.

Q. And if he did not assent? A. Then I suppose it was to be offered to him.

Q. Was that the agreement — that if Frank did not consent that Joe should be State's witness, he should be State's witness him-

---

[22] This question, though repeated several times, is not very important in itself. It unreasonably assumes that even in the excitement and worry of the moment everything would have been carefully arranged. Webster is using the question to embarass and confuse the witness.

self? A. I understood that Joe was determined not to assent to the proposition unless Frank were willing.

Q. How was it arranged that Mr. Colman should find out about Frank's attitude when you left Joe's cell? A. I don't recollect.

Q. Where were you when Mr. Colman told you not to take the club? A. Before the door of Joseph's cell.

Q. Did you hear anything said about the daggers in Frank's cell? A. Nothing.

Q. Did you hear anything said about it being a hard case for Joe to have the privilege of being State's witness, since the whole thing was done for his benefit? A. I did not.

Q. Did he say it was hard for Joe to have the privilege? A. He said nothing about that; he said it was hard to choose.

Q. Will you swear that he did not?[23] A. I will not swear that he did or did not; I don't recollect.

Q. Was anything said to that amount? A. I do not recollect.

Q. Will you swear that nothing was said about melting the daggers? A. I will swear that I did not hear anything.

Q. Was there any secret conversation? A. No sir.

Q. Have you any doubt but that you heard all that was said? A. No sir.

Q. Did Frank say he told Joe it was a silly business? A. No sir.

Q. That he told Joe it would bring them into trouble? A. No sir.

Q. Anything about the time at which Frank went home on the sixth? A. No sir.

Q. How near were you to the prisoner? A. I was sitting beside my brother. Mr. Colman stood up.

Q. And nothing was said about the time of night at which the murder was committed? A. No sir.

Q. I want you to state these matters over again as you mean to stand by them. You have taken back all that you once said. When you went into Frank's cell did you tell him that Joseph had determined to confess? A. I don't remember; I have no knowledge of having said so.

Q. Can you swear that you did not say words to that effect? A. I shall not swear that I did not.

Q. Did Frank say that it was hard that Joseph should have the privilege of confessing? A. I will not swear that it was not said.

[23] Webster is taking advantage of the fact that a witness, although he is swearing all the time, will in many cases flinch when asked, "Will you swear?" Coming from Daniel Webster, the question was probably terrifying.

Q. Did not Frank tell Mr. Colman he went home that night after the murder? A. He did not.

Q. About the time the murder was committed? A. There was none.

Q. Did Mr. Colman ask him at what time it was committed? A. I think not.

Q. About the dirks? A. Nothing was said about them, and nothing about the club.

Q. Did you hear anybody say anything to Mr. Colman that day about the bludgeon? A. I did not; I had it from him.

Q. Where did he tell you? A. In the entry.

Q. You had heard nothing about it in Joe's cell? A. I am not certain.

Q. Then how came he to say he trusted to your honor not to get it? A. Because he wished to get it himself.

Q. How came he to make such a remark, implying that you knew where it was? A. He might have supposed I knew.

Q. How did you understand him then, when he said he relied upon your honor not to take the weapon? Where did you get your knowledge that there was a club under the steps? A. I think I must have got it from somebody in Joseph's cell.

Q. Then you heard it mentioned by someone — where was it? A. I do not recollect whether I heard it there or from Mr. Colman.

Q. Did you derive this information before you went into the cell? A. I do not recollect.

Q. Then you heard it there? A. I think I must.

Q. Did you learn there under what particular steps it was? A. I never knew under which flight.

Q. Where did you go from Frank's cell? A. To my office.

Q. Where did Mr. Colman go? A. He said he would go and see the committee.

Q. When did he say he should go and see the attorney general? A. After we came from Frank's cell.

Q. If it was understood that Frank's assent was necessary, how came it that Mr. Colman was not to go to Frank? A. I was to go myself.

Q. Was anything said in Frank's cell about the person who perpetrated the murder or how many there were in the chamber at the time? A. There was not.

Q. Do you know what Mr. Colman has testified? A. Not a syllable.

Q. What did you expect him to testify? A. The truth.

Q. Did you expect your testimony would differ from his? A. I did in the point about the club.

Q. Mr. Colman told your brother that his only hope was in confessing? A. He did.

Q. Mr. Colman said he was authorized to offer the pardon to either? Did he offer it to Frank? A. He did.

Q. Did he say, "If you don't choose, Joseph shall not be State's witness?" A. He said he left it to them to agree.

Q. Had it been agreed that Joseph should have the privilege? A. It depended upon Frank's consent.

Q. You met Mr. Colman on the turnpike on Saturday morning and he thought he might have been misunderstood by Mr. Stephen White about the club. Did you not ask Mr. Colman not to tell that Frank had informed where the club was? A. No sir.

Q. Did you read the note he wrote? A. I did not.

Q. Did you look upon it as a matter of some importance to correct Mr. White's misapprehension if there was one? A. Yes sir.

Q. What did you know about your father's house having been broken open? A. I heard something about it.

Q. Did you hear the prisoner say anything? A. He said he found the doors and desks open.

Re-direct examination. Q. (Gardiner) What business led you to Boston on the day you met Mr. Colman? A. I went to see counsel.

Q. What pressed you to get back to Salem? A. I wanted to see Mr. Colman before he went to see my brothers.

Q. What church does the defendant belong to? A. Dr. Flint's.

Re-cross-examination. Q. (By Webster) What was the haste [in returning to Salem]? A. I wished to go with Mr. Colman.

Q. Were you afraid to trust Mr. Colman? A. No sir; they had no counsel and I chose to be present.

Q. Did you come with directions from counsel to instruct them to say nothing? A. I did not.

Q. Did Mr. Colman agree not to see your brother till you came back? A. He did.

Q. Which one? A. Joseph, I think.

Q. What reason did you give? A. Not any; I had my reason.

Q. What reason had you for wishing Mr. Colman should not see

Joe till you came back? A. Because I wished to see the business conducted fairly.

Q. Then merely for your own satisfaction you wished to be present when the pledge was offered to Joe? A. Yes sir.

Q. And on your return you found Mr. Colman there? A. I did.

William F. Gardiner

I live in the next house to Captain White's. I passed there twenty or thirty minutes after ten. I was coming from Mr. Daland's, which is the next house to Captain White's on the other side and on the corner of Essex and Newbury Streets. There was a party there that night which was just breaking up at that time. I heard no noise nor anything which attracted my attention. Mr. Daland's windows look into Captain White's front yard. There were three persons with me.

Stephen D. Fuller

The plan made by me is correct. The distance from Essex Street to Brown Street through Captain White's garden is about three hundred feet.

There is a small passage through from Captain White's garden to Brown Street, but the fence at one end is 7½ feet high.

Nothing could be seen of White's house from the ropewalk steps, nor from the post by Mrs. Shepard's house, nor from the post by Captain Bray's house, nor from any part of the space between the two posts on the south side of Brown Street with one exception: through a small opening between Mr. Potter's and Mr. Henderson's houses, a part of the rear of Captain White's house could be seen, but not the part in which he slept.

Grafton G. Page

I saw the prisoner on the sixth of April about seven o'clock in Essex Street near the Salem Hotel. Forrester, Burchmore, Balch, and I were together and he asked us into the hotel to take some refreshments. We stayed there about five minutes, then came out and I left them.

I am a student of Harvard College. Glazed caps were at that time worn by almost all the students who belong there. Our caps were mostly bought in Boston. Sixteen of my Salem classmates have them. Camlet cloaks are also very common among students.

Cross-examination. Q. (Webster) What makes you recollect that the night you met Frank Knapp was the night of the murder? A. I heard of the murder the next morning and remembered where I was.

Q. What made you remember? A. I accounted to myself next morning, as it was natural for a person after such an event to think where he was.

Q. Have you ever had any doubt about it being the night before the murder that you saw the prisoner? A. I had when I was first called upon.

Q. If you fixed the time in your own mind the next moring, how came your doubts to arise? A. I didn't recollect at first.

Q. Have you ever said you were not positive about the evening? A. No sir.

Q. When you were first summoned as a witness, did you say you were not positive? A. I said I wished some time for consideration.

Q. Very well, Mr. Page, we will not detain you from your studies. A. It's vacation, sir.

The witness subsequently stated that he came from college on Saturday, spent the evening at home, that he could not have met Frank on Sunday evening, that it must have been Monday or Tuesday evening, and that it was cloudy.

Moses P. Balch

I live on Lynde Street. On the evening of the murder I think, but I am not positive, that I was with the prisoner and Burchmore and Page and Forrester. I first saw him in Essex Street between six and seven o'clock. I was with him three-quarters of an hour. I saw him again between eight and nine, he came into Remond's in Derby Square. Burchmore, I think, and Forrester and Page were with me when he came in. We left the prisoner at the corner of Court and Church Streets about ten o'clock to go home.[24] I was with him all the time from nine until near ten. Forrester left us at the corner of the Franklin Building.

Cross-examination. Q. (Webster) Do you undertake to say that this took place on the evening before or after the murder of Mr. White? A. I cannot say positively that this was on the night of the murder. It was either on Monday or Tuesday evening. I cannot tell any nearer.

[24] Court Street appears to have been the older name of Washington Street. The Franklin Building was at the northeast corner of Essex and Newbury Streets, the present site of Hotel Hawthorne.

GARDINER: What was the weather on Tuesday evening? A. The evening on which we were walking was dark and cloudy.

Q. (Webster) What were you doing at Remond's? A. Smoking.

Q. What sort of a place is it? A. A sort of oyster bar.

Q. How are you able to fix the time at which Frank left you at ten o'clock? A. When I went home all the folks were abed.

Q. And because when you went home all the family were in bed, that makes you swear right off that it was ten o'clock when you left Frank, does it? A. It was after ten.

Zachariah Burchmore, Jr.[25]

On the evening preceding the murder, I went with the prisoner and Page and Forrester to the Salem Hotel about seven o'clock. We stayed there about a quarter of an hour, and the prisoner left us. About an hour after, Forrester, Balch, and I were sitting and smoking at Remond's when he came in—about half-past eight. We all went out together just before nine. I don't remember whether Forrester went out with us or before. We walked in Essex Street about half an hour, and I left about half-past nine at the Franklin Building or opposite.

Cross-examination. Q. (Webster) What night was it? A. To the best of my belief it was on the night of the murder.

Q. Was it on the night of the murder? A. I only remember by its being the night I went to the hotel with Page and Balch.

Q. How does that make you recollect? A. I never went there with them at any other time.

Re-direct examination. Q. (Gardiner) Are you sure whether it was before or after the murder? A. No sir; I believe it was the same night.

Re-cross-examination. Q. (Webster) Can you say anything more concerning the time on which you saw the prisoner than that it was the same evening you were with Page and Forrester? A. I can only recollect that it was an the evening that we were in the hotel that I saw the prisoner. I don't remember what the weather was. It is my impression that it was the night of the murder.

---

[25] Hawthorne pays a tribute to Burchmore in the introduction to *The Scarlet Letter*.

John Forrester, Jr.[26]

I took a walk with the prisoner, I think, on the evening of the murder. I met him in company with Balch, Burchmore, and Page, and was introduced to him. This was about seven o'clock. I was with him about twenty or thirty minutes. We went to the Salem Hotel. He left us and I saw him again in about an hour at Remond's.

Cross-examination. Q. (Webster) What place is Remond's? A. It's an oyster shop.

Q. Did you find spirits there for sale? A. Yes sir.

Q. Were you drinking? A. No sir.

Q. What were you doing? A. We had been eating.

Q. Were you smoking? A. Yes sir.

Q. And you were in a hotel drinking at seven o'clock in the evening, were you? A. Yes sir.

Q. How do you fix the time on which this took place? A. I recollect it was before the murder; it was an unpleasant evening.

Q. Do you recollect the day of the month? A. No sir.

Q. Do you know the month? A. It was in April, I believe.

Q. What part of April? I don't remember.

Q. Was it near the twenty-first or twenty-fifth? A. I don't remember.

Q. Was it nearer the end than the middle of the month? A. I don't remember, but it was before the murder.

Q. Do you remember whether it was the night before or the same night of the murder?

The witness finally concluded that he could not state whether it was the evening after, the same evening, or the evening but one before the murder. He did say, however, "I never walked with them all but once."

Captain Joseph J. Knapp[27]

I am the father of the prisoner. I made an assignment of my property on the sixth of April. I was at home that night a little before ten. I came from Mr. Waters' house in Derby Street.

[26] He was a nephew of Stephen White, of Justice Joseph Story, and of the chairman of the committee of vigilance, Dr. Gideon Barstow. He was a cousin of Nathaniel Hawthorne.

[27] The appearance of Captain Knapp (1773-1847) on the witness stand was one of the high points of the trial. Bennett said that during the examination of Captain Knapp and his son Phippen "an affecting sympathy for the peculiarity of their relative positions towards the prisoner was visible amongst the auditors."

I saw the prisoner just after ten. He entered my front northern parlor about five minutes after ten and asked me if he should bolt the door. I told him no, for Phippen was out and I should wait for him. I told him that I was very glad that he was at home in good season. He asked me if I wanted any assistance; I told him no. I asked him how the weather was and he said that it blew fresh from the east. I asked him if he knew the time, and he told me it was just ten. I did not go to bed till after two o'clock. His chamber was in the west end of the third story. There is only one staircase up to the third story. My door opens into the entry. To come out of Frank's chamber, one must pass my door.

No person moved in the house that night except Phippen when he came in. I saw Frank again the next morning between seven and eight o'clock when he came from his chamber. His usual hour of coming home was about ten, as that was the strict rule of the house. He was very regular. He will be twenty years old next month.

My son Phippen was with me until near ten. I left him at Mr. Waters' house. I again saw him about twenty or twenty-five minutes after ten when he came in to take the key. He was assisting Mr. Waters in making an assignment of my property, and he rejoined me just after one o'clock. He went to bed before I did, and at about two, immediately after he came in. I did not see either of my sons in the chamber that night.

Cross-examination. Q. (Webster) Did you see Michael Shepard that night? A. I did — last at my son's office a little after nine.

Q. You did not see him later than that? A. I did not.

Q. What place had you gone from last when you went home? A. From Mr. Waters' dwelling house. I left there about ten minutes before ten.

Q. How do you fix that time? A. I know the clock had not struck ten when I left my son with Mr. Waters.

Q. When did you see Michael Shepard next? A. The next day.

Q. Where? A. I am not certain, perhaps it was at his dwelling house in the fore part of the day.

Q. Had you any conversation with him as to Frank's being at home the preceding evening? A. No sir.

Q. When did you see him next? A. The next day at the Mercantile Insurance office.

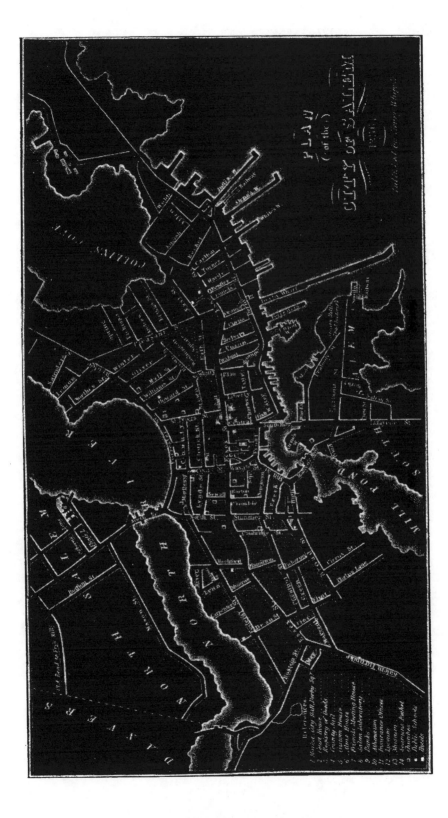

CAPTAIN JOSEPH J. KNAPP, SR.
(From Salem Marine Society painting)

Q. Had you then conversation as to the time your son came home? A. **No.**

Q. When did you see him next? A. Near the Asiatic Bank on the same evening.

Q. Had you then conversation as to the time? A. I had. I told him Frank was at home and abed before half-past ten o'clock. He asked if he could credit what was in circulation.

Q. What did he refer to — the suspicions concerning your son? A. Yes sir.

Q. The arrest had taken place then? Who had been arrested? A. Joseph and Francis.

Q. Had the Crowninshields been arrested? A. They had been before.

Q. Were the circumstances so fresh that you could recollect and tell Mr. Shepard what you have stated? A. Yes.

Q. Did you state what you knew just as you have stated it? A. No — there is some error — I have mistaken the question.

Q. What corrections do you wish to make? You have stated that you saw Mr. Shepard the evening after the murder at the Asiatic Bank. Is that right? A. Yes, I saw him.

Q. Was there anything said about the time Frank was at home the night before? A. No sir.

Q. When had you the first conversation with Michael Shepard about this? A. The day of the arrest, or the day after, I had conversation with him.

Q. Where was this conversation? A. Abreast the Oriental Insurance office.

Q. Who was present? A. No person.

Q. Was that the only conversation you ever had with him on the subject of your son's going home that night? A. It was.

Q. Who introduced it? A. Mr. Shepard. I told him Francis was at home and had retired that evening before half-past ten.

Q. Did you tell him that, as near as you could fix it, it was about five minutes after ten when Frank got home? A. Yes.

Q. Did you tell him you recollected about Frank's asking whether he should bolt the door? A. Yes.

Q. Have you had conversation with Mr. Treadwell on this subject? A. I have no knowledge of ever having had any.

Q. Did you ever tell Mr. Treadwell that you did not know what time Frank was at home; that the folks said it was about half-past ten? A. I have no knowledge of having any conversation with Mr. Treadwell.

Q. Had you been much occupied during the evening of the sixth? A. I did nothing till Mr. Shepard went away.

Q. Who was your assignee? A. Mr. Shepard. I had been talking with him that evening about it.

Q. Why were you up so late? A. To prepare a little schedule of property.

Q. What time was the assignment brought to you and executed? A. Wednesday, the day after.

James H. Savory

I work for the Salem and Boston Stage Company. I was in the street on the morning of the seventh of April. I went about twenty minutes before four o'clock from the Lafayette Coffee House to the stable in Union Street. I saw some person turn out of Captain White's yard and come up the street towards me. He came as far as Mr. Gardiner's yard and then turned and ran. I was then between the two Peabody houses. I saw him running down as far as Walnut Street. As far as I can judge, he was a man about my size. It was dark and misty. He had on a dark dress.

Silas Walcutt

I was out on the morning of the seventh between three and four. When I was going up the court, I saw a man nearly opposite Mr. Prince's house in Derby Street. He was walking easterly when he saw me. He then turned and walked back westerly seven or eight rods off. The last I saw of him was when he was just above Mr. Prince's house. He was a middling sized man. The morning was pleasant enough though rather foggy.[28]

Warwick Palfray, Jr., was recalled. He testified that he had published in his paper of Monday an account of the finding of some flannels in Danvers. They had been found on the Saturday before publication. Mr. Palfray thought that Richard Crowninshield, Jr., hung himself the next Wednesday.

John McGlue recalled. At the time of the murder he owed Richard Crowninshield, Jr., some money — perhaps thirty or forty dollars —

---

[28] If the man seen by Savory went down Walnut Street to Derby Street and walked east, he might have been the man seen by Walcutt. He would also have been near the lower end of Union Street, at the head of which was the Knapp home.

for caps and turned axletrees that had been made at the chaise factory. Richard had asked McGlue for the money before and after the murder, and on the Friday before Richard was arrested, McGlue had paid him seven dollars.

Witnesses for the Prosecution

George Wheatland

The day before the Crowninshields were arrested, Phippen came to my office. I asked him to tell me about the Wenham robbery. "Why," said Phippen, "there have been a number of circumstances, such as breaking houses, to excite suspicion. Just before starting to Wenham, which was a little before half-past eight or nine, they talked jocosely about being robbed, and said they might be attacked by robbers. Frank took a sword cane. They started and came back and made a parade about taking pistols, but went without them."

A few days after the murder, Phippen said that on the night of the murder, he saw a light in Captain White's chamber. He said he could not tell when it was he saw the light, as he passed Captain White's house four times.

At another conversation, he spoke of the interview between himself, Mr. Colman, and the prisoner. I asked Phippen why Mr. Colman went to Frank's cell. He stated that Mr. Colman was a very intimate friend of the family, and had married Joseph; that he [Phippen] went to Joseph's cell and Mr. Colman told him that he was engaged then. He said that when he went in, Joseph had been telling Mr. Colman everything, and he [Phippen] told Mr. Colman they must go and tell Frank what they had been about. He said he mentioned to Frank that Joseph was going to confess; that it would be better as Joseph had a family, and Frank, if convicted, would stand a better chance to get a pardon.

I asked Phippen if Mr. Colman had asked Frank any questions. He said he did ask some and that Frank answered. I don't recollect what the question was, or the answer. I told him that I thought it would be enough to make Frank a principal. I told him that the confession was premature. He said that it made no difference, as they had evidence enough already to convict Dick as a principal.

Cross-examination. I don't remember[29] the question Mr. Colman

---

[29] It is odd that Wheatland, a young lawyer much interested in the case, should have such a poor memory.

asked. I don't know whether it related to the weapon being found, or his being in Brown Street, but I think it did relate to one or the other. Phippen told me that Frank was in Brown Street, but I do not know whether he got it from Frank or Joe.

I do not know the reason why I thought it would prove him a principal.

I cannot swear it was one of those things which I have stated. . . . I can't positively say whether I have expressed a hope that the prisoner would be hung, but I think I have. I have said they were guilty.

Henry Colman, recalled

Q. (Webster) Did you hear the testimony of Mr. N. P. Knapp? A. I did.

Q. Was anything said which brought to your recollection anything which you wish to alter? A. Nothing.

On my return from Boston on May 29th I met Mr. Phippen Knapp near the Halfway House. He asked me if I had said anything as coming from Frank. I told him I was apprehensive I had, but I would correct it. I wrote a note in pencil to Mr. White requesting him to consider Joseph as authority for what I had told him.

Mr. Knapp desired that I would not go to see his brothers till his return. I promise to wait till one o'clock. I did wait until three, and then went.

Cross-examination. As we came out of the jail, Mr. Phippen Knapp went to the cell of Joseph to tell him, as I supposed, that Frank had assented — I thought so.

Michael Shepard

Soon after the murder of Captain White, being with Captain Knapp, Sr., I asked him whether his son now associated with the two young men who were mentioned. He replied that his son did not, that he hept remarkably good hours of late, and that on the night of the murder he was in bed at half-past ten o'clock, so Phippen told him. He did not mention the time as within his own knowledge. This was before the arrest of his own sons, and I believe before the arrests of the Crowninshields.

Q. (Webster) Did he tell you that he was at home and knew when Frank came in? A. No sir.

Q. Did he tell you that he himself came home about five minutes past ten? A. No sir.

Q. Did he tell you he knew the clock had not struck ten when he left Mr. Waters' house that evening? A. No sir.

John W. Treadwell recalled

On Friday morning, the twenty-eighth of May, I had a conversation with Captain Knapp, Sr. I then put the question, "At what time did Frank come home?" He said, "I don't know, but I believe at the usual time."

Witness for the Defense

Elizabeth Benjamin

I am a domestic at the senior Captain Knapp's.

I heard of the Wenham robbery and know that Joseph and Frank went away on the night of that robbery after dark. There was nobody at home when they went.

The Attorneys Summarize

Throughout the trial great crowds who cannot force their way into the courtroom, jam the square in front of the building. And now that all the evidence is in on both sides, everyone feels that he is about to witness the great climax of the trial in an oratorical battle between the two chief attorneys. Dexter, who started the trial as the underdog, has gained in stature; but Webster is still the favorite. During his address to the jury, the streets are crowded and the treetops as well. Inside the little courtroom it is hot and uncomfortable.

Dexter uses six hours, beginning at 3:30 in the afternoon on Tuesday, August 10, and speaking until adjournment at 7:00; the next morning he speaks from 9:00 to 11:30. Then Webster begins for the prosecution and speaks until 1:00, from 2:30 to 7:00, and from 9:00 to 11:00 the next morning, making a total of eight hours. Fourteen hours of speaking would ordinarily be hard to take, but many listeners enjoy every minute of it.

Both attorneys drew high praise from all who heard them. Dexter's argument was thought to be "worthy of his high reputation as an able reasoner and an enlightened and powerful lawyer." It was said that if Webster's argument could be accurately reported, "the annals of bar eloquence would not contain its superior."

Unfortunately, neither of the speeches was accurately reported, and it is impossible to make a satisfactory reconstruction of them.

We pass over Dexter's speech and come to a few passages from Webster's summation which students of the orator may like to compare with the speech Webster published about two months later.

It was . . . with some regret that I heard the learned counsel for the prisoner assert that I was brought here to hurry the jury beyond the evidence and against the law. Gentlemen I am sure that no man can hurry you against the law. I am satisfied that no man in this court will be permitted to hurry you against the law.

It has been said that there exists an excitement! Gentlemen there is cause for excitement. True, *you* should not be excited; you must act upon the testimony and come to the consideration of this cause with minds and consciences freed, unshackled, and unprejudiced. But there is an excitement, there ought to be an excitement which should rouse the faculties and call into operation all possible assistance, even of the dullest apprehension.

It was a cool, desperate, concerted murder. It was neither the offspring of passion nor revenge. The murderer was seduced by no lionlike temptation; all was deliberation; all was skillful.

And now that all is known it appears more atrocious than was ever apprehended. The murderer was a cool, business-like man, a calculator, a resolute and determined assassin.

The object was money, the crime murder, the price blood. The tale of silver was counted out, the price fixed. Here is the money, there is the victim — grains of silver against ounces of blood.

Under our New England example, murder has received a new character. Let the painter beware how he exhibits the murderer with the grim visage of Moloch. Let him not paint the bloodshot eye beaming with malice and red with revenge, but the cool face of an infernal spirit of another stamp about his ordinary business. Let his features be smooth and unruffled — all calmness, coolness, and deliberation. Not human nature in despair nor in paroxysms — no rushing of the blood to the face, no fiendish distortions, but calm and unagitated smoothness.

At the blessed hour when of all others repose is soundest, the murderer goes to his work. In the silence and darkness he enters the house. He does not falter, there is no trembling of the limbs, his feet sustain him. He passes through the rooms, treads lightly through the entries, ascends the stairs, arrives at the door. There is no pause. He opens it. The victim is asleep, his back is towards him, his deaf ear is uppermost, his temples bare. The moonlight plays upon his silver locks.

One blow, and the task is accomplished!

Now mark his resolution, his self-possession, his deliberate coolness! He raises the aged arm, plunges the dagger to the heart — not once but many times — replaces the arm, replaces the bedclothes, feels the pulse, is satisfied that his work is perfected and retires from the chamber. He retraces his steps. No eye has seen him, no ear has heard him. He is master of his own secret, and he escapes in secret.

That was a dreadful mistake. The guilty secret of murder never can be safe. There is no place in the universe, no corner, no cavern where he can deposit it and say it is safe. Though he take the wings of the morning and fly to the uttermost part of the seas, human murder to human vision will be known. A thousand eyes, a thousand ears are marking and listening, and thousands of excited beings are watching his bloodstained step.

The proofs of a discovery will go on. The murderer carries with him a secret which he can neither carry nor discharge. He lives at war with himself; his conscience is a domiciled accuser that cannot be ejected and will not be silent. His tormentor is inappeasable, his burden is intolerable.

The secret which he possesses, possesses him, and like the evil spirit spoken of in olden times leads him whithersoever it will. It is a vulture ever gnawing at his heart; he believes his very thoughts to be heard.

His bosom's secret overmasters him, subdues him — he succumbs. His guilty soul is relieved by suicide or confession, and suicide is confession.

Webster pronounced his concluding words in a voice and manner that one listener described as "less solemn than easy and tranquil":

I can wish nothing better for you gentlemen than that you should go home with confidence in the right discharge of your duty. It has been truly said that this will be a day long to be remembered. It will be long remembered because it is a day full of important duty to be performed or neglected. It will follow you, gentlemen, it will follow us all, as duty accomplished or as duty neglected; and if there is anything which is at all times and everywhere present, it is the consciousness that we have discharged ourselves well of every important trust. If we could take the wings of the morning and fly to the uttermost parts of the East, the sense of memory would be present there. This recollection will follow us in life, and be with us in death. It will be with us in light, and ever near us when darkness covers us. At the close of life it will be with us; and at that solemn hour, the consciousness of duty discharged or duty neglected will be there to afflict us if disregarded, or to console us if under the will of the Almighty, it has been performed.[30]

The Jury Disagrees

The cause was placed in the hands of the jury at about half-past one on the afternoon of Thursday, August 12. At ten o'clock the next day the jury reported that they had not agreed upon a verdict.

[30] The passages quoted come largely from the Dutton and Wentworth pamphlet with occasional phrases or sentences from the Boston *Courier* and from the report by Whitman.

The foreman stated that the difficulty was in the presence of Knapp, and the purpose of that presence in Brown Street. The court replied that those were matters of fact and evidence belonging to the jury. The jury was again instructed that if the defendant was in Brown Street at the time of the murder, according to a previous agreement, performing his part in aiding and abetting, he would be implicated and liable under this indictment as much as if he had been in the chamber of Captain White. If the jury were satisfied that he was there, not for the purpose of aiding and encouraging, but only for the purpose of receiving information that the deed was accomplished or from curiosity, then the law said he was not present.

At three o'clock, after more than twenty-five hours of deliberating, the foreman stated that they had been together so long that they were nearly worn out. He said that there was not the least probability that they would ever reach an agreement. In spite of the court's stern insistence that a verdict be reached, the jury maintained that it was impossible. The court then discharged the jury.

It was rumored that two and possibly three of the jury had opposed conviction, and it was not long before a newspaper of Newburyport insisted that the names of those "to whom Frank Knapp is indebted for his escape," be made public. The Boston *Courier* referred with contempt to those subtle gentlemen of the bar "who prefer that a rogue should entirely escape, than be punished contrary to technicalities." The Lynn *Record* said, "We are strongly inclined toward the belief that lawyers are productive of more evil than good, and that it would be better in all cases of deviation from the laws, that the cause should be submitted to the judge and jury, which is all that is required to obtain a just verdict."

The *New Hampshire Patriot and States Gazette* remarked: "It would be a sad joke if the immortal Daniel, who, it was said a few days since, was 'swinging a ball around his head, ready to settle it upon the forehead of his victim,' should not succeed in getting a culprit hanged who everyone knows deserves it."[31]

After the jury was discharged, the solicitor general moved that

---

[31] It is interesting to notice the silence of writers regarding the jury's disagreement. Introductory notes to the speech usually fail to mention the disagreement; it is the same with most biographies of Webster. S. L. Knapp's *Memoir of the Life of Daniel Webster*, published in 1831, did mention the disagreement, but we believe that no biography of Webster from that time until Fuess wrote his *Life of Daniel Webster* in 1930 mentions the fact that the case had to be tried the second time; yet the standard form itself shows that there were two trials.

a jury be impaneled to try the prisoner again on the same indictment.

The counsel for the prisoner objected, and moved a postponement until the regular fall term of the court because an important witness was absent and would not return from sea until that time. The motion was supported by several affidavits that stated the facts to which the witness was expected to testify.

The counsel for the government admitted that the witness, if present, would testify to the facts set forth in the affidavits, and the court then ordered that the prisoner be put on trial again immediately.

CHAPTER 8

THE SECOND TRIAL OF JOHN FRANCIS KNAPP

Saturday, August 14

ON SEVERAL OCCASIONS during the first trial the court had insisted that there be no publication of evidence until the case was closed; but before the second trial got started, several pamphlet reports of the evidence were placed on sale and a number of newspapers devoted an entire issue to the testimony that had been given. In the second trail, therefore, each witness knew what testimony had been given by others. The Yeoman's *Gazette* of Concord suggested that "street fever" infected the nerves of some of these witnesses. "A few witnesses *knew positively* facts at the second trial on which they were *silent or doubtful* at the first trial."

The government called fifteen new witnesses and the defense called twelve.

In presenting the testimony at the second trial, we shall, in the main, limit ourselves to what appears to be new evidence or variations from evidence given before. In fact, not much more was reported.

In this trial the government was represented by Solicitor General Daniel Davis and Daniel Webster; the prisoner by Franklin Dexter and William H. Gardiner.

WITNESSES FOR THE PROSECUTION

It appears that Benjamin White, John P. Saunders, Lydia Kimball, John C. R. Palmer, Jr., and William H. Allen gave the same testimony as at the first trial. We do not have Leighton's testimony in this trial, but Dexter in his summation notes a variation.

Dr. Oliver Hubbard

Our report of Dr. Hubbard's testimony is not satisfactory. According to the Boston *Courier*, he said that he assisted Dr. Johnson in the examination of White's body. He expressed his opinion at that time, and saw no cause to change it, that the murder had been committed before twelve o'clock.

A notebook kept by Robert Rantoul carries these words from Dr. Hubbard's testimony, "Some blood from wounds then dripping —idea of time from heat of body—blood not quite dry and cold."

Monday, August 16

In the course of the day the following witnesses for the government gave essentially the same testimony they had given at the first trial: Rev. Henry Colman, Stephen C. Phillips, Nathaniel Kinsman, Warwick Palfray, Jr., Nehemiah Brown, Peter E. Webster, John A. Southwick, Ezra Lummus, Mrs. Lummus, David Starrett, Henry R. Daland, Daniel Marston, George Smith, John McGlue, John W. Treadwell, and Dr. Gideon Barstow.

The counsel on both sides agreed that in order to save time the evidence given at the former trial to prove the alibi of George Crowninshield should be read to the jury. Webster read from his notes the testimony of Richard Burnham, Benjamin Newhall, Thomas W. Taylor, Joseph Anthony, and Mary Jane Weller.

Dexter endeavored to have Mr. Colman's evidence of Frank's confession ruled out. The court, however, were unanimous and gave their opinions severally in favor of its admission. No record of the arguments or of the opinions has been preserved. Since it became clear from Colman's testimony in the first trial that Frank did consent to Joe's confessing, it would seem that the court must have based their ruling on the ground that Frank made his own confession prior to giving his consent to Joe's confessing.[1]

Stephen Mirick

The witness elaborated his former testimony by saying that he had never pretended to identify the prisoner as the man he observed; but from his own observation made subsequently and from the description of the defendant given by others, *he had no doubt* that the man at the corner and the prisoner at the bar were one and the same person. He said that he would not have offered this opinion entirely from his own observation, but he thought that if the

---

[1] The opinions of the justices must have squelched Dexter very effectively, for we find no attempt in his final summation to argue that Colman's testimony as to Frank's confession was to be disregarded, although it is apparent in Webster's argument that he had expected such an attempt.

defendant were now dressed as the man at the corner was dressed, he should not hesitate to say that they were the same. The description of others merely confirmed his general impression.·

Mrs. John A. Southwick

She said that when Mr. Southwick first entered the house, he told her that he had seen Frank Knapp on the steps of the ropewalk.

The jury requested permission to view the premises of the late Captain White, and the prisoner's counsel expressed their approval of the request. This permission, which had been denied to the first jury, was granted.

Captain Bray

The witness added to his testimony given at the previous trial by saying that he had no doubt the prisoner was the person whom he first saw in Brown Street and pointed out to Mr. Southwick, and he thought he stated the same when he first saw the prisoner in jail. He said that when he followed one of the men past the cemetery on Howard Street, he thought he might be a resurrection man [one who steals bodies from graves to sell to medical students].

Judith Jaques

On Friday evening, the second of April, about ten o'clock, I was passing down Brown Street. When I got to Captain Kinsman's house I saw a group of men standing by the ropewalk steps and one of them was pointing towards Captain White's house. As I passed by Mr. Downing's gate I saw that there were three persons, one sitting down and one standing on each side of him. The one on the eastern side had something in his hand. I could not tell what it was. As I passed, the one sitting down took it out of the hand of the other and put it behind his back. The two persons standing had on glazed caps, cloaks or wrappers with capes, and the one sitting had on a hat and a surtout without a cape. I could not tell what the instrument was. I thought it a bugle, but did not observe it particularly.

Cross-examination. I told of it the next day and have mentioned it something like a hundred times. I was not summoned to attend the former trial of this cause.

Phillip Chase added the following to his former testimony. He visited Palmer in prison, in the room directly under Richard Crowninshield. While there a string was let down through the ceiling with a lead pencil attached. Soon after a piece of paper with two lines of poetry was let down with a request that if the occupant of the cell was acquainted with the poetry, he should complete the verse and send it back. Mr. Chase pulled the string and it was pulled back. Then he heard a shrill whistle which satisfied him that Palmer knew who was above. All these attempts failing, the person above called in a hard whisper, "Palmer, Palmer."

Lewis Endicott

I had a conversation with Joseph Knapp, Jr., in January last, about the time that Captain White had an ill turn. He said if he had been in town, Mrs. Beckford would not have sent to Boston for Mr. Stephen White, for he could destroy all his own notes. He said that Captain White made a will and that Mr. Stephen White was not executor, but John W. Treadwell alone. He said that black and white would not lie; that Mr. Lambert who was dead was the only witness. I asked him if he had seen the will and he said that he had. I asked him if Captain White did not keep his will locked up. He said yes, but there was such a thing as two keys to a lock.

Miss Sanborn testified that on the morning after the murder a cloak was left at Captain White's house by a young man whom she did not know, who said, "This is my brother's cloak," J. J. Knapp, Jr., took the cloak soon after when he was going to Wenham.

Miss Catherine Kimball testified to the same effect.

Webster said the government desired to prove that the house of Captain White had been entered and a will destroyed a short time before the murder. In this connection he attempted to introduce a part of Joseph Knapp's confession, but the court ruled it inadmissible.

In addition to the testimony given at the first trial, *Hart* said that on Sunday, the twenty-fifth of July, Leighton told him, "Thomas, they're coming down to take me if I don't tell all I know about it." Hart asked, "What'll they do with you?" Leighton replied, "Put me in prison, I suppose." Leighton then repeated what he had overheard at the gate between Joseph and Frank Knapp.[2]

---

[2]. This was presumably the first time that Leighton told his story; it was two days before the time first set for Frank's trial. It was not until the following Saturday that he told it to Waters, Choate, and Treadwell.

Tuesday, August 17

John Chadwick testified as to the state of the weather on the night of the murder. He said that there were passing clouds and that it was a light evening but very dusty. He had recognized the two Saltonstalls at three rods' distance.

Nathaniel Saltonstall testified that the weather was thick and hazy but light.

THE DEFENSE

William H. Gardiner then opened the defense. His address to the jury followed for the most part the general lines of his opening in the first trial.

In the course of the day the following witnesses gave the same testimony they had given at the first trial: Alfred Welles, Nathaniel P. Knapp, Asa Wiggin, Israel Ward, William Peirce, Solomon Giddings, Stephen Osborne, and James W. Webster.

Gardiner read from his notes the testimony given at the first trial proving the alibi of George Crowninshield. The witnesses were John Needham, Sally Needham, Benjamin Selman, Clark Reed, and Matthew Newport.

Witnesses were called for the purpose of showing the notoriously bad character of Palmer.

William Babb

Q. (Gardiner) When did you see Palmer? A. Well, I'm not certain.

GARDINER: State to the best of your knowledge.

WITNESS: Well, I'm not positive.

GARDINER: You are not required to be positive.

WITNESS: I believe it was on Friday night, the ninth of April.

He produced the receipt of Green.

In *cross-examination* Webster asked Babb if he was certain whether it was Friday the ninth or Tuesday the sixth. Babb was not certain. "If a man's life depended on it," asked Webster, "would you swear it was one day or the other?" "No sir," replied Babb, "I couldn't be positive."

Daniel Potter

I have conversed twice with Leighton about the murder. Once last Friday afternoon while the jury was out. Leighton then said that Frank Knapp came to Wenham *soon after breakfast* on the day that he overheard the conversation between Frank and Joseph. As I questioned him, someone told him to stop talking. I saw him again two hours afterward. He said Frank was viewing the farm that morning.

Cross-examination. Potter said that he had bet upon the outcome of the last trial.

Q. (Webster) Have you no bet upon this trial.? A. No sir.

Q. You don't speculate on this occasion? A. No sir, I have not heard the whole trial.

I dare say, responded Webster, your opinion will be better formed when you have heard the whole trial.

Stephen Field, Jr., testified that he overheard the conversation between Leighton and Potter, and it was as Potter had testified.

Octavius Pickering[3]

The witness said that he heard the testimony of Leighton at the former trial and took notes of it, but was not certain what Leighton had said about remembering, while in Waters' office, the conversation between the Knapps. Mr. Pickering believed that Leighton said that he did remember, but told Mr. Waters he did not.

The witness said he had heard Bray's testimony in the first trial and recollected that Bray did not say he believed the person in Brown Street was Frank Knapp.[4]

Edward G. Prescott[5]

The witness was asked regarding Bray's testimony in the first trial. He said that Bray testified that he could not swear the prisoner was the man in Brown Street, but that he was about the same height.

He said that at the former trial Mirick said he thought the man in Brown Street was the prisoner partly from his own observation and partly from the report of others. Mirick had been asked if he could speak from his own observation and he said that he could not.

---

[3] From 1822 to 1840 he was reporter for the Supreme Judicial Court of Massachusetts, and many volumes of the Massachusetts reports bear his name.

[4] It is clear from Pickering's testimony and also from the testimony that follows that no stenographic report of the evidence was made. The court remarked that the regular procedure was to prove former testimony by witnesses who were present.

[5] At the time of the trial, he was a law partner of Franklin Dexter. He was a younger brother of the historian, William Hickling Prescott.

Mr. Prescott stated that Leighton testified that he did not remember the conversation between the Knapps while he was in Waters' office.

He said that Burns testified at the former trial that Frank's dagger had a white plated handle.

James Savory

The witness testified, as at the first trial, that he saw a person go out of Captain White's yard between three and four o'clock on the morning of the seventh of April. This person turned and ran as soon as he saw the witness.

Cross-examination. Q. (Webster) Have you ever seen that person since? A. I think I have seen a person walking in the street whom I suppose to be the same.

Q. Who was it? A. I can't swear, but I suppose it to be Frank Knapp.

The witness testified that when he was carrying a person to overtake the Boston Stage a few days after the murder, he saw Frank and mentioned to his passenger — whom he did not know — that Frank was the same person he saw come out of the gate.

The witness said he did not think it was Frank when he saw him come out of the yard. He had known Frank for many years.

Dexter asked if it would be proper for the defense to introduce witnesses to contradict the evidence brought out by this examination.

Webster thought they could disprove the fact, but could not discredit their own witness.

Moses P. Balch. In addition to his former testimony, Balch said, "Frank told us at seven he was going out of town to see a girl, and when he met us about nine, said he had been out on horseback, about a twenty minute ride."

Webster said that Frank had a saddle horse from Mr. Osborne late on the evening of Saturday the third, but none on the evening of Tuesday. Webster thought that this might dispose of the facts previously stated by the witness.

Cross-examination. The witness said that he was first called by Mr. Waters, and he told Waters that he could not fix the night. He was next called on by Phippen Knapp, and he told him the same. Balch and Burchmore had compared their recollections in Mr. Rantoul's office and they told him that they could not swear to the time.

Phippen Knapp told Balch that Frank said it was the night of the murder.

Zachariah Burchmore added to his former testimony the statement that he told Mr. Waters that if he had not sworn positively enough the first time, he would the next. He was first called on by Mr. Waters and he told Waters he could not swear positively as to the night.

Wednesday, August 18

Captain J. J. Knapp, Sr., gave the same testimony he had given at the first trial.

John F. Forrester added to his former testimony the statement that Phippen Knapp and Robert Rantoul came to Andover to question him concerning the evening with Frank. They told him that Frank said it was the night of the murder, and that Page, Burchmore, and Balch thought so too. The witness could not fix the time; he had an impression but nothing more.

John Chapman, a new witness, testified that the weather on Monday evening before the murder was very pleasant. It was a clear moonlight night. There was a public meeting at the South Meeting House. It was a very full meeting.

Samuel Knapp[6]

With the consent of the prosecution, Gardiner read an affidavit concerning the testimony that would be given by Samuel H. Knapp if he were present. In this affidavit Frank Knapp swore that his brother Samuel, if present, would testify as follows: On the night of the murder Frank came home about ten o'clock and opened Samuel's chamber door and spoke to him at ten minutes after ten; Samuel heard Frank go immediately to his own room and, as he supposed, to bed.

Robert Rantoul, Jr., swore that he was present at Justice Savage's examination of the prisoner, and that it was not thought necessary that Samuel Knapp should postpone his voyage to South America on account of this trial. His evidence was not thought necessary because the prisoner was then accused as an accessory and not as a principal.

Ebenezer Shillaber testified at the former trial that he asked Southwick whether the man he saw in Brown Street might not have

---

[6] Samuel was a brother of the prisoner.

been Richard Crowninshield and the man who joined him the prisoner, to which Mr. Southwick replied that for aught he knew it might have been so. Mr. Shillaber now added that he did not ask Southwick that question until he understood that Southwick had said it was Frank Knapp who was in Brown Street.

WITNESSES FOR THE GOVERNMENT

Michael Shepard, John W. Treadwell, George W. Teal, and Stephen Brown gave the same testimony as at the first trial.

Thomas Taylor, a new witness, said that he was employed at the jail. He testified that Mr. Colman went two or three times to Joseph's cell; that Phippen once went to the door of the cell and was at first refused but afterwards admitted by Mr. Colman; that they were there four of five minutes and then went to Frank's cell.

Colonel Perley Putnam

On Friday, week before last, I asked Burchmore if he was positive that he saw Frank on the evening of the murder. He said he could not swear that he had.

Rev. Bailey Loring

John Forrester, Jr., has lived with me at Andover a year. A week before the trial commenced, two gentlemen whom I understood to be Mr. Robert Rantoul, Jr., and Mr. N. P. Knapp came to my house to see Forrester. I said to him, "Do you know anything about the murder?" He said that about the time of the murder he was in Salem and walking with Frank Knapp and some other young men. I asked him if he could recollect what night it was. He said it was on that night or about that night. I asked him if Page could not recollect the night. He said he could not. He said that the gentlemen who came up wanted him to go to Salem to meet the others to bring up some circumstance to refresh their recollection. They told him that if he did not come they would summon him.

John Felt Webb said that he conversed with Samuel Knapp before he went to sea. The conversation was on the eighth of June. Webb asked Samuel if he knew when Frank was at home on the night of the murder, and he said no. He said that Frank was not at home when he went to bed.

Joseph White

I know Charles Page; we are both members of college. I have conversed with him about the murder. He said that it was Monday or Tuesday or Wednesday evening that he was with the defendant and he could not tell which.

Dr. Abel L. Peirson

On Thursday, the eighth of April, I was requested to examine the body of Captain White. Dr. Johnson, some of his pupils, and several spectators were present. It was the first time that I had seen the body after the murder.

On examination, we found two groups of wounds on the body. There were six stabs three inches from the left pap and near together, measuring exactly half an inch in length. Each gaped about a quarter of an inch and resembled somewhat the figure made by a parenthesis. About six inches farther down there was another series of wounds, seven in number. These wounds were all mere slits, not gaping at all. One of them was three-quarters of an inch in length, the others varied from one-half to three-quarters. These two series of wounds differed in so many particulars that I inferred that they were made by different instruments. The instrument by which the ribs were probably broken must have been about five inches in length, as the ribs were probably broken by the guard or hilt, and it did not appear to have been long enough to reach so far as the instrument that passed through the diaphragm.

Joseph Dewing testified that he had heard Frank Knapp say he could get out of his father's house at any time without letting the family know it, and had done so frequently.

John Felt Webb was recalled. He testified that Frank Knapp had frequently told him he could go in and out of his father's house in the night without anybody knowing it.

Jesse Smith, Jr.

Moses Balch has told me at two different times that he could not tell the time of night that he left the prisoner. He once said it was about twenty or thirty minutes after nine, but he could not tell. The second time he said it must have been about ten o'clock, but he was not certain. All he knew was that he was walking with the prisoner on Monday or Tuesday evening; he did not know which.

Cross-examination. Balch said Charles Page was with them and he could not tell. Since the last trial, I have told Balch what he told me before — that he left the prisoner about half-past nine — and he said he did not recollect it. He said he had always said it was about ten. He has said since that his recollection agreed with that of the prisoner.

WITNESSES FOR THE DEFENSE

Dr. Samuel Johnson recalled. He said he did not observe such a difference in the appearance of the wounds as to lead him to believe that more than one instrument had been used.

The counsel for the prosecution admitted that the testimony given by Miss Sanborn and Miss Kimball regarding the cloak at Captain White's house was of no importance.

DEXTER'S ADDRESS TO THE JURY

Gentlemen of the Jury:

You have now heard all the evidence on which you are to form your judgment of life or death to the prisoner. He stands before you for that judgment under terrible disadvantages. . . . You see around you proofs of the power against which the accused has to struggle in his defense. You see the extraordinary array of counsel, active and inactive, brought in aid of the government or withdrawn from the reach of the prisoner. You have witnessed the efforts that have been made by those who could take no other part in the prosecution, to fasten upon him the evidence of guilt; and you may anticipate the power and eloquence with which the case is to be closed against him.

Gentlemen, why is all this? . . . If there is legal evidence against the prisoner, can there be a doubt that he will be convicted? And if there is not, is a verdict of condemnation to be wrenched from you by talent and eloquence which the ordinary course of a criminal trial would fail to procure? . . .

There is, however, a more dangerous influence in this case. . . . We care less for the array of counsel than for the array of the community against him. . . . We have greatly feared the effect of this hostile atmosphere on the testimony. We have feared, and found, that in such a state of excitement no man could take the stand an indifferent witness. He is to be esteemed a public benefactor on whose testimony the prisoner is convicted, and he who shrinks from the certainty expected of him, does it at the peril of public displeasure and reproach. If proof of this were needed, it might be found abundantly in the variance of the evidence on the two trials of this cause . . . and this last reinforcement of evidence is but proof of what had been done for the conviction of the prisoner.

After all that has been said abroad we fear that it may even seem strange that we should claim for the prisoner that presumption of innocence which the law affords every man. But it is not the less your duty to extend it to him. . . . You must be satisfied by the evidence in the case, beyond reasonable doubt, of the truth of the whole and of every material part of the charge as it is here laid against him.

I say this, gentlemen, because a new doctrine of the law has been advanced to meet the difficulties of this case. We have been told that the prosecution will contend that if the general guilt of the prisoner has been established, there is a presumption of law that he is a principal offender; that the burden is thrown on him to show that he is guilty in a less degree. It is enough for us to say that this is a doctrine subversive of the very foundation of all criminal law; that it strikes at the root of that humane provision that no man's guilt is presumed; and that it is unsupported by any authority which has been or can be adduced.

What then is the crime of which the prisoner stands indicted? It is that he was present, aiding and abetting in the murder. Not that he is guilty of the murderous intent or that he procured the murder to be committed, but that he was present at the perpetration of it and gave his assistance to the murderer.

But we admit the law to be well settled that an actual presence is not necessary to constitute the prisoner a principal. We admit that any place from which actual physical aid can be given in the commission of the murder is presence within the meaning of the law. . . . To make a man an aider and abettor in a felony he must be in such a situation at the moment when the crime is committed that he can render actual and immediate assistance to the perpetrator, and that he must be there by agreement, and with the intent to render such assistance. . . . No previous consent or inducement, no encouragement at the moment short of the hope of actual and immediate physical assistance is sufficient for that purpose. . . .

Was the prisoner, with such intent, under such an agreement, in such a situation that he could render actual aid at the moment when the murder was committed? . . .

Sensible of the weakness of the evidence of the prisoner's presence

in Brown Street (specially as it stood on the first trial), the prosecutors have relied much on the aid of the conspiracy. . . .

If then, as the prosecutors contend, the evidence of Leighton is
sufficient to indicate the object of the conspiracy; if the words he
so ingeniously overheard can, as is said, mean nothing but that the
two Knapps and Richard Crowninshield had agreed that the latter
should murder Captain White, then all the remaining proof of the
conspiracy is superfluous. The only object for which it could legally
be used was accomplished at the first step.

The Wenham robbery, the robbery of the Knapps' house, the
preceding letters of Joseph Knapp to Stephen White and to the
committee, and other circumstantial stuff that has been introduced,
may be used to aggravate the general appearance of the whole transaction, but they have no bearing on the case of the prisoner. The
letters may be proof that Joseph Knapp was guilty, but what is
that to the prisoner? He is not to stand or fall by the subsequent
and independent acts of Joseph. Why are these evidence against
him, more than Joseph's confession given to Mr. Colman? They are
but confessions made after the fact and without the knowledge of
the prisoner. As to the robbery, it may have been real or pretended.
But whether real or pretended, what has it to do with the murder
of Captain White? Not a particle of extrinsic proof of its falsehood or
of its connection with that event has been produced.

Some other circumstances may be dispatched in the same manner.
The conspirators wore daggers; the proof is that the Crowninshields
habitually wore them before the murder and that the prisoner never
had one until long after. And whether he then wore it for murder
or in boyish bravado, you may judge of Leighton's account of the
manner in which he used it upon him. Pleased with his new weapon,
"he pricked me bull calf till he roared."[7] And how much of Leighton's testimony is to be ascribed to that is matter of no great consequence, so incredible is the whole.

So of the five-franc pieces. The proof is that Joseph received five
hundred on the twenty-first of April, and that George and Richard
Crowninshield spent nine between that time and their arrest — nine
five-franc pieces! Richard was to receive, according to Palmer, one
thousand dollars for the murder, and we are called upon to account
for nine of these pieces when the whole five hundred would not be

---

[7] *Second Part of Henry The Fourth*, III, ii, l. 181. *Falstaff.* Come, pricke me
Bulcalfe till he roare againe. (First Folio.)

half of the price agreed to be paid. And why should not the whole five hundred have been paid? And if they were, why are not more than nine traced to the Crowninshields? The coin, besides, is no uncommon one; they carry no earmarks. The witnesses tell you they pass currently, commonly, here. . . .

But suppose it otherwise; how does this prove Frank Knapp guilty of this murder? Is he shown to have any of this pernicious coin? All the evidence about them is of the nine spent by the Crowninshields, and that Joseph Knapp gave Hart three to buy meal for the family.

Besides, the proof of any communication between Joseph and Richard after the murder completely fails. . . . The whole evidence is that about the last of March, Richard Crowninshield stopped at Lummus' tavern with a stranger who asked if Captain Knapp had been there lately; they left their chaise and walked away together. Afterwards, about the twentieth of April, Richard and another person stouter than the prisoner, called at Lummus' in the evening and spent a five-franc piece. Hart and Leighton testify that somewhere about that time Frank Knapp came in a chaise to Wenham with a stranger who sat in the chaise at the door an hour or an hour and a half. They differ very much in their accounts of the transaction; but neither pretends to know or believe that the stranger was Richard, or that any money was paid. In fact, money could not well have been paid at that time in five-franc pieces without observation. All they knew was that there was a long conversation between the two Knapps in the house and between them and the stranger at the door. . . .

One word about George Crowninshield. . . . He came to Salem with Selman and Chase on other business. It seems to be the object of the government to show that he could not be the man in Brown Street; but we think it material to show you also that neither was he anywhere in the neighborhood of Mr. White's house at the supposed time of the murder.

Much use was made at the former trial of the testimony and books of Osborne, the stable-keeper. It appears by them that the prisoner was in the daily habit of riding, and often to Danvers and to Wenham, early in the month of April; that he went to Danvers on the second of April as testified by Palmer and Allen, and afterwards on the same day hired a chaise to go to the Springs; that on the sixth of April he went to Danvers, and after that did not ride until the nineteenth. We see little that can fairly be inferred from this but that there was a frequent intercourse between the prisoner and the Crowninshields, a circumstance undoubtedly unfavorable though slight, and between him and his brother Joseph's family, a matter from which nothing can be inferred.

Two or three circumstances, however, attending these rides have been selected as highly suspicious. In the first place the frequency of them just previous to the time of the murder and the interruption of them just after. If the books are examined it will be found that these rides are as frequent in the months of February and March as in April, making due allowance for the difference of weather. The prisoner returned from sea in January and he appears to have hired Osborne's horses almost every day from that time until the sixth of April. That evening was marked by the failure of his father as well as by the murder of Captain White, a circumstance quite sufficient to account for the discontinuance of his visits to the stable, and also for another fact somewhat relied upon.

The place, it seems, for which the chaise was hired on the sixth of April is still blank in the book. Now Mr. Osborne testified that it was the habit of the prisoner to fill out and rectify the charges against him by his own memorandum book. . . . The chaise was hired for *The Springs*, but those words were afterwards struck out and *to ride* put in their place in the prisoner's handwriting. But the first words are not so erased as to be concealed. They are merely crossed out with a single line of the pen. . . .

One circumstance more and I have done with these minor points. It is thought very strange that on the sixth the prisoner ordered his chaise brought to the courthouse instead of getting in at the stable. A hundred innocent reasons may be imagined for that, while it is hardly possible to think of one in any way connected with the murder. He was much more likely to be noticed if seen getting into a chaise in Court Street than at the stable, because one was a usual, the other an unusual thing. The fact that he had a chaise was as much known at the stable; and if he wished to conceal the direction in which he rode . . . why did he not start the contrary way and drive round the town until he could escape unnoticed? . . . It is so simple a thing that any reason is enough, and none need be sought for. But the most indifferent acts of the prisoner have been traced out with inquisitorial diligence and magnified into proofs of crime.

Is there anything in all these circumstances inconsistent with the prisoner's innocence? It is not enough that they are consistent with his guilt. Before circumstantial evidence can amount to proof, it must be impossible to explain it without supposing guilt. . . . It seems to be enough if the prisoner can be found anywhere or doing anything on the day of the murder which might by any supposition connect him with it. A thousand suspicions, it has been well said, do not make one proof. And what are these but possibilities? . . . A thousand such possibilities would hardly make one suspicion.

But one thing that has a little more show of proof, or rather of suspicion, must be disposed of before we come to the direct evidence of the conspiracy. I mean Mr. Burn's story. Burns is a Spaniard; and although I would not discredit him on that ground alone, I cannot have the same confidence in his oath I should have in that of one of our own citizens. He hardly speaks English intelligibly, and there is some doubt whether he was finally understood as he meant. His story is intrinsically improbable, and he has discredited himself by his own contradictions. He tells you the prisoner called at his stable and asked if he were alone. Being assured that no one was there, he wished to be yet more private and asked if he could speak with him in the chamber. And all this secrecy was to tell Burns that the committee had heard that Burns was out on the night of the murder and that they suspected him; that if he saw any friends that night, he had better hold his tongue about it; and that Joseph Knapp and the prisoner were his friends. And then follows an idle tale about the prisoner's accusing Stephen White of the murder, and then threatening Burns with his dagger because he would not believe it. Now what possible object could the prisoner have in all this but to bring himself into suspicion? No one had at that time whispered a suspicion against him. . . .

But, it may be asked, what motive could Burns have to fabricate this story? It is vain to deny that three is a sufficient motive. We have seen the operation of it on more than one witness, and that Mr. Burns is above its influence I see no special reason to believe. You observed the manner in which he testified; how zealously he defended Mr. Stephen White from the aspersions of the prisoner, and how impossible it was for the counsel to obtain anything from him but impertinence by the mildest cross-examination. Such a man as Burns well understands what is the source of favor in this trial. . . .

But be his story ever so probable, you cannot believe it. He swore positively on the first trial that this happened after the Wenham robbery, and on this he has sworn positively that it was nearly three weeks earlier. He has described the prisoner's dagger as totally unlike any one he ever had, and differently at his two examinations. Let him and his story go for what they are worth. I trust that the prisoner is in no danger from them.

I come now to what is called the direct evidence of the conspiracy. It rests on two witnesses, Leighton and Palmer — or rather it rests on Leighton alone, for without his testimony that of Palmer would not be admissible. Palmer pretends only to have heard a conversation between the two Crowninshields in the absence of the prisoner. Now to make this admissible against Frank Knapp, a conspiracy must first be established between him and the Crowninshields. For that purpose Leighton overhears the two Knapps tell each other the whole story while he listens behind a stone wall. Now it may be supposed that this very deficiency in Palmer's story is proof of its truth. Not so. Palmer's story was first told and put in writing to convict Richard Crowninshield, and it would well enough stand alone on that. But when Richard was out of the way and Frank became the principal, a connecting link was wanting; and to furnish this is Leighton's office.

And what is Leighton's story? Of all the gross improbabilities that ever were laid at the foundation of a cause, this is the most gross. It is just the clumsiest contrivance of a play, where the audience is informed of what has taken place behind the scenes by the actors telling each other what they have been doing together. If it were told with the utmost consistency, could you believe it for a moment? Why, gentlemen, do but listen to it. He tells you that Frank Knapp came to Wenham about ten o'clock (and Potter says he told him he came there immediately after breakfast, which would be about seven), that he and Joseph were together all morning in the fields, and that after dinner he left them together talking at the gate by the house while the witness went down the avenue to his work. There was abundant opportunity, then, for them to talk in private about what most concerned them. But after the witness had passed through the gate at the end of the avenue and taken his place behind the wall, he heard voices in the avenue. Without rising he peeped through the gate and saw the two Knapps *about twenty-five rods off* coming towards him; that they ceased talking until they arrived within three feet of the wall and then began this dialogue: Said Joseph, "When did you see Dick?" "This morning." "When is he going to kill the old man?" "I don't know." "If he don't do it soon I won't pay him." And they then turned up the avenue and walked away, and this is all the witness heard.

Now is anything more than a bare statement of this story necessary to show its falsehood? For what purpose, under Heaven, could the Knapps have postponed all conversation on this most interesting subject till that very time? They had been together all morning; they were plotting a murder, and Frank had been that very day to see the perpetrator; and yet neither Joseph had the curiosity to ask, nor Frank the disposition to speak of the matter until just as they reached the place of Leighton's ambuscade. And there, in an abrupt dialogue of one minute's duration, they disclose the whole secret and walk back again. Not a word more is heard by the witness. The conversation evidently began and ended with these words. Really it is too miserable a contrivance to deserve much comment.

But there is a remarkable mistake about this story which stamps it with falsehood. Leighton fixes the conversation on Friday, the second of April. And why on that day? Because he knew, as well as every person who had read the newspapers, that on that day Frank did see Richard. But unluckily he fixes him at Wenham at the very hour in which it now appears, from the testimony of Allen and Palmer, that he was at Danvers. Leighton says that Frank came to Wenham at ten, and said he had seen Dick that morning; but it now appears that Frank did not go to Danvers until two o'clock, and at that very hour Leighton pretends to have heard this conversation at Wenham.

Again, Palmer tells you that at that interview at Danvers, the plan was first proposed to the Crowninshields, that George spoke of it to Richard and himself as what he had just heard from Frank; and yet from this dialogue at Wenham it seems that Joseph was impatient at the long delay of Richard. "When is Dick going to kill the old man?" "If he don't soon I won't pay him." How are these things to be reconciled?

Leighton tells you, too, that he never mentioned this conversation until after the murder. And why not? Why, forsooth, he did not think of it. He had heard a plan, palpable plot of murder contrived by his own master, and yet he did not think of it! He did not tell it to Mr. Davis when he joined him at his work, nor to Hart who slept in the same room with him. And when he hinted after the murder to Starrett, at two different times, that he knew something and had overheard something about the murder, Starrett had not the curiosity to ask him what it was! He is directly contradicted by Hart, both as to time when he told of it and as to the circumstances of Richard's supposed visit to Wenham. Hart says he never heard of this conversation until after Leighton's examination at Salem and that Leighton told him the committee brought out a warrant to commit him to jail if he did not tell what he knew—facts both of which Leighton denied on the stand.

Now what account does he give of the manner in which his evidence was brought out? He says he was summoned to attend court, taken out of the field when he was at work and carried to Mr. Waters' office. He was kept there, forenoon and afternoon, more than four hours, closely questioned and threatened; but he told nothing. Why did he not tell? On the first trial he swore he remembered well enough but he did not choose to tell. To be sure he swore both ways about it, but he finally said he did remember and would not tell; and on this statement a most ingenious argument was built by the counsel in his favor: "He would not betray his employer; improper as it was to deny what he knew, he had fidelity enough to refuse." But on this last trial he takes all that back; he swears positively he did not remember a word about it. Equally regardless of his own oath and the argument of counsel, he denies the whole. He says it all came into his mind about two days after his return to Wenham — the very words. What brought it to his mind he cannot tell. Now what credit can you give to this boy and his story?

But one of the most remarkable improbabilities of it is yet to come. He says he told the gentlemen at Mr. Waters' office that if they would come to Wenham the next day he would tell them all he could remember. That was on the twenty-second of July. Now do you believe if that were true they would not have gone? . . . And yet he tells you he heard nothing from them until ten days after that time. Then they came to Wenham and he told them about it. Now, gentlemen, if you had seen as much as we have of the diligence of the committee and sub-committee in looking up testimony in this cause, you would not think this the least improbability in Leighton's story.

Consider how important his testimony is. Without it, Palmer's and the whole evidence of the conspiracy would be useless. It is the very cornerstone of the prosecution. And yet it was not thought worth looking after for ten days immediately preceding the trial.

Again, we shall be asked, what motive has Leighton to swear falsely? And we answer, fear, favor, and hope of reward. He was told at Waters' office he should be made to remember; he said he was threatened with a warrant; and he knows of the immense rewards that have been offered. He remembers the pricking with the dagger, and he swears now to you that if Knapp escapes hanging, he expects he will kill him.

Under all these circumstances, I put it to your consciences to say if you can take this boy's word against the life of the prisoner. If you disbelieve it, then you must wholly reject Palmer's testimony and all evidence of what was said and done by anyone but the prisoner or in his presence. There is absolutely no other evidence to connect the prisoner with Joseph or the Crowninshields in this matter.

But who is this Palmer, this mysterious stranger who has been the object of so much curiosity and speculation? He is a convicted thief. We produce to you the record of his conviction of shopbreaking in Maine. He is an unrepenting thief, for he tells you on the stand he cannot speak of the stealing of Mr. Sutton's flannels in Danvers, committed since his discharge from the State prison, without incriminating himself. Mr. James Webster tells you his character among his neighbors in Belfast is as bad as it can be. He tells you himself that he has passed in his wanderings from tavern to tavern, sometimes by the name of Palmer, sometimes that of Carr, sometimes that of Hall (the alias of the notorious Hatch), and sometimes that of George Crowninshield. The latter name he gave at Babb's house when he was called on to settle his bill; and whether he settled by a note he *cannot remember,* but Mr. Babb remembers that he did and signed that note *George Crowninshield!*

And how came Mr. Palmer a witness before you? He was arrested as an accomplice in the murder at Prospect, committed to Belfast jail, brought up by land from Belfast in chains, put into a condemned cell in Salem, remained in jail two months, neither committed for trial nor ordered to recognize as a witness, but kept for further examination at his own request until he is brought out and made a free man on the stand.

Now what it this man's credibility? If his conviction had been in Massachusetts he would have been incompetent; he could not have opened his mouth in court. But the crime is the same, the law violated is the same, the infamy and punishment are the same in Maine as in Massachusetts, and his credibility is the same. Add to that conviction, his subsequent theft, falsehood, and forgery, and you have left in him but a bare possibility that he may speak the truth. As to his temptation to testify against the prisoner, you see how he was brought here, under what liabilities he stands, and what is the price of his discharge. He tells you himself that, though a disinterested love of public justice first moved him to inquire into the matter, he thinks he deserves some little pecuniary reward for his exertions, and doubtless he thinks that reward will depend something in the success of them.

But what is his story? It is that being himself concealed at the house of the Crowninshields in Danvers, he saw Frank Knapp and Allen come there on Friday, April 2, about two o'clock; that Frank and George walked away together, and after their return Frank and Allen rode off; that the Crowninshields then came into the chamber where he was, and George detailed to him and Richard the whole design and motive of the murder as a matter then for the first time communicated.

Now perhaps there is nothing intrinsically very incredible about this story, except its too great particularity. If it be false, it is so artfully engrafted on the truth that Frank Knapp was there at that time and had an interview with George alone, that it would be almost impossible to detect it. Palmer, too, must be allowed the credit of ingenuity, whether his story be true or false. It is impossible for anyone in his situation to have testified with a more artful simplicity. And I admit too that he has had the good sense to tell no unnecessary falsehood. The only instance in which he has tripped is his saying that George Crowninshield told him on the ninth of April that he had melted the daggers the day after the murder for fear of the committee of vigilance, whereas the committee was not appointed until late in the evening of the ninth. . . . But this conversation is too particular. Like Leighton's, it goes too much into all that the case requires. Why should the Crowninshields tell all this to Palmer without first sounding him? He says he rejected their offer immediately. Would they risk detailing the whole plan to him before securing any indication on his part of

assent? Nay, after having communicated it to him and after he
had refused to have any part in it, would Richard have gone on to
execute it? He is not a man to trust his life to the keeping of such
a witness as Palmer, who had refused to become an accomplice. . . .

Is Palmer corroborated? In the immaterial circumstances of his
story in which he had the sense to tell the truth and no temptation
to lie, he is confirmed by other witnesses. But on the only important point he stands alone and unconfirmed. The conversation between him and the Crowninshields rests, and must of necessity rest,
on his single statement.

But it has been said that his letter corroborates his story. How
can that be? Would he be such a fool as to swear now to anything
inconsistent with his letter of which we had a copy? . . . But does
that letter contain anything which he might not well have known,
whether his story be true or false, and which is now confirmed by
any other witness? Not a word. It states that he knew what J.
Knapp's brother was doing for him on the second of April, that
he was extravagant to give a thousand dollars for such a business,
and that is all. The rest is but vague and unmeaning menace. Now
it is undoubtedly true that Frank Knapp was at Danvers on the
second of April and had a private conversation with George, and
that Palmer was at Danvers and saw him. And that single fact is
the only one contained in the letter which is corroborated by any
other witness. That he was there to engage the Crowninshields in
this business and that they were to have a thousand dollars, comes
from Palmer himself and from him alone. Even Leighton's story,
though intended to corroborate it, contradicts it by inconsistency
in time and in the age of the plot. He says nothing of the thous-
and dollars. But why should Palmer venture to mention a
thousand dollars if that were not the sum offered? And why should
he have written the letter at all if he knew nothing about Frank's
business at Danvers?

The solution is easy. It supposes, indeed, some skill in Palmer, but
we have seen enough of that. Consider when this letter was written.
Not until after the arrest of the Crowninshields. If he had really
heard this plot laid, why did he not give information of it immediately on hearing of Captain White's death, and of the immense
rewards offered for the discovery of the murder? He tells you he
wrote that letter to bring the matter to light, from a pure love of
public justice. Public justice has been a rather hard mistress to

Palmer, but he is not the less faithful to her. Now why did not that love of public justice induce him to inform against the Crownin-shields and Knapps before anybody else suspected them, and while public justice had some thousands of dollars to give him to obliterate the remembrance of her castigations? He had the whole matter in his own breast. He had heard every word of the plot. If they were guilty he had information enough to lead to their detection. Yet he waits five weeks after the murder and a fortnight after the arrest of the Crowninshields and then writes this letter to Knapp demanding money, but in fact, as he tells you, to get evidence against them. But what led him to suspect the Knapps? What was more easy? He probably knew that J. Knapp's mother-in-law was an heir of White; he saw Frank Knapp in private conversation with George Crowninshield four days before the murder and he saw in the papers that the Crowninshields were arrested as the murderers. It required less than Palmer's shrewdness to put these things together. As to the thousand dollars it may be his own pure invention; there is no other evidence of it. Or it may be that he heard the Crownin-shields say after Frank left them that they expected a thousand dollars without saying from what source. His letter is therefore no corroboration at all. It does not contain a fact proved by anybody but himself except that Frank was at Danvers on the second. Nor is Palmer's story on the stand corroborated by any other witness in a single fact that had not been published in every newspaper in the State weeks before he testified.

This is the evidence of the conspiracy. I have but two remarks to make on it. If you could believe it on such evidence, the only effect of it would be to show that Frank Knapp was an accessory, and it makes nothing said or done by Joseph Knapp or the Crowninshields evidence against the prisoner. The very proof relied on to establish the fact of the conspiracy proves equally well all that of which such acts and declarations are legal evidence; that is, the design and object of the conspiracy. The most, then, that can possibly be inferred from this evidence, bad as it is, is that the prisoner was an accessory before the fact; and that if he were in Brown Street at the moment of the murder, and in a situation in which he could give assistance, there would be a presumption that he was there for that purpose. We are willing to meet the government on that ground. We deny that he was there and we deny that the man who was there could by possibility have given any assistance.

Two men were seen in Brown Street at half-past ten, of whom one is alleged to have been the murderer and the prisoner the other. But what proof is there that the murder was committed at that hour? If that fails the whole case fails. Was there anything in the conduct of the men to show it? One was seen waiting half an hour in Brown Street. A little before eleven he was joined by another who came up either from the Common or from Newbury Street, and might as well have come from one as from the other as he was first seen in the middle of the street. The man that came from the east-ward did not run; he walked directly up to the other and held a short conference with him; they moved on together a few feet, stopped again, talked a few moments, and then parted — one step-ping back out of sight and the other running down Howard Street. Of the two witnesses that saw them, Bray thought they were about to rob the graveyard; Southwick suspected, but what to suspect he did not know, and his wife suspected that he had better go out again to watch them. A murder was committed that night in the next street, and this is all the proof that these were the murderers. A club, indeed, was afterwards found in Howard Street, but neither of these men had any visible weapons.

What say the doctors? Dr. Johnson says he saw the body at six and then thought it had been dead between three and four hours. Dr. Hubbard now thinks longer, but says at the time he agreed with Johnson. There is pretty strong proof that the murder was in fact committed about three o'clock.

Savory saw a man, between three and four, come out of Captain White's yard and walk up Essex Street, but meeting the witness he turned about and ran down as far as Walnut Street. Walcutt, about the same time and near the lower end of Walnut Street, met probably the same man coming towards him. On seeing him, he turned about and walked the other way. Now which was most likely to be the murderer — the man who might have come either from Newbury Street or from the Common at eleven, or the man who was actually seen to leave White's yard at half-past three, and twice turned back and once ran away to escape observation?

But here we are met with a dilemma on the second trial. What I have stated was the whole of Savory's testimony on the first trial. He was then asked whether he had ever heard of that man since, and he said no. Now he is asked whether he has seen that man since, and to the utter amazement of everyone, after giggling like an idiot, he says he thinks it was the prisoner! And this is seriously taken up by the counsel for the prosecution, and Dr. Peirson is examined to prove that the stabs were made with different instruments. You have heard his reasons for it. His opinion is that some of the lower wounds, being longer than the upper, must have been made by a broader dagger or sword cane. These lower wounds were oblique and of various lengths, but he thinks that a dagger, however sharp at the edges, driven obliquely into the body, will not make a wound longer upon the surface than the breadth of the dagger. This seems very much like saying that the human skin may be pierced but cannot be cut. It is certainly contrary to common observation if not to common sense. Dr. Johnson says he saw no proof of more than one sharp instrument.

But for what possible purpose, if Frank Knapp had met the murderer in Brown Street and heard that the deed was done at eleven, should he have gone into the house again and stabbed the dead body? Like another Falstaff did he envy the perpetrator the glory of the deed and mean to claim it as his own? Or was it for plunder? No, for the money was not taken. The two suppositions that the prisoner was engaged in the murder at half-past ten, and that he visited the house at half-past three, are totally irreconcilable. We deny that he was in Brown Street, and we will take the risk of Savory's testimony.

This is but one of the many examples of the rapid growth of evidence in a popular cause. Savory's first story was true; he had told it so from the first day after the murder, and it was confirmed by Walcutt. But this last edition of it is as foolish as it is wicked, and needs no refutation or comment to those who saw and heard him on the stand. The manner was as indecent as the matter was absurd.

The government must satisfy you beyond reasonable doubt that either the murder was committed at half-past ten, or that the prisoner was the man who left the house at half-past three. You cannot believe both; and can you say that you are satisfied of either? Is there not a great, a very reasonable doubt of both? You must not convict the prisoner between the two. You must be as well satisfied of one as if the other did not exist. Which then will you take? That he was the man seen by Savory? If Savory were honest and credible, you would have but his opinion from a glance in a dim and misty night, for it grew more dark and cloudy towards morning — a thing certainly not to be relied upon, standing alone as it does. Was the murder committed at half-past ten? What is the proof of it? And what was the man doing in White's yard at half-past three? And why did he run when he was seen? Which acted most like a murderer, the man that came into Brown Street or the man that ran from the yard? Which was the hour most appropriate to so horrible a deed? That at which a party was breaking up at Mr. Daland's, the next house to Mr. White's, or the still hour before daylight when no person was abroad but by accident? And what is the fair result of the doctor's opinion on the view of the body? All these things concur to fix the murder on the man who left the yard in the morning. If you believe that was Frank Knapp, if you can say on your oaths that Savory's testimony satisfied you of it beyond a reasonable doubt, be it so; but it will satisfy nobody else. I have no fear of it.

There remains then, only the supposition that the murder was committed at half-past ten; and then the question is: Was the prisoner the man in Brown Street? On this point we have the most deplorable examples of the fallibility of human testimony, and of the weak stand that even common integrity can make against the overwhelming current of popular opinion. The witnesses are four. Webster and Southwick swore the same on both trials; Bray and Mirick have varied most essentially. As it now stands, Mirick and Webster are of little importance. Mirick saw a man in a frock coat, who he now thinks was the prisoner, standing on the corner of Brown and Newbury Streets from twenty minutes before to twenty minutes after nine. The man appeared to be waiting for someone, and when any person approached his post he walked away and then turned and met him. He did this several times. Now whether that was or was not the prisoner is not in itself of any importance. It is hardly to be believed that a man who was to be engaged in a murder at half-past ten would be seen lingering near the spot for forty minutes at the early hour of nine. It would, if true, be no unfavorable circumstance. For what purpose connected with the murder was he there at that hour? Did the murderers take their measure so ill that one was on the watch for the other at a public corner near the scene of the murder an hour and a half before the time?

Besides, where are the persons whom Mirick saw meet the prisoner at the corner? He spoke to several. Why are they not found and produced? It is impossible they should not be found. We have been loudly and gravely called upon to produce the man in Brown Street if Frank Knapp was not he. It is thought very strange that if it were not he, some friend of justice should not come forward and own himself to be the man, at the risk of taking the prisoner's place at the bar as a principal in the murder. So, too, it was asked, if Richard Crowninshield was not the man that joined him in Brown Street, why don't the prisoner show where Richard was? And yet we are told that the prisoner stood half an hour at a corner and was met by various persons, but not one of those persons is produced to prove it when it is the very question whether it was the prisoner or not, and Mirick tells you himself that others saw him where they certainly would have recognized him. Now it is a principle of law that no evidence is good which of itself supposes better in existence, not produced. Mirick's evidence, then, is good for nothing until those who met the prisoner at the post are produced.

Besides, how did Mirick recognize him? He had never known him; he never knew him until he was brought up for trial nearly four months after the night of the murder, and in a different dress. He was then told by a bystander which was Frank Knapp. Being asked at the first trial who he thought the man at the corner was, he said he thought it was the prisoner, not from what he had observed alone, but partly from what he had heard about him. Now this was obviously no evidence at all. What a man thinks from what he hears is nothing. What he hears is no evidence; and still less what he thinks about it. But at this trial Mr. Mirick makes another step. He says he thinks it was the prisoner from his own observation alone, making allowance for the difference of dress. Now, how much of an allowance that is depends on how much the appearance of a man, seen four or five rods off by a perfect stranger, in a light but cloudy evening, consists in his dress. It can consist of nothing but dress, figure, and manner. Mr. Mirick's evidence, therefore, amounts to this and no more: "I think the prisoner's figure and manner the same as those of a man I saw four months ago, under the circumstances above described." This is so slight that the difference in his testimony is not worth mentioning, except to show the growing tendency of the whole evidence.

About the time that Mirick leaves the prisoner in his frock at the corner, Mr. Webster overtakes him in Howard Street in a wrapper. He passed him without much observation; he did not see his face, but he thinks it was the prisoner. The probability, from the change in dress, is that it was not.

And this reminds me of a remark made on the last trial, that such differences and sudden changes of dress were to be expected for the purposes of disguise when such business was on foot. With great deference to the learned counsel, it seems to be highly improbable.

What is the evidence on this point? The prisoner is supposed to have had on his usual frock and cap at the corner from a quarter before to a quarter after nine; at half-past nine to have walked in Howard Street in the same cap and wrapper; to have sitten [sic] on the steps of the ropewalk in his own cap and camlet cloak at half-past ten; and five minutes after to have been seen in the same street in his frock.

Now I agree with the learned counsel that on such occasions disguise is to be expected, and farther, that it is entirely incredible anyone should go undisguised. But what disguise is here? The wrapper does not, indeed, correspond to any known dress of the prisoner; but in every other situation in which he is seen, he is recognized by his usual dress and by that alone. Now it is incredible enough that a man should, in a light evening, be out in his usual dress to commit murder in his native town; but that he should think to disguise himself by putting on and off his own cloak, as well known as his own coat, and thus be seen in two of his habitual dresses, is a little too much to ask you to believe. Why not assume one effectual and complete disguise? Or, if he feared being seen too often in one dress, why not put a strange cloak over a strange coat? And why wear his own cap the whole evening? The counsel has said that this was a murder, planned with great skill; nothing could be more unskilled than the prisoner's part if he was there.

But let us come to the more material part of this testimony. Mr. Southwick swears positively to having seen the prisoner on the ropewalk at half-past ten in his own cap and cloak; that he passed him three times and watched him twenty minutes. He has known the prisoner from childhood. He did not speak though he felt very suspicious of him. He went into the house and took off his coat and came out again, and the man was gone. He met Mr. Bray, who pointed out a man standing at Shepard's post on the other side of the street in a frock and cap like the prisoner's. Bray and he stopped and observed him till he left Shepard's post, walked down the opposite side of the street, and passed them and stood at the post under Bray's window. They then crossed over and entered Bray's house, passing within twenty feet of him. Southwick says he did not recognize the man in the frock coat, but supposed him to be the same he had seen on the steps because there was no other person in the street, and because he had the same suspicions of him!

Now this testimony of Mr. Southwick is open to two or three important objections. In the the first place, if Frank Knapp were on the steps to aid in a murder at that moment in execution, and expecting to be joined by the murderer, would he have permitted Southwick to pass him three times and watch him twenty minutes? He knew Southwick as well as Southwick knew him. Southwick says he dropped his head each time he passed him so that he could not see his face.[8] So there is a foolish bird that puts its head in a hole and thinks itself safe if it cannot see its pursuers. Murderers are apt to be more cautious.

He says he knew it then to be Frank Knapp, and told his wife so. But though he thought the man he and Bray saw was the same, and both wondered what mischief he could be about, he never told Mr. Bray who he thought it was. Is that possible? Yet both he and Bray agree in it.

But the greatest impossibility of all is that he should not have recognized the prisoner, if it was he, in his usual dress, while walking down the opposite side of this narrow street. [The street is about twenty feet wide.] Chadwick tells you it was so light he easily distinguished Mr. Saltonstall farther off the same evening. Now how inconsistent is this story with the supposition that that was the prisoner. He knew Frank Knapp familiarly; he saw him and recognized him in his cloak on the steps; he saw a man on the opposite side of the street five minutes after, who he, for some reason not connected with his appearance, thought was the same. And yet, though that man wore the usual dress of the prisoner, and walked down the street by Southwick when it was light enough to distinguish persons across the street, and though Southwick passed

---

[8] In Dexter's summation in the first trial he said that if anything further was wanted to discomfit this incredible witness, the fact was before them. "He swore that there was no fur on the cap, that the person accused dropped his head each time Southwick passed. Think you, gentlemen of the jury, that he could not have seen fur if it had been on the cap when he dropped his head? Here is the cap—and here is the fur! What excuse now?"

within twenty feet of him to go into Bray's house, he did not recognize him as the prisoner.

Again, he thought the man in the frock was the same as the man in the cloak. He knew the man in the cloak was Frank Knapp, yet he and Bray wondered who the man in the frock could be; and Southwick never thought of telling Bray it was Frank Knapp.

Now if Southwick's testimony were believed, it not only would not prove that the prisoner was the man at the post, but it would prove almost conclusively that it was not. It is impossible that Southwick should not have known him if it were he, and should not have told Bray if he knew him on the steps.

Besides Southwick is contradicted by Mr. Shillaber. He told Shillaber that "for aught he knew the man in Brown Street might be Richard Crowninshield, and Frank Knapp the other — he could not tell who they were." And how does Southwick explain this? He says Mr. Shillaber's question was, "Might not the man that came from Newbury Street be Richard Crowninshield?" A probable question indeed for Richard's counsel to ask!

But one word more with Mr. Southwick. When Chase and Selman were indicted for this murder, he went before the grand jury as a witness at Ipswich. He there swore that the man he saw in Brown Street was about the size and height of Selman and said not one word about Frank Knapp! On this testimony, and that of Hatch, the convict, was Selman indicted and imprisoned as a felon eighty-five days, until another grand jury assembled and, as Hatch's oath was inadmissible and Southwick had turned his testimony against Knapp, Selman was discharged.

Now when was there anything more abominable than this, except in form? It is not, to be sure, within the reach of the law, but how is it in conscience? He swears now that he then knew it was Frank Knapp, and yet he indirectly swore then that it was Selman. And what is the contemptible evasion by which he tries to escape? Why, that it is true that he was about the size of Selman, and he was not asked whether it was Frank Knapp! If he tells truth now, he knew then that by one word of truth he could clear Selman of all suspicion of being in Brown Street. He wilfully *suppressed that truth.* Now why is he a more credible witness than if he had been convicted of perjury?

It is said he told his wife it was Frank Knapp. She says so and it may be true, but it is not the very best corroboration. It is not of one half the weight of the fact that he did *not* tell it to Bray.

Still that only goes to the identity of the man on the steps. It leaves the man at the post still nameless, and that is the important question. Southwick does not pretend to identify him.

Now this — with the addition of a statement from Bray that he could not tell who the man in Brown Street was, though he was about the size and shape of the prisoner and wore a cap and full skirted coat such as the hatters and tailors say Frank Knapp and a hundred others wear — was absolutely all the evidence on the first trial that the prisoner was in Brown Street. Two remarkable facts have happened since. One is that Mr. Bray, one of the most honest witnesses in the cause, has in this trial, to the same question, answered that he had no doubt the man he saw in Brown Street was the prisoner. Now I have no disposition to accuse Mr. Bray of any intentional misstatement or overstatement, but here is a direct and flat contradiction. One week he says, "I have seen the prisoner in jail and in court, and I cannot say he was the man in Brown Street"; and the next week he says, "I have seen him in jail and in court, and I have no doubt he is the man."

Nay more; though he said that he had thought more of it since the trial and become more certain — a strange way of correcting an opinion formed on what was seen four months ago — he said too that when he first saw the prisoner in jail he recognized him by his dress and motions. Now there is no reconciling these things, let them be explained as they may. Both cannot be true. Which will you believe? That he does or does not recognize him?

Mr. Bray is one of the committee of vigilance; let that go for what it is worth and no more. But which is more likely to be right — his first testimony, the result of the reflection of three months, before he knew what would be the event of the trial, or that result corrected by the revision of a week, when he knew that the first trial had failed on that very point? I repeat that I accuse Mr. Bray of no wrong, but I cannot acquit him of that subjection to the power of imagination which has brought others here, as honest as himself, to swear positively to things that never did and never could happen. . . .

The other of the two remarkable facts which I have mentioned is a most wholesome lesson as to the credibility of the testimony in this case, and of the value of circumstantial evidence. It is worth hours of argument and peals of eloquence. It is a fact, a stubborn fact, and there is no explaining it nor getting away from it. Miss Lydia Kimball and Miss Sanborn, two elderly respectable females, as credible persons as any that have testified, have, under the influence of the madness that seems to have possessed almost everybody in Salem, testified distinctly and positively to a thing as within their own knowledge which is absolutely impossible. They both swore that on the morning after the murder, a person whom they did not know, brought into Captain White's house an old cloak and left it, saying, "This is my brother's cloak." Miss Kimball can't say it was the prisoner who brought it, for neither of them knew him at that time; but Miss Sanborn thinks he had a cap on, and Miss Catherine Kimball says that Joseph Knapp afterwards took the cloak as his own. Now here seemed to be strong confirmation. Here was the prisoner, driven by the folly that always attends guilt, carrying into the very house of the murder the disguise he had worn the night before. How perfectly this corresponded with the testimony of Burns that Joseph Knapp left his cloak at the stable, and with the suggestion of counsel that Frank Knapp had gone there to get it as a disguise! How wonderful is the force of circumstantial evidence! Men may lie, but circumstances cannot!

Now what is the fact about that cloak? It was Joseph's cloak. Stratton, Stephen White's coachman, went out to Wenham with a chaise that morning to bring in Mrs. Beckford, and she brought that cloak in with her. Stratton left Mrs. Beckford at Joseph White's, but by accident carried the cloak to Stephen White's in the chaise. He afterwards folded it up and carried it to Joseph White's house. He was the stranger with the cap that did not say, "This is my brother's cloak"; for how could he say so? He knew it was Joseph Knapp's cloak. Now what becomes of the truth of Miss Kimball's and Miss Sanborn's story and the force of circumstances? "Circumstances cannot lie"; but women and men too that swear to them may be mistaken, and with the help of a heated imagination and a few leading suggestions, may honestly invent the most outrageous fictions.

Now this was detected by mere accident. . . . We called Stratton . . . and then the whole matter was distinctly admitted. And this is the way that evidence is got up against the prisoner, and how much more of equally plausible testimony might be explained away in like manner we shall never know. Not a single fact in the cause is better vouched than this, few so well; and yet the only material part of it is utterly false.

Now take Bray and Southwick, the only material witnesses; make what allowances for error you think ought to be made, and can you say you are satisfied that the prisoner was in Brown Street? . . .

But let us look for a few moments at the proof of the prisoner's alibi. It is applicable to two different times. The first between seven and ten, the second after ten. The first depends on the testimony of Page, Balch, Burchmore, and Forrester. Now Page says he knows it was Monday or Tuesday evening; he said on examination he knew it was not Saturday because he came home from college that day and spent the evening at home. Burchmore is positive it was on Tuesday; and though uncertain before, has since remembered that he told William Peirce so the day or day but one after the murder. We offer Peirce as a witness to the fact. Balch and Forrester both strongly believe that it was on Tuesday, and all agree it was cloudy though light, and Monday was fair and bright.

Now what is there against this? It is said they have expressed doubts and uncertainty heretofore. There is no contradiction; three of them give now only their belief but it is a very strong one in all. Burchmore, however, is positive, and he gives a good reason for it and good proof of his correctness. Here stands William Peirce ready to swear that Burchmore told him so the next day or the day after. We cannot examine him, and the prosecutors will not. We have a right then to take it as proved by Peirce.

But it is said that on the evening spoken of Frank said he had a horse from Osborne's, and none is charged on that evening and one is charged on Saturday evening; and this is thought sufficient to overthrow the whole testimony. But he may have had a horse and not be charged with it, or he may have told a falsehood when he says he had one. You remember the purpose for which he said he was going out of town. Perhaps he chose to make a pretense of riding, the better to conceal his motions. It all depends on the accuracy of Osborne's books. Osborne was not examined on that point. But, after all, it is of no importance except to show that Mirick and Webster are mistaken, and they are not very material witnesses.

The other branch of the alibi is more important because it embraces the supposed time of the murder. Captain Knapp, the father, swears that he went home a few minutes before ten, and that Frank came in and went to bed a few minutes after. And there is a particularity about this account that marks it either as truth or as wilful and cunning perjury; and Captain Knapp's character is enough to shield him from such a charge. He says he commended Frank's return at the prescribed hour; that Frank asked him if he should bolt the door, and he said no, that Phippen was out; that Frank, seeing him looking over his papers (for he failed the very night) asked him if he should help him, then threw his cap on the window seat near his own hat and went up to bed. Captain Knapp sat up till after one, and Phippen returned at that hour and sat up for the rest of the night. Samuel H. Knapp's evidence is that a few minutes after ten, the prisoner opened his chamber door, spoke to him, and then went into his own room; and nobody heard him leave the house afterwards. He came down to breakfast as usual in the morning.

Now this is impeached by testimony of certain conversations and statements of Captain Knapp and Samuel H. Knapp. It is said Captain Knapp told Shepard that Frank came home and went to bed before half-past ten "as Phippen told him." If he said, "as I told Phippen," that would corroborate instead of contradicting him. And it is said further that he told Treadwell that he did not know what time Frank came home but believed about the usual hour.

Now these are not contradictions, and their apparent inconsistency depends wholly on the accuracy with which these conversations are remembered and reported. Of all kinds of evidence, reports of conversations are the most uncertain. You have seen in this very case that neither counsel nor the reporters nor even the judges agree as to the words used by the witnesses on the last trial of this cause, only a week since, although the greatest attention was paid and careful notes were taken. Then what is the probability that accidental conversations which took place two or three months ago can now be accurately stated? Which is the more probable, that Captain Knapp remembers the facts he states so circumstantially, or that Shepard and Treadwell remember his words? And he is confirmed by Phippen Knapp and Eliza Benjamin as far as they could know.

But there is one piece of evidence that meets all the deficiencies of this case with a wonderful felicity. Whatever the government cannot otherwise prove, Mr. Colman swears the prisoner has confessed and nothing more. Of half an hour's conversation with the prisoner, he cannot remember a word but what turns out to be indispensable to the case of the prosecution. I no more mean to accuse Mr. Colman of wilful misstatement than I do Mr. Bray or Miss Kimball or Miss Sanborn. But he is ten times as likely to be mistaken as either of them. The old cloak story was, until exploded, ten times more credible than Mr. Colman's account of the confession. The witnesses for aught we know are equally respectable in character, and the testimony intrinsically more probable. What but the contagion of an unexampled popular frenzy could have so deluded those women? They have not been exposed to it more than others; but Mr. Colman has been living in its focus and breathing its intoxicating air for months. No man in the community has been so excited by this horrible event as Mr. Colman.[9] No man has taken a more active part in inquiring into its mysteries. Shall he then claim an exemption from the power that has either prostrated the integrity or strangely confounded the memory of witnesses as credible as himself? He had visited Joesph's cell three times that very day before he went into Frank's, and the last time passed directly from one cell where he had received a full verbal confession, to the other where he now thinks he heard what he has testified. To a man so excited as he was, and is to this day, here is ample cause for confusion and mistake.

The witness is a clergyman, and whatever credibility that office may claim for him, I am willing he should enjoy. In my mind it is no more than belongs to any man of honest reputation; and on one account something less, for I cannot think the clerical office so well fits a man to endure and resist the excitement to which the witness has been subjected, as a secular employment. It is the experience of the world that clergymen, when they mingle in worldly business, are more powerfully acted upon by it than others.

Now every material word of his testimony is contradicted by Mr. N. P. Knapp, the prisoner's brother. He went into the cell with Mr. Colman and must have heard all that was said. He had not been in Joseph's cell during any part of his confession, and was not therefore liable to any misunderstanding. His attention was early called to it by a dispute with Mr. Colman about the club, and by consultations with counsel for his brother's defense. He has always borne an unsuspected character. Mr. Colman himself testifies to the propriety of his conduct before the trial. He trusted him with the

---

[9] In later years the London *Times,* in a review of one of Colman's books, referred to him as "this unnecessarily agitated man."

knowledge of the place where the club was hidden and depended on his honor not to remove this witness of his brother's guilt, and the trust was not betrayed. Now there stand two witnesses, equal in character, directly opposed to each other on a matter known only to themselves and to the prisoner.

It is said Mr. Knapp is contradicted by Mr. Wheatland; that is, Mr. Wheatland swears that in casual conversations held some months ago, Mr. Knapp made statements to him contrary to what he now swears. I have already remarked on the value of this kind of evidence. It depends on the thing least of all to be depended on, the accuracy with which words are remembered. The change of a word changes the whole meaning. Make the case your own. Can you pretend to remember casual conversation held with your neighbors three months ago so that you can now swear to them? And if they should swear to the facts differently from your present recollection of those conversations, would you charge them with perjury? Or do you think if we had an investigating committee of twenty-seven, and the whole bar and population of Salem, looking up evidence for the prisoner, we could not find witnesses who understood or misunderstood Mr. Colman to give accounts different from what he now swears to? With such means, any man may be contradicted. But Mr. Wheatland candidly tells you on this trial that he cannot speak with certainty as to those conversations— how much related to what was said by Joseph and how much to what was said by Frank. That once admitted, the whole force of the contradiction is gone.

Mr. Knapp cannot be mistaken about this matter. It is impossible that, after having employed counsel for the defense before the magistrate, and being himself a lawyer and understanding the danger of such evidence, he could have heard Frank confess away his life without remarking and remembering it. I say confess away his life; for though these confessions, if true, cannot harm him as a principal, he was then chargeable as an accessory, and on such a charge they would have been fatal.

Mr. Colman, on the contrary, is most liable to be mistaken about it. Having had repeated conversations with Joseph, before and after on the same subject, it would be wonderful if he could accurately report, as he pretends to do, the very words of Frank. It would be wonderful if he could separate the substance of the interviews. He did not, as he says, expect to be called as a witness against Frank.

Mr. Knapp did expect to be examined because he had early intimation of Mr. Colman's mistake about the club.

Now take the contradiction of Mr. Knapp, such as it is, by Wheatland on the one hand, and Mr. Colman's liability to error on the other; put equal characters into the two scales, and which will preponderate? One must be wrong. It is unnecessary and would be wicked to charge either with perjury; but there is a mistake between them that no supposition can reconcile. If you are not already satisfied which was most liable to err, look at the intrinsic probability of the stories.

The prisoner is a young but not a timid man. You have seen enough of his bearing on this trial to judge whether he would be likely to be surprised into a confession; and he was not surprised, for he had been examined and had counsel. Mr. Colman was a perfect stranger to him, not even known by sight. Now one of these witnesses tells you that the prisoner disclosed his whole guilt to a perfect stranger at first sight, without reluctance or hesitation, in direct answer to as many questions, and without threat, promise, or encouragement; while the other says he only said it was hard that Joseph should make any confession about him, but that he had nothing to confess and should stand his trial. Which of these things is the more probable? And is it probable that N. P. Knapp, a lawyer, who was then providing for the defense of his brother, should have permitted him to make these confessions without interferring?

I have said that Mr. Colman heard confessions of the exact facts which the case required and no more. See how that is, and how probable it is. The prisoner makes no general confession, claims no right, and expresses no hope to be admitted State's evidence. But to four distinct questions respecting the details of murder, he gave four distinct answers criminating himself.

Now what were those answers? That the murder was committed between ten and eleven, a fact as you have seen wholly without other sufficient evidence but all important to the case; that Richard Crowninshield was the actual murderer, a thing without the shadow of other proof except that McGlue saw him the evening before near White's house and looking away from it; that the club was hidden under a certain step of the Branch Meeting House, the only proof that that club had anything to do with the murder; that the dirk was worked up at the factory; and lastly that Frank was absent from home at the time, to fortify the Brown Street evidence and destroy the alibi. . . .

But is it not remarkable that so little should be remembered of a half hour's conversation, and that so very distinctly? Is it not re-remarkable that, finding Frank so communicative, Mr. Colman should not have gone on to verify Joseph's whole confession in the same way? He tells you he has Joseph's confession covering nine sheets of paper; and yet, though Frank answered so freely, he had the curiosity to ask him only these four questions. It is truly incredible.

Now what improbability is there in N. P. Knapp's account of this interview? Not the least. He agrees with Mr. Colman that Frank said it was hard that Joseph should confess, and he cannot positively swear that what Mr. Colman adds as to its being done for Joseph's benefit, did not follow, because he remembers the first part of the sentence and he may have forgotten the rest. But he swears that to the best of his belief, it was not so. And to the four questions and answers, he swears positively that no such things were said, because, if said, he must have remembered them. And is not this a perfectly proper distinction? His account too of the conversation with Mr. Colman on the turnpike and in Central Street of the note to Mr. Stephen White, and of all the other circumstances relating to the subject, is perfectly consistent, natural, and credible.

But what is the amount of all these confessions? If true, they prove indeed that he knew too much of this guilty deed. But they imply no presence at it. All but his absence from home are facts that he might, and some that he must have learned afterwards from others. And what does the fact that he was absent from home prove? At most, it is but a circumstance corroborative of the Brown Street evidence. He may have been there or he may have been elsewhere. The form, indeed, in which we have the con-fession from Mr. Colman might imply that he was absent, knowing of the deed — "I went home afterward." But, obviously, this all depends on the exactness with which the words are re-membered. Suppose only a slight change, and the dialogue to run thus: "When was the murder committed?" "Between ten and eleven." "Were you at home then?" "No, I did not go home until after that time." Now this would contradict the alibi, but would not contain any implication of his partaking in or knowing of the murder at the time. And when an implication depends on such slight differences, it is no evidence at all. And I repeat: What is the probability, if any confessions were made, that they were made in the words now delivered, when Mr. Colman has forgotten both words and substance of all the rest of the conversation?

One point only remains; but it is the great and important one. Believe the prisoner — if you will believe anything on such testimony as Leighton's and Palmer's — a conspirator and a procurer of the murder; believe him in Brown Street at half-past ten, and that the murder was committed at that hour — against the manifest weight of all the evidence but the confession; believe the confession, too, and the whole of it — improbable and contradicted as it is; and, whatever the prisoner may deserve in your moral judgment, he stands as clear of this indictment as a principal, aiding and abetting, as Joseph Knapp does, who was in bed at Wenham.

And here, gentlemen, if you ever come to this part of the case, you are to be tried as well as the prisoner. He is to be tried for his life, and you for a character which will last as long as life. The time will soon come when this trial will be coolly and impartially examined. . . .

Let us go back to the acknowledged law of the case. No matter what the prisoner has done or agreed to do, if he was not at the moment when the murder was committed in a place where he could give actual assistance, and there for that purpose, then he was not a principal in this murder. It has indeed been contended that it is enough that the parties thought the place a proper one for the purpose. Such is not the law; but here it is the same thing, for how can you judge that they thought it a fit place unless you yourselves think it so? . . .

Could the man in Brown Street give that help to the murderer, without the hope of which the murder would not have been committed? This is a question of fact for you to try on the evidence and the view. You must be satisfied of this beyond any reasonable doubt, or your verdict of guilty will be against yourselves. Now what assistance did the case admit? It was a secret assassination. If the prisoner had been actually present in the room or in the house, that alone would be enough. . . . But when you find but one accomplice, and him at a distance in another street, you must inquire why he was there. You must be satisfied that he was posted there with some power, and therefore with a purpose to aid. It becomes material to inquire particularly what aid he could afford. The late lamented chief justice, in his charge which has been read to you, delivered with special reference to the facts in this case, says if he was there to prevent relief to the victim, to give an alarm to the murderer, or to assist him to escape, then he was present, aiding and abetting. . . .

Was he there to intercept relief? If so, he would have taken a post where he could be aware of its approach. But did he do so? It is said the murderer entered the house at half-past ten. At that hour and for twenty minutes after, the prisoner is said to have been sitting wrapped in a cloak on the steps of the ropewalk, not watching others but hiding his own head from observation. From that time until five minutes before he was joined by the murderer, he was still farther off, leaning on a post at Shepard's house. How could he know whether relief was approaching or not? He could not see the house from any one spot where he was seen that evening. Anyone who passed him would have to turn two corners before he would be near White's house. Now he could see nothing but Brown Street and nobody but those who passed through it. If anyone passed there, what was he to do? Was he to knock him down upon the possibility that he might be going to turn into Newbury Street, and then might turn into Essex Street, and then might go up that street toward White's house? On such a possibility was he to protect the murderer by an act that would infallibly create alarm to no purpose? The supposition is absurd. He could not intercept relief because he was not where he could be aware of it.

Could he give an alarm? An alarm of what? You see that he could not know of the approach of danger. If the enterprise had failed, Richard might have been discovered, overpowered, and removed before his accomplice could have been aware of any difficulty.

But if it had been his object to intercept relief, or to give an alarm if he could not intercept it, where would he have been? At that point from which relief might be feared, and where early and certain intelligence of it might be had. Where was that? Certainly in Essex Street. Who would come to the relief? The inmates of Captain White's own house, or of the adjoining houses of Daland and Gardner, or of the opposite houses, or some casual passenger. Now against all these, the post of observation was in Essex Street and near the house. Or, if he wanted to watch the adjoining streets, why not stand at the corner of Newbury Street? Why not anywhere but at the places where he was seen during the whole time?

But one thing remains. Could he in Brown Street help the murderer to escape? If he had been waiting with a swift horse to convey him away, that might do. But one man on foot can no more help another to run away, than one can help another to keep a secret. One could only embarrass and expose the other. Was he then to defend him in his flight? Resistance was not to be depended on or expected; besides, the accomplice was unarmed, and of what avail would he have been in Brown Street where no force could be expected unless the alarm had become general. (Much of this argument consisted of reference to the plans, and cannot be reported.)

Now we call on the prosecutor to satisfy you of some one_mode in which aid could be afforded. On the former trial two ways only were suggested. First, that Richard might have gone into the garden early in the evening and waited for a signal from Frank in Brown Street to indicate the time when the lights were extinguished in Captain White's house. And, second, that Frank was in Brown Street to see that the coast was clear in Howard Street, so that Richard might go there to hide the club. Now these things, absurd as they seem, were really said and insisted on. And they are the best hypotheses that the best of counsel can make for the government. We want no better proof of the utter weakness of the point. If Richard was in the garden under the very windows, would he want Frank to tell him when the lights were put out? He could have watched every inmate of the house to his bed. He could have tracted every light up the stairs until they were extinguished in the chambers. He could have heard every noise and known when it ceased in the sleep of those within.

As to Frank's watching Howard Street, it would be enough to say that he was watched all the time and that he did not once look down Howard Street. Frank had been standing from five to ten minutes at Bray's post where he could not see a foot into Howard Street; and then Richard, having finished his conference, without any caution or examination, started and ran into that street with the speed of a deer. Did this look like watching? And for what purpose was Howard Street to be watched? That Richard might hide his club in a particular place selected, a club that nobody had ever seen and that could not be traced to him if found?

For what purpose then was the man in Brown Street? We are not bound to prove or to guess. But if it was the prisoner, and if the stories of the plot are true, he might have been there to know in season whether the enterprise had succeeded. Its failure might have been most material to be known to the contrivers before inquiry had gone far. If plunder was expected, he might have been there to share it. Neither of these things would make him a principal, for neither would be aiding at the time.

And now, gentlemen, as the last question in this cause, you are to say on your conscience: Are you satisfied beyond a reasonable doubt that the man in Brown Street, wherever he was, could have given any effectual aid in the actual commission of the murder, and selected that as the most proper place for that purpose? If you doubt about that upon the whole evidence, do your duty and acquit the prisoner. Such is the law; let it answer for its own deficiencies, if it be deficient, and trust that those who have that power will amend it if it needs amendment.

Gentlemen, of the jury, these are the prisoner's last words; his counsel have done and said all that they have found to do and say in his behalf. The rest is for the government, the court, and for you. You are to be assailed with a powerful argument by the learned counsel who is to follow me. Admire the eloquence, admire the reasoning; but yield nothing to it but admiration, unless it convinces your understanding that the evidence you have here heard, without regard to anything said or written elsewhere, ought to satisfy you of the fact that the prisoner was where he could aid in this murder, and by such presence did aid in it.

The prisoner is very young to be placed at the bar for such a crime. But, young as he is, I ask no mercy for him beyond the law. For every favorable consideration and sympathy consistent with the law, I would urge upon you his youth, his afflicted family, and the seduction of the evil example of others. By these, and all good motives, I would urge you not to sacrifice him against the law, that those more guilty than himself may be reached through him. His life is in your hands and in the hands of each one of you. May you, and each of you, give no verdict and consent to none but such as your hearts can approve now and forever.[10]

<hr>

[10] Dexter's argument was printed in the Boston *Evening Transcript*, part on September 11, and the remainder on September 13. It was, no doubt, reported by Lynde M. Walter, first editor of that newspaper. Probably Dexter had a chance to revise Walter's report. The *Transcript's* version was published some six weeks later in the *Appendix to the Report of the Trial of John Francis Knapp*. The argument is in *American State Trials*, vol. VII.

WEBSTER SUMMARIZES FOR THE GOVERNMENT

When Webster began his argument to the jury the courtroom was more than filled. A reporter wrote: "The throng of ladies has been so tremendous that even the poor devils of reporters who have sweated through nearly twenty days of drudgery, confinement, and impure air have not been allowed to retain their places at this feat of eloquence. . . . If the shoe falls off or the hat drops, it is lost irrecoverably. To stoop is annihilation; bob your head and it is gone."

There was one reporter, however, who managed to get what seems to be the only reasonably good report of Webster's speech. He was Lynde M. Walter, editor of the Boston *Evening Transcript*. Late in July, after issuing three trial numbers of the *Transcript,* he found that it was being ignored both by the public and by the competing newspapers. Obviously something sensational was needed to put the young paper on its feet, something so interesting that the *Transcript* could no longer be ignored. Walter found his answer in the second trial of Frank Knapp. He had made a good though brief report of the first trial for Dutton and Wentworth. He took down the closing arguments of Dexter and Webster, and on the twenty-eighth of August the *Transcript* reappeared. The entire issue, published sixteen days after Webster concluded his speech, was devoted to Webster's summation. There was not a single news item, article, editorial, or advertisement. The *Transcript* made a well recognized hit with the public by publishing the speech, and, says Joseph Chamberlain in his book, *The Boston Transcript,* with the help of a murder trial, "the little paper went smoothly on its way."

Walter's report seems not to have been noted by any of the commentators on Webster's speech, and no other adequate report has been discovered.[11] Some weeks later, of course, Whitman's *Appendix to the Trial of John Francis Knapp* was printed in Salem, and it contains the speech that appears in Webster's collected works; but we shall see that this speech is, in part, a revision of Walter's

---

[11] There was a brief summary of the first hour and a half of Webster's speech in the Salem *Gazette* of August 20, and apparently some commentators have accepted this summary as covering the whole speech. Claude Fuess in his excellent *Daniel Webster* (II, 296) says that this address was inferior to Webster's speech in the first trial. It was largely given to a reply to the complaint that the prisoner was the victim of persecution, and also stressed the prisoner's folly. Mr. Fuess then cites a passage which seems to have come from the *Gazette,* since, so far as we know, the passage is not found, in exactly these words, in any other report: "He only walks safely who walks uprightly. Guilt always stumbles. No road is smooth enough, no turnpike broad enough for the guilty man."

report, and also a compilation of various reports of speeches given at the first as well as at the second trial, and of Webster's own notes.

How faithfully Walter reports Webster's actual language, it is impossible to say; but there is reason to believe that it comes closer to Webster "in the raw" than most of the speeches that appear in the standard edition of his works. Whether Walter practiced shorthand we do not know; but he might not have needed more than such a system of abbreviations as any reporter invents for himself, for there is evidence that Webster ordinarily spoke very slowly.[12] Walter's version is much shorter than the speech Webster later released for publication.

A part of Mr. Walter's report follows:

Gentlemen of the jury:

Whatever additional labor may be imposed on the committee of vigilance, or upon the court, or others connected with the criminal trial now proceeding on a second examination, it will not all be regretted, if this second examination should tend to establish the truth by fixing the guilt of the prisoner, if it should succeed in removing all doubts whether he is justly amenable to the law he is alleged to have broken.

His learned counsel have said, with great propriety, that it is your single and individual duty to weigh the law and the testimony, and singly and individually to determine his guilt or innocence. If the discussion on the part of the defense had been conducted throughout in a spirit corresponding with that remark, I should proceed at once to an examination of the testimony in the case; but, gentlmen, you have heard, by way of preliminary and concluding remarks, so many things not bearing on the evidence, so much wholly disconnected with the guilt or innocence of the prison-

---

12 In extemporaneous speaking Webster's speaking was sometimes not only slow but halting. Harriet Martineau wrote, "It is something to see him moved with anxiety and the toil of intellectual conflict . . . to watch the expression of laborious thought while he pauses, for minutes together to consider his notes, and decide upon the arrangement of his argument." William Davis, who heard Webster many times, said that it was his habit to stop and scratch his right ear until the right word came. George Frisbee Hoar said that Webster had a wearisome habit of groping after the most suitable word and trying one synonym after another until he got the one that suited him best. A newspaper account of a speech delivered in Boston in 1830 tells how Webster "wound himself up in a sentence from which he seemed unable to extricate himself" until a voice from the audience supplied the missing word. "Mr. Webster echoed it, and the hall resounded with thunders of applause."

er, that I do not feel at liberty to proceed to the examination with this matter undisposed of.

It cannot have escaped your remark that a tone of complaint has prevailed in the defense, as if the prisoner was in danger of public feeling more than of pressing justice. You have been told of the getting up of the pursuit tending to the apprehension of the criminals, of the current of feeling bending against the prisoner, as it were, to destroy their last hopes of escape. Is this a time to talk of hopes of escape, when the whole community is roused and startled by unparalleled iniquity, when every man's safety depends upon his personal exertions to discover the perpetrators of the outrage? You have heard of wicked combinations to overwhelm the guilty, of the time and adventitious circumstances under which he is brought to trial. You have heard of foul testimony; of a private prosecutor; and all in a tone of complaint, beginning at the begining and ending at the end of the arguments for the defense.

Although all this is foreign to the case, it deserves notice — short notice — and shall receive it. I do not know that in all my practice, I have heard it made a subject of complaint what counsel were engaged in a cause. The efforts of the defendant's counsel have generally been directed to a defense and not to complaints that counsel was engaged. I recollect, in one of the last capital trials in this county, that I was concerned for the defense; and, in addition to the ordinary prosecuting officers, the respectable head of the Suffolk Bar, Mr. Prescott, was brought down from Boston to aid in behalf of the government.[13] The counsel for the prisoner then contented themselves with answering his arguments, as they were able, and not with carping at his presence.

It is complained that rewards were offered. Does it ever happen otherwise when a secret crime, even theft, is perpetrated, that those interested do not offer rewards for the detection of the offenders? Rewards were offered in the case to which I alluded; handbills were issued from here to Virginia; and every means taken to lead to detection. The community was nearly as much excited as at present.

But the height of the offending here, is that a combination was formed, a committee appointed. There was also a committee

---

[13] The Trial of Levi and Laban Kenniston for robbery, Ipswich, Mass., 1817; 14 *American State Trials*, 237. (The word *capital* should be *criminal*, although robbery had been a capital offense not many years before.) After other reputable lawyers had refused to take the case, because they considered it hopeless, Webster appeared for the defense and succeeded in clearing his clients.

appointed then. Is the human mind perverted; have we lost so much of moral sense as to be quiet under scenes like this? Has it come to this, that men cannot lift their hands without having it said they have combined? That they cannot stir without these remarks are boldly to be made to mark them with disgrace?

Again, it is said that the forms of ordinary justice were found too slow; and it is complained that a special session was appointed for these trials. The legislature is drawn in as a part of the conspiracy against this prisoner; and because the private prosecutor was a member of the senate, it is said to be all by his instigation! Does not everybody see that this session was absolutely necessary? Does not everybody know that in a capital trial the whole court must be present, and that the whole court can sit but one week in a year in this county? Under the ordinary sessions these prisoners could not have been tried in three years. The act was passed from public necessity and was drawn by the late chief justice for the accommodation of his court. Who supposes that the extra session ought not to have been appointed, when the ordinary sessions in three years could not have dispensed justice in these cases?

This prosecution of the prisoner as a principal is said to have been an afterthought. When Richard Crowninshield died, neither had been indicted; and it is asserted without the slightest authority, that the idea of prosecuting the prisoner as a principal never arose till after the death of Richard. The prosecuting officers had not then determined on the course to be pursued.

The counsel say they are concerned for the law rather than for the defendant. The law is in no danger except from their interpretation. I rather rely on you, gentlement, and on the court; and I doubt not that under your administration it will be fully and faithfully maintained.

You are told, in a tone of admonition, that your verdict will be a precedent. I hope it will be a precedent; a precedent to show that a jury can justly and truly discharge their duty to the prisoner and firmly uphold the law.

It is truly said that the law is not established so much to punish the guilty as to protect the innocent. But who are the innocent? Who are they whom the law is framed to protect? They are the honest, the industrious, the peaceful, the innocent sleepers in their own houses. The law is established, that those who live quietly in the fear of God by day, may sleep quietly in his peace by night.

The gentleman can think of none who are innocent but those who are placed at that bar, yet unconvicted.

And who are the guilty for whom the law provides its punishment? They are those who break in upon the silence of repose, and the helplessness of repose, to murder the innocent sleeper in his bed. It is of them that the law says, they are worthy of an ignominious death and must suffer its penalty.

You, gentlemen, are sworn to administer that law. You must do it without fear. If you, through mere unreasonable doubts and scruples, let the guilty escape, the law fails of its purpose; public security ceases, and men must rely on their own strength for their own safety. The jury must entertain no cavils, no studied evasions, no contrivances how they may suffer the escape of a prisoner; they must discharge their duty in saying whether he is guilty or innocent, and leave the consequences to another department of the government.

You will consider, gentlemn, how much consideration is due to the complaints about the manner in which the perpetrators of this murder have been detected; whether it makes any difference to the guilty, by what means his crime is brought to light; whether it is any cause of injury to be complained of, that he is found out. The counsel, taking a lofty flight of sentimentality, complain that even Palmer has betrayed his bosom friends! They complain that Palmer has been seduced; and they thought it a great hardship that he had been produced as a witness for the government. But why don't they meet the case? If a fact is out — no matter whence it comes — why don't they meet that fact? Do they mean to deny that Captain White is dead? I thought it would come to that.

Is there proof of a conspiracy? If there is, it does not remove that fact that Palmer was knowing to it. It don't prove it, to be sure, but it does not remove it; and when established as a fact, the testimony bears with great cogency upon the case. Instead of stating that the thing is proved by such a witness, why not deny the fact? Why not assert that there was no conspiracy, instead of carping at the mode of proof? Over this point the counsel continually hover; they neither fly away nor light; they neither deny nor assent. But they will find it necessary to come to somewhat closer quarters. The inquiry is into the truth of the fact. Instead of complaining that the prisoner had been detected by such means as Providence allotted, would it not have been better if they had asserted his entire innocence and denied all his guilt? Instead of complaining that he had been proved to be in Brown Street, would it not have been better to have shown that he was somewhere else? This style of complaint had been carried to great extent against disinterested and respectable witnesses, as if it were as bad to have had a hand in the detection of the murderers, as in the perpetration of the crime; as if to have known anything of the murderers were an act of the most flagitious and exquisite wickedness. And it would seem that because the crime has been detected by extraordinary exertions, the man accused ought to be mildly and calmly judged.

Much has been said about prejudice against the prisoner. There is nobody that I know of who has a particle of wish to his injury, further than may and ought to fall in the just dispensation of the laws. Nobody among those who conduct the prosecution feels a particle of displeasure with Frank Knapp; there is nothing of seeking revenge, nothing of persecution against him. It is not to be endured that honest indignation should be turned from the criminal against those who have detected him. The community are unfit to live under protecting laws if, in a case like this, they would not rise unitedly to see them enforced. The members of the committee were actuated by a desire to detect the murderers, not to fix the crime on A, B, C, or D. Every man felt an honest burst of feeling against the criminals; he would cease to be a man who did not; but no man labored to turn prejudice against the prisoner. The public feeling of the community is misrepresented; it is represented as if it pursued its zeal for blood to the head of the defendant. This is entirely wrong; the only zeal felt on this occasion is that men may not be exposed to murder in their own houses unarmed, and that they should be quiet in the pursuit of their daily toil. And that feeling will exist to the end, until the law in its just interpretation has visited the perpetrators of this atrocious crime, whoever or wherever they may be.

I doubt not you will administer the law truly, as far as you have anything to do with it. The consequence of your verdict is not for your consideration. It is for you to say, in your own department, whether the prisoner is or is not guilty; and if it should appear, as has been represented, that on account of his youth or other circumstances, he may be deserving of a pardon, it is for others to say so.

In order to see what the evidence in the case does prove, we must ask if Captain White was murdered in pursuance of a conspiracy. This is the first question, since the prisoner is charged in the indictment in three ways as a principal. He is charged as a principal; first, as having done the deed with his own hand; second, as an aider and abettor to Richard Crowninshield who did the deed; and third, as an aider and abettor to some person unknown.

You have already heard of two remarkable circumstances attending this trial. One is that Richard Crowninshield, generally supposed to have inflicted the blow, has gone, by the act of his own hand, from the tribunals of this world to the tribunals of eternal justice in another. He is called the perpretrator to distinguish him from those who were otherwise aiding to commit the murder, who are called principals in the second degree. Another is that the main instigator of the murder, he at whose hiring and procurement and for whose benefit it was committed, who has made a confession of all the circumstances attending its commission, is not now a witness; he has refused to testify and, with the other accomplice, is yet within the reach of the law. Your decision may, therefore, affect more than the life of the defendant. If he is not convicted as a principal, neither he nor anyone else can be convicted of any participation in the crime; such is the nature of the law, and the result will be on the community. This has no tendency to prove his guilt, and it is only mentioned to show you the full consequences of your verdict. The fate of the whole depends upon this verdict; and it is for you, gentlemen, to determine whether this and the other prisoners are guilty and should suffer according to the law.

Now let us begin at the beginning; let us see what we know, independent of any evidence — of any direct evidence. This case depends mainly upon circumstantial evidence; secret crimes ever do, midnight assassins take no witnesses. There are very important circumstances in the case wholly independent of any direct testimony. This has been called, by the learned counsel for the defense, *circumstantial stuff*. It is stuff; but not such stuff as dreams are made of! It shall be my business to weave this stuff into a web, and see what may be made of it. The circumstance of Palmer's letter from Belfast is more than stuff; the circumstance that Joseph Knapp, Jr., wrote certain letters is more than stuff; the fact that the housekeeper was away is another circumstance and a piece of that same stuff; the facts that the doors were unbolted, the windows unbarred and opened, leading the way to the bed of the sleeping victim — this is stuff! No, gentlemen, this is weighty matter; conclusive matter which comes, if unexplained, with terrible force against the prisoner at the bar.

Let me invite your attention to those facts that tend to show how the murder was perpetrated — whether by conspiracy and in pursuance of a preconcerted plan. The appearance of things the morning after the murder showed that it was the work of a conspiracy. No stranger had done the deed; no one unacquainted with the house and the habits of its inmates. This was not an act of violence in the open streets nor in the house; somebody within had opened for those without; somebody who knew, had described to the murderer the situation in which all would be found; somebody who had access to the house had prepared it and made ready for the work. This shows a band of men in execution of their purpose.

And when the murder was perpetrated, the house was not alarmed. The assassin entered without fear or alarm; there was no riot, no violence. He found the way made plain before him. He found the window shutters unbarred and opened, the window fastening unscrewed, the sash thrown up. There was a lock on the chamber door but the key had been taken out and secreted, so that by no accident contrary to his usual custom could the victim preserve his life. The path of the murderer to and from the house was marked. The plank by which he ascended the window was brought from the garden gate, and his retreat was shown by drops of blood and footprints in the earth. That is evidence of conspiracy, combination, and preconcerted arrangement. The house must have been prepared by somebody within to afford easy access to those without, or somebody must have gone to the perpetration blindly and in the face of difficulty and detection. These are circumstances independent of all direct evidence. Here was evidence of a prepared, concerted, conspired murder.

Can it be doubted who made this preparation? Can it be supposed that Richard Crowninshield went groping in ignorance, in the dark, to find his victm? Can it be doubted that this originated with Joseph Knapp, Jr.? And when it is proved that the conspiracy was formed by the two Knapps and the two Crowninshields; when it is proved that the deed was to be done in the absence of the housekeeper; when it is proved that some of the conspirators were lurking suspiciously about the place at the time of the murder; when it is proved that Joseph Knapp, Jr. was in the house in the afternoon before the murder, can it be doubted that they, or some of them, have been the murderers of Captain White?

The posture of the family affairs at the time: the old gentleman reputed to be rich, with no children nor any wife; no heirs but nephews and nieces, the wife of Joseph Knapp being the daughter of his niece and housekeeper and the granddaughter of his sister. Mr. Stephen White was the son of a brother of the deceased and, it was generally supposed, would be the principal inheritor of his property by a will. It became an object to the other heirs at law to destroy the will; for according to a very prevailing though erroneous belief, the property would, if Captain White died intestate, descend equally to the children of the sister and the children of the brother. In this situation the murder was discovered. It alarmed everybody. Suspicion turned upon everybody interested in the death of Captain White. The enormity of the crime raised suspicions too horrible for utterance. If the object had been to steal the will, it did not succeed, for the will was found, a will that was good and complete. Suspicion turned at once from the heirs at law to the heirs under the will, as the only persons interested in the immediate death of the testator. Here the counsel carry their argument to the extent of ridicule. There is evidence to show that the Knapps tried to fix the suspicion upon Stephen White; but the counsel insist that the Knapps found suspicion turned upon him and only tried to strengthen it. They say the Knapps are not very criminal in this matter because they only strengthen, they did not originate the suspicion. Good God! What do the counsel mean? Did they not originate the suspicion when they killed Captain White? It is a good apology, indeed, that they only fomented a flagitious excitement which they had caused! It was not quite so wicked to write the letters—as if there had been no previous suspicions! Who made the original cause of suspicion but the murderers with their own poniards?

Gentlemen, if we are not right now regarding the perpetrators of this murder, then there is not the least thing known about it. The community is as ignorant as at the hour of its committal.

The counsel thought they might admit that Richard Crowninshield was the perpetrator; and yet they say let it be proved. But the question is: Why did Richard Crowninshield kill Captain White? He did not murder without motive, without inducement. If he slew, who paid? He was not a gratuitous assassin. There is no going piecemeal in this case; you must come to the opinion that here is the truth, the whole truth, or that nothing whatever is known of the murderers. You must believe that you know the whole extent of the conspiracy.

Let us inquire: What is the conspiracy? Joseph Knapp was the discoverer and destroyer of a certain will; and if he could prevent Captain White from making another will, he would have a larger share of his fortune. He hired a ruffian; gave him aid to get into the house; the murder was committed. The two Knapps and the two Crowninshields were implicated by undeniable proof. Joseph Knapp had confessed but refused to testify. Of those four, one — the perpetrator — has gone to another account, and the prisoner is indicted as his aider and abettor in the commission of the fact.

This conspiracy began as far back, at least, as January. Endicott testifies to a conversation with Joseph Knapp on the seventh of January. Joseph said that Captain White had made a will and that Stephen White and Mr. Treadwell were executors. When asked how he knew, he said, "Black and white don't lie." He said it gave the bulk of the fortune to Stephen White, and when asked how he knew it, he repeated, "Black and white don't lie." When asked if the will was not kept in a trunk he said, "Yes, but there is such a thing as having two keys to the same lock." Here is evidence from J. Knapp's own intimations, that he had seen and could see the will whenever he chose. At the same time he said, "If I had been in town when the old man was taken violently sick, Stephen White would not have been sent for to Boston." This is in January.

But the most important part of the evidence of the conspiracy is told by Palmer. He begins on the second of April. Palmer is said to be a totally incredible witness. I shall not attempt to purify his reputation or uphold his character either as a man or as a witness. He is before you, bad enough, gentlemen — as bad perhaps as they represent him — I am willing to leave it so. The prisoner's counsel say, and say truly, that such a witness is not to be believed without strong confirmation; but if his story is confirmed, you must believe him and must act accordingly. If he were an accomplice turned State's witness — a very discreditable situation — and standing supported in some parts of his testimony, you might believe him for the whole. If his story is credible and consistent, and wholly unsupported except by testimony to other circumstances you may even then believe him. Much depends on circumstances, as to the credibility of such a witness. As to the complaints that the government have brought foul testimony, it is only to be said that the government do not select their own witnesses; they take such as have been chosen and furnished by the criminals. The defendant's counsel say Palmer was the bosom friend of some of the conspirators — surely it is not hard to judge a man by the testimony of his bosom friend!

The testimony of Palmer is competent for the government to use; it is before you and must pass for what it is worth. He stands, of all the witnesses in this case, the most entirely absolved from contradiction, either in his own story or by the testimony of other witnesses. His story is throughout consistent and credible; no one has attempted to detect any, the slightest, inconsistency in its details. Every part of his testimony to the conspiracy has been completely supported; they have not attempted with success to impeach him even in unimportant particulars. Babb has been brought in to contradict him, but he could not undertake to disprove the testimony of Palmer. He did not recollect, he could not fix the time when Palmer was at his house. He at first thought it might have been Friday the ninth instead of Tuesday the sixth that he went there. Palmer testified that he was there the Tuesday night of the murder, the sixth, and it is entirely and satisfactorily proved that he was at Danvers on the ninth and not at Babb's. In this attempt to contradict him, therefore, he is proved correct. So far as he is consistent with himself and credible in connection with the testimony of others, and so far as he is directly supported by others, so far he may be believed. The question is: Is his story true? We did not make the witness; he is such as we found him, such as the conspirators had chosen to confide their secrets with; if he sees fit to reveal what he learned in their company, he is fairly used for that purpose and is fairly believed so far as the jury see fit to believe him.

Palmer's testimony is important in fixing the conspiracy, if it is believed. He testifies to a ride of Frank Knapp to Danvers on Friday the second of April. At this time the project had been long in contemplation; this was not the first visit of Frank to the Crowninshields — Allen has testified to one in March. Palmer is here corroborated by Osborne's book — the best evidence because they fix the times of events. These books show that Frank had a saddle horse in the afternoon and a horse and chaise in the evening, as stated by Palmer. He is also supported by Allen who went with Frank to Danvers. He then goes on to state the conversations which took place between him and the Crowninshields after Frank came away. They told him of the proposal of the Knapps, and offered him a partnership in the crime and the profit. Frank had told them that Captain White had gone to Danvers alone in his wagon, and it would be easy to waylay him — overturn his wagon, and so to kill him. And they finally said the housekeeper would be away when the deed was to be done. How is this supported by other evidence? It is proved that Captain White on that day did ride alone to Danvers; that Frank Knapp did hire the horse and chaise in the evening; that the housekeeper was out of the way when the murder was committed.

Above all, the truth of Palmer's story is made manifest in the letter from Belfast. That letter is a most important piece of corroborative testimony. It was not written after the facts were known; it was not an afterthought got up to match the occasion. It was written long before the Knapps were suspected, and bears internal and conclusive evidence of knowledge on the part of the writer. The letter begins, "You may be surprised to be addressed by a perfect stranger" — he was a stranger, there is no evidence that he had ever seen Joseph Knapp; and Frank had not seen him, for at the time of the visit he was secreted at the Crowninshield's. It then makes a demand of money — send me money. It is a threatening letter, and afterwards says, "I know your plans; I know your brother Franklin and the business he was upon on the second of April." How could Palmer, in Belfast, before the Knapps were suspected, have fixed upon the second of April if he had not possessed knowledge of what transpired on that day? Every line of it bears confirmation to the truth of his story.

Take now the testimony of Endicott, of Palmer, and add to them the facts known in the case, and see if you doubt for a moment that Captain White was murdered according to the plan of a conspiracy; see if you doubt that these four were the conspirators.

Do you doubt Leighton? In manner he is a very bad witness; in some circumstances of his testimony he is a bad witness; all is against him in appearance; but do you think, notwithstanding all this, that he tells the truth? If you do, his testimony has a momentous weight in this case — it is not necessary but it is of great importance. He tells you of a conversation which he says he overheard between the brothers Knapp at Wenham. He heard Joseph ask Frank, "When did you see Dick?" Frank replied, "This morning."

Joseph asked again, "When is he going to kill the old man?" Frank said, "I don't know." And Joseph then remarked, "If he don't kill him soon I won't pay him." There is no doubt about the meaning of this; it is all clear. If you believe the witness, you cannot doubt that "Dick" meant Richard Crowninshield, and "the old man" Captain White.

But do you believe him, gentlemen? He seems to have been dragged here a reluctant witness, unwilling to testify against his employers. The day after the murder he said that he knew something, but checked himself, thinking he might go too far. He tells you that he was fearful for his own safety if the prisoner should escape; what reason he had to fear, you will judge. Certain it is, from undoubted testimony, that he had felt the dagger's point of the murderer of Captain White. If his story be true, he had ample cause for fear.

But it is said to be extraordinary that the conversation should happen there, at the end of a lane, just in hearing of the witness. Gentlemen, it is extraordinary that such a conversation should happen anywhere. The time and place of all such facts seem extraordinary when they are made known. It is no more wonderful that such a conversation should happen where it did, than that it should happen anywhere else; and if the witness happened to be within hearing, it is not extraordinary that he should hear it. There is nothing incredible in the circumstance if you believe the witness. It is said that it is dangerous to take a part of a conversation, when that part might be qualified by what preceded or followed it. You will perceive that this conversation might either stand alone or be connected with previous conversation on the same subject, and yet be wholly incapable of qualification. It is the same whether as a whole or a part, and cannot be misunderstood. A different accent, which the witness could not give, would make it seem either distinct or connected with something else; but nothing could change its meaning.

The fact is, the whole current of testimony bears with overwhelming force against the prisoner. When Palmer said that Dick was to kill the old man, and that Joseph Knapp, Jr., was to give him a thousand dollars for it, a hundred facts disclosed themselves, before unnoticed. The story of Leighton is altogether true or altogether false; and you will consider if he had power to put together such a conversation even if he had the will. It is simple, clear, distinct. Nothing is so plain as truth; there is nothing that bears with so much cogency as truth, nothing that exposes itself like truth. It is not pretended that the story was made for him, and there is nothing so difficult in believing its truth, as in believing that he was its fabricator.

Let us now look at the acts of the parties themselves. Palmer's letter was directed to Joseph Knapp instead of Joseph Knapp, Jr. By the way, that mistake about the name, though a slight circumstance, goes to establish the credibility of the witness. This letter, thus directed, fell into the hands of the father. Now let us keep a steady eye on this piece of *circumstantial stuff*, and see what we can weave it into. This letter fell into the hands of the father. He was utterly ignorant of its import, and carried it to his sons at Wenham on Saturday. They had a hearty laugh about it. How could anyone on the Penobscot River know their plans and doings? They advised their father, unsuspecting man, to carry it to the committee of vigilance. He did so, and all hope of concealment for the guilty was lost. Between the time of laughing at the letter on Saturday and Sunday morning, an occurrence took place to change the complexion of the letter. One of the Knapps had seen one of the Crowninshields, and learned that one Palmer who had gone to the eastward, did possess the knowledge of their guilty secrets. Then all was terror and alarm; and on the day following, Sunday, they wrote the letters to Stephen White and the committee of vigilance. The letter to the committee, accusing Stephen White, was written by Joseph Knapp, Jr., most certainly with the knowledge and concurrence of Frank. Was ever known a piece of more gratuitous, unqualified, inexcusable villainy? Merely to explain the apparent mysteries of that letter from Palmer, they engendered the basest suspicions of a man who, if they were innocent, they had no reason to believe guilty; and who, if they were guilty, they most certainly knew to be innocent. Joseph Knapp, Jr., told Allen that a fellow down East knew all their plans, and had written, demanding money; and that their father had put the letter into the hands of the committee. "I wish you to put these letters into the post office," said he, "because I wish to nip this silly affair in the bud."

Now mark the destiny of crime! Every page, every word, every letter of that criminal attempt to conceal crime, is brilliant with the light of disclosure. Joseph Knapp, Jr., wrote that letter to turn suspicion from himself and fix it upon Stephen White, and every line of it preaches that he was the murderer. If it were not rather the direction of an all-wise Providence, I should say it was the silliest piece of folly that ever possessed the head of a fugitive from justice. Crime is ever obliged to resort to such subterfuges; it trembles in the broad light; its vision is distorted; it needs no springing tempest to shake it into disclosure; its evil genius adheres to it and leads it wherever it will. Who, for a moment, beholds this letter and doubts his guilt? The constitution of nature is made to inform against him. There is no corner dark enough to conceal him; there is no highway, no turnpike smooth enough and broad enough for him to bear along his guilty load. All occasions inform against him. Every step proclaims his secret to every passenger. His own acts come out to fix his guilt. In striving to turn away suspicion, the murderer writes his own confession; he declares the truth to every eye. In striving to place himself in the attitude of conceal-ment, he bares his black bosom to the detestation of mankind. To do away with the effect of Palmer's letter, signed Grant, he writes his own condemnation, and affixes to it the name of Grant. Do you doubt this? Who could have written that letter to the commit-tee, signed Grant, but one who had seen this from Belfast, signed Grant? And who had seen this but the Knapps? The moment that letter was read, the whole truth was discovered.

At this point of the argument, the court adjourned until after-noon, when Mr. Webster resumed; but because of the immense crowd, and the unfortunate politeness of the sheriff, who took away the reporter's chair to accommodate a lady, it was found impossible to take notes. "The afternoon speech, therefore," says Walter, "is written from memory, and done as faithfully as a tolerably good memory will allow."

The part already set down proves the importance of Walter's report. We pass now to its conclusion, which shows that the perora-tion of the standard edition of Webster's argument was not drawn from the speech we are now considering, but is a revision of the closing of his address to the first jury.

Gentlemen, I shall detail you no longer. I think you can have no more doubt that the two Crowninshields and the two Knapps were conspirators for the murder of Joseph White. I think you cannot doubt that the murder was committed between ten and eleven on Tuesday evening of the sixth of April; that it was perpe-trated by the hand of Richard Crowninshield; that somebody was in Brown Street to aid in the murder of Captain White; that that person must have been the defendant. The other two are accounted for; Joseph Knapp was at Wenham, George Crowninshield was with his companions at Salem. Where were the defendant and Richard Crowninshield? I think you will believe the confessions; and if you do, there is no getting rid of the inference that arises. The confessions prove beyond all doubt that he was there. He could not have gone there to expose himself for any idle motive of curiosity. He went there to abet the murderer, by appointment and agreement. He did abet; he did follow his agreement; and thus has exposed himself to public justice.

Gentlemen, of all the evidence you are the judges. The law will be stated by the court, and you will feel bound by their decisions. No doubt you will judge the defendant fairly and reasonably, according to the evidence and the law. If any reasonable doubt of his guilt should arise, you will acquit him. You will judge individually and collectively. His life is in your hands. All our trust is that you will remember that, while you owe him a duty, you also owe the public a duty. There cannot be any more important truth to be disclosed relative to this crime; you cannot doubt that you now know all that will hereafter be known. You cannot fear that anything will arise to make you regret your verdict, neither can you fear that any mistake in testimony remains to be rectified. No one rushed in to give proof of his guilt. The witnesses have been cautious and considerate. If he is convicted, and not pardoned, he must suffer death. You have sworn to administer the law, and you cannot take into your hands the prerogative of mercy. If his youth is in his favor, the power to pardon rests with the executive government of the commonwealth. Your duty is, if you find him guilty, to say so. I have no doubt your hearts will incline you to mercy; but you will remember that you stand here for your country, and you cannot shut out the weight of testimony from your minds. The demand of public justice is — and it is ordained by Providence as well as by human law — that if a man is charged with the crime of murder, and found to be guilty, his life shall be forfeit to the community.

We would all judge in mercy, but we must move steadily in the light of truth and justice. Doubts may arise in your deliberations, but you must not make them merely to let the prisoner escape. Very little can it matter to him, or to the rest of the unhappy men who are charged with participation in his crime, that the sentence of the law should be avoided. Poorly is he supported, poorly are they all supported, if the mere effort is to escape the penalty which separates them from the tribunal of another world. It is as if one should strive to avoid wetting his feet with the dewdrops of the morning, who had arrived at the brink of the whole ocean.

The kindest wish we can have for him is that he may have a devout sense that his only hope depends on the goodness of Almighty God, and that his prayers may reach the throne of Divine Mercy.

The kindest wish we may have for you, gentlemen, is to wish that you may, by the assistance of God, be enabled to do your duty to the prisoner at the bar firmly and consistently; that you may do justice to him, and maintain the public law and the safety of the community.

The Judge's Charge

We must pass over the charge of Justice Putnam to the jury. To our "unturtored minds" it seems like a good speech for the government, tempered with judicial mercy. But we bow to the statement of a contemporary of Putnam: "He had no zeal that was not matched by his fairness." We are especially impressed by his zeal. We accept the defense of an eminent judge of today that "judges do that sort of thing." We agree that some judges do.

The cause was submitted to the jury at one o'clock on Friday afternoon, the twentieth of August. At six o'clock the jury returned a verdict of guilty.

The *Essex Register* said that the scene was affecting. Several of the jurors and many others in the courtroom "discovered evident emotion"; but the prisoner remained unmoved.

On Saturday Justice Putnam pronounced the sentence. He asked the prisoner if he had aught to say why sentence of death should not be pronounced against him. The doomed man replied: "I have only to say that I am innocent of the charge alleged against me."

Jutisce Putnam then addressed the prisoner at some length, urging repentance. He concluded: "That you be carried from hence to the prison from whence you came, and from thence to the place of execution and there be hanged by the neck until you are dead. And may God in his infinite grace have mercy on your soul."

The *Evening Transcript* said that "Frank's eye was firmly fixed on Judge Putnam when he was pronouncing sentence. There was every appearance of rigid determination in his look. The only change was when at last the Judge burst into tears. His eye sunk, and he appeared for an instant to be overmastered by his feelings, but an additional rigor was imposed upon his muscles. . . . He raised his eyes again and conquered." The *Essex Register* added this: "When he received this awful sentence . . . he took from his pocket his quid of tobacco and placed it in his mouth with as much unconcern as if he had been the most disinterested spectator in the solemn scene.

Many of the people of Salem were pleased with the verdict and editorial opinion was generally favorable to the outcome of the trial. The Newburyport *Herald* agreed with others that expediency played some part in the conviction, but contended that necessity required the conviction. And, it may be added, this has been the contention of later writers who have defended Webster and in general the course of the prosecution. Two such guilty men as Joe and Frank could not be allowed to escape through the niceties of the law.

But some newspapers protested the conduct of the trial and the hysteria of the community that threatened to weaken the safeguards of orderly court procedure. The *Yeoman's Gazette* of Concord said:

The opinion was often expressed by judicious professional men . . . witnesses of the state of feeling in Salem, that a conviction would be obtained on the second trial, *because the street discussion* of the evidence would weigh against the prisoner. . . . One would almost suppose that the jury threw all *doubts* in the scale against the prisoner. . . . The strongest safeguard of life — we mean a trial by jury — becomes a solemn mockery.

The *Literary Subaltern*, of Providence, denied that it was an apologist for Knapp, but contended that he had not had a fair trial:

An exasperated public seemed determined that someone should be offered a sacrifice for the deed whether guilty or not. . . . The talents of Daniel Webster were employed, and by the nature of Mr. Webster's employment, that distinguished man was bound to make use of every effort and talent he possessed to convict his victim of the crime of Murder, right or wrong, whether he was guilty or innocent.

At half-past eight on the morning of December 28th Frank Knapp was hanged. He kept up a brave front to the end. That evening his body was buried in the Howard Street cemetery, next to the grave of his mother and not far from the grave of Captain White.

CHAPTER 9

WEBSTER WRITES A SPEECH FOR POSTERITY

IN DISCUSSING with a friend the task of preparing his speeches for the press, Webster once remarked, " A very large part of my life has been spent in 'scratching out.' " It is a fairly well known fact that most of his published speeches — occasional, legislative, and legal — were carefully revised after delivery, either by himself or by some of his friends, before they received his final approval. His letters contain many references to the labor that he sometimes spent in revising speeches before they appeared in the press or in pamphlets. In 1851, when he was planning the publication of a six volume edition of his speeches, he wrote to Edward Everett, "I propose certainly to write over everything which has not been revised by myself."

Webster's revision of the speech we are considering appeared on October 28 in the *Appendix to the Report of the Trial of John Francis Knapp*. Webster's motive in making this revision at that time is clear. He was preparing for publication his first volume of collected speeches, and he wished to print this argument in as effective a form as possible. The volume, *Speeches and Forensic Arguments*, the title of which was copyrighted in November, 1830, was prepared with the help of his nephew, Charles B. Haddock, professor of rhetoric at Dartmouth College. With the exception of a few very minor changes, the text of the speech in this edition is identical with that in the *Appendix*. When the six volume edition of his speeches was printed in 1851 with the title, *The Works of Daniel Webster*, with the editorial assistance of Edward Everett and George J. Abbott, the speech in the Knapp trial underwent numerous, although usually minor, changes. The National Edition of *The Writings and Speeches of Daniel Webster* was published in 1903 in eighteen volumes and was edited by James McIntyre; but as far as the speech in the Knapp trial goes, it follows the 1851 edition.

We give you the *Appendix* version on the assumption that it represents Webster more closely than do the later revisions. For the same reason we retain his paragraphing and his very liberal use of italics. Those who like may compare the textual variations that have been made in later printings and consider to what extent they are improvements. It seems that Everett, whose own rhetoric Wendell Phillips said was "faultily faultless," could not bear to have Webster use a colloquial word or construction. For convenience, we shall refer to the speech in *Speeches and Forensic Arguments* as the Haddock edition and the speech in the *Works* as the Everett edition.

Webster's reconstruction of his speech follows.

Gentlemen of the Jury:

I am little accustomed, gentlemen, to the part which I am now attempting to perform. Hardly more than once or twice has it happened to me to be concerned on the side of the government in any criminal prosecution whatever; and never, until the present occasion, in any case affecting life.

But I very much regret that it should have been thought necessary to suggest to you that I am brought here to "hurry you against the law and beyond the evidence." I hope I have too much regard for justice, and too much respect for my own character, to attempt either; and were I to make such attempt, I am sure that in this court nothing can be carried against the law, and that gentlemen intelligent and just as you are, are not, by any power, to be hurried against the evidence. Though I could well have wished to shun this occasion, I have not felt at liberty to withhold my professional assistance, when it is supposed that I might be in some degree useful in investigating and discussing the truth respecting this most extraordinary murder. It has seemed to be a duty incumbent on me, as on every other citizen, to do my best and my utmost to bring to light the perpetrators of this crime. Against the prisoner at the bar, as an individual, I cannot have the slightest prejudice. I would not do him the smallest injury or injustice. But I do not affect to be indifferent to the discovery and punishment of this deep guilt. I cheerfully share in the opprobrium, how much soever it may be, which is cast on those who feel and manifest an anxious concern that all who had a part in planning, or a hand in executing, this deed of midnight assassination, may be brought to answer for their enormous crime at the bar of public justice.

Gentlemen, it is a most extraordinary case. In some respects it has hardly a precedent anywhere; certainly none in our New England history. This bloody drama exhibited no suddenly excited, ungovernable rage. The actors in it were not surprised by any lion-like temptation springing upon their virtue, and overcoming it, and overcoming it before resistance could begin. Nor did they do the deed to glut savage vengeance, or satiate long-settled and deadly hate. It was a cool, calculating, money-making murder. It was all "hire and salary, not revenge." It was the weighing of money against life; the counting out of so many pieces of silver against so many ounces of blood.

An aged man, without an enemy in the world, in his own house, and in his own bed, is made the victim of a butcherly murder for mere pay. Truly, here is a new lesson for painters and poets. Whoever shall hereafter draw the portrait of murder, if he will show it as it has been exhibited in an example where such example was last to have been looked for — in the very bosom of our New England society — let him not give it the grim visage of Moloch, the brow knitted by revenge, the face black with settled hate, and the blood-shot eye emitting livid fires of malice. Let him draw, rather, a decorous, smooth-faced, bloodless demon; a picture in *repose*, rather, than in *action*; not so much an example of human nature in its depravity, and in its paroxysms of *crime,* as an infernal nature,[1] a fiend in the ordinary display and development of his character.

The deed was executed with a degree of self-possession and steadiness equal to the wickedness with which it was planned. The circumstances now clearly in evidence spread out the whole scene before

[1] Speaking of the Loeb-Leopold case, Clarence Darrow says in *The Story of My Life:* "Loeb is a good-natured, friendly boy. I realize that most people will not be able to understand this, and perhaps will not believe it. Some may remember Daniel Webster's address to a jury in a murder case. He pictured the accused: his low brow, his murderous eye, his every feature proclaimed him a fiend incarnate. One would suppose from Daniel Webster's foolish argument that the defendant would be recognized as a murderer wherever he went. A part of this tirade was published in the old school-reader, and we used to 'speak' it on the last day of the term. We youngsters wondered why the Lord needed to put a mark on Cain's brow, for after reading Daniel Webster's receipt we could go out on the street and pick out killers everywhere, for all seemed to be marked. But Daniel Webster was not a psychologist; he was a politician and an orator, and that was enough for one man."

It is apparent that Darrow's memory was somewhat faulty. But regarding Webster's psychology, it may be noted that Wigmore in his famous work, *The Principles of Judicial Proof,* picks out the passage leading up to "there is no refuge from confession but suicide, and suicide is confession" for special commendation, saying that it is well endorsed by experience. It may be noted, incidentally, that writers generally credit Webster with being a statesman, but a woefully poor politician.

us. Deep sleep had fallen on the destined victim, and on all beneath his roof. A healthful old man, to whom sleep was sweet, the first sound slumbers of the night held him in their soft but strong embrace. The assassin enters, through the window already prepared, into an unoccupied apartment. With noiseless foot he paces the lonely hall, half lighted by the moon. He winds up the ascent of the stairs and reaches the door of the chamber. Of this he moves the lock, by soft and continued pressure, till it turns on its hinges, and he enters, and beholds his victim before him. The room was uncommonly open to the admission of light. The face of the innocent sleeper was turned from the murderer, and the beams of the moon, resting on the gray locks of his aged temple, showed him where to strike. The fatal blow is given, and the victim passes, without a struggle or a motion, from the repose of sleep to the repose of death! It is the assassins' purpose to make sure work, and he yet plies the dagger, though it was obvious that life had been destroyed by the blow of the bludgeon. He even raises the aged arm, that he may not fail in his aim at the heart, and replaces it again over the wounds of the poniard! To finish the picture, he explores the wrist for the pulse! He feels it, and ascertains that it beats no longer! It is accomplished. The deed is done. He retreats, retraces his steps to the window, passes out through it as he came in, and escapes. He had done the murder. No eye has seen him; no ear has heard him. The *secret* is his own, and it is safe!

Ah, gentlemen, that was a dreadful mistake! Such a secret can be safe nowhere. The whole creation of God has neither nook nor corner where the guilty can bestow it and say it is safe. Not to speak of that eye which glances through all disguises, and beholds everything as in the splendor of noon, such secrets of guilt are never safe from detection, even by men. True it is, generally speaking, that "murder will out." True it is that Providence hath so ordained, and doth so govern things, that those who break the great law of Heaven by shedding man's blood seldom succeed in avoiding discovery. Especially in a case exciting so much attention as this, discovery must come, and will come, sooner or later. A thousand eyes turn at once to explore every man, every thing, every circumstance connected with the time and place; a thousand ears catch every whisper; a thousand excited minds intensely dwell on the scene, shedding all their light, and ready to kindle the slightest circumstance into a blaze of discovery. Meantime the guilty soul cannot keep its own secret. It is false to itself, or, rather, it feels an irresistible impulse of conscience to be true to itself. It labors under its guilty possession, and knows not what to do with it. The human heart was not made for the residence of such an inhabitant. It finds itself preyed on by a torment which it does not acknowledge to God or man. A vulture is devouring it, and it can ask no sympathy or assistance, either from heaven or earth. The secret which the murderer possesses soon comes to possess him, and, like the evil spirits of which we read, it overcomes him, and leads him whithersoever it will. He feels it beating at his heart, rising to his throat, and demanding disclosure. He thinks the whole world sees it in his face, reads it in his eyes, and almost hears its workings in the very silence of his thoughts. It has become his master. It betrays his discretion, it breaks down his courage, it conquers his prudence. When suspicions from without begin to embarrass him, and the net of circumstance to entangle him, the fatal *secret* struggles with still greater violence to burst forth. It must be confessed, *it will be* confessed; there is no refuge from confession but suicide, and suicide is confession.[2]

Much has been said on this occasion, of the excitement which has existed and still exists, and of the extraordinary measures taken to discover and punish the guilty. No doubt there has been, and is, much excitement, and strange indeed were it, had it been otherwise. Should not all the peaceable and well-disposed naturally feel concerned, and naturally exert themselves to bring to punishment the authors of this secret assassination? Was it a thing to be slept upon or forgotten? Did you, gentlemen, sleep quite as quietly in your beds after this murder as before? Was it not a case for rewards, for meetings, for committees, for the united efforts of all the good to find out a band of murderous conspirators, of midnight ruffians,

---

[2] This passage is praised for its dramatic quality and its chief purpose is overlooked. Since Frank is being tried as aiding the perpetrator, it is necessary to convince the jury that Dick Crowninshield did the murder; but proof of that fact is not of the best. It is possible that one or more jurors may reject Frank's confession, and there is no other proof that Dick was even in town on the night of April 6. In the words of Albert E. Pillsbury, one time attorney general of Massachusetts, "Webster, spurning argument from beneath him, . . . strips the veil from the murderer's soul, . . . by a lightning-flash shows the guilt confessed." But we should not let Pillsbury's words conceal the fact the passage is argument—disguised.

We may, however, ask ourselves how far Webster's description of the murderer's struggle corresponds to what we know of Dick Crowninshield's conduct. Webster had a vivid imagination.

and to bring them to the bar of justice and law? If this be excitement, is it an unnatural or an improper excitement?

It seems to me, gentlemen, that there are appearances of another feeling of a very different nature and character, not very extensive, I should hope, but still there is too much evidence of its existence. Such is human nature that some persons lose their abhorrence of crime in their admiration of its magnificent exhibitions. Ordinary vice is reprobated by them; but extraordinary guilt, exquisite wickedness, the high flights and poetry of crime seize on the imagination, and lead them to forget the depths of the guilt in admiration of the excellence of the performance, or the unequaled atrocity of the purpose. There are those in our day who have made great use of this infirmity of our nature, and by means of it done infinite injury to the cause of good morals. They have affected not only the taste, but I fear also the principles, of the young, the heedless and the imaginative, by the exhibition of interesting and beautiful monsters. They render depravity attractive, sometimes by the polish of its manners, and sometimes by its very extravagance, and study to show off crime under all the advantages of cleverness and dexterity. Gentlemen, this is an extraordinary murder, but it is still a murder. We are not to lose ourselves in wonder at its origin, or in gazing on its cool and skillful execution. We are to detect and to punish it; and while we proceed with caution against the prisoner, and are to be sure that we do not visit on his head the offenses of others, we are yet to consider that we are dealing with a case of most atrocious crime, which has not the slightest circumstance about it to soften its enormity. It is murder; deliberate, concerted, malicious murder.[3]

Although the interest of this case may have diminished by the repeated investigation of the facts, still the additional labor which it imposes upon all concerned is not to be regretted if it should result in removing all doubts of the guilt of the prisoner.

The learned counsel for the prisoner has said truly that it is your individual duty to judge the prisoner; that it is your individual duty to determine his guilt or innocence; and that you are to weigh the testimony with candor and fairness. But much, at the same time, has been said, which, although it would seem to have no distinct bearing on the trial, cannot be passed over without some notice.

[3] Up to this point Webster has been drawing from his speech in the first trial. Webster appears to follow rather closely the Dutton and Wentworth pamphlet which was probably prepared by Lynde M. Walter, the young man who reported the second trial summation that appeared in the Boston *Transcript*.

A tone of complaint so peculiar has been indulged as would almost lead us to doubt whether the prisoner at the bar, or the managers of this prosecution, are now on trial. Great pains have been taken to complain of the *manner* of the prosecution. We hear of getting up a case; of setting in motion trains of machinery; of foul testimony; of combinations to overwhelm the prisoner; of private prosecutors; that the prisoner is hunted, persecuted, driven to his trial; that everybody is against him; and various other complaints, as if those who would bring to punishment the authors of this murder were almost as bad as they who committed it.

In the course of my whole life, I have never heard before so much said about the particular counsel who happen to be employed; as if it were extraordinary that other counsel than the usual officers of the government should be assisting in the conducting of a case on the part of the government. In one of the last capital trials in this county, that of Jackman for the "Goodridge robbery" (so called), I remember that the learned head of the Suffolk bar, Mr. Prescott, came down in aid of the officers of the government. This was regarded as neither strange nor improper. The counsel for the prisoner in that case contented themselves with answering his arguments, as far as they were able, instead of carping at his presence.

Complaint is made that rewards were offered in this case, and temptations held out, to obtain testimony. Are not rewards always offered when great and secret offenses are committed? Rewards were offered in the case to which I alluded, and every other means taken to discover the offenders that ingenuity or the most persevering vigilance could suggest. The learned counsel have suffered their zeal to lead them into a strain of complaint at the manner in which the perpetrators of this crime were detected, almost indicating that they regard it as a positive injury to them to have found out their guilt. Since no man witnesses it, since they do not now confess it, attempts to discover it are half esteemed as officious intermeddling and impertinent inquiry.

It is said that here even a committee of vigilance was appointed. This is a subject of reiterated remark. The committee are pointed at as though they had been officiously intermeddling with the administration of justice. They are said to have been "laboring for months" against the prisoner. Gentlemen, what must we do in such a case? Are people to be dumb and still, through fear of overdoing? Is it come to this: that an effort cannot be made, a hand cannot be lifted, to discover the guilty, without its being said there is a combination to overwhelm innocence? Has the community lost all moral sense? Certainly, a community that would not be roused to action upon an occasion such as this was — a community which should not deny sleep to their eyes, and slumber to their eyelids, till they had exhausted all the means of discovery and detection — must indeed be lost to all moral sense, and would scarcely deserve protection from the laws. The learned counsel have endeavored to persuade you that there exists a prejudice against the persons accused of this murder. They would have you understand that it is not confined to this vicinity alone, but that even the legislature have caught this spirit; that, through the procurement of the gentleman here styled "private prosecutor," who is a member of the senate, a special session of this court was appointed for the trial of these offenders; that the ordinary movements of the wheels of justice were too slow for the purposes devised. But does not everybody see and know that it was a matter of absolute necessity to have a special session of the court? When or how could the prisoners have been tried without a special session? In the ordinary arrangement of the courts, but one week in a year is allotted for the whole court to sit in this county. In the trial of all capital offenses, a majority of the court, at least, is required to be present. In the trial of the present case alone, three weeks have already been taken up. Without such special session, then, three years would not have been sufficient for the purpose. It is answer sufficient to all complaints on this subject to say that the law was drawn by the late chief justice himself, to enable the court to accomplish its duties, and to afford the persons accused an opportunity for trial without delay.

Again, it is said that it was not thought of making Francis Knapp, the prisoner at the bar, a *principal* till after the death of Richard Crowninshield, Jr.; that the present indictment is an afterthought; that "testimony was got up" for the occasion. It is not so. There is no authority for this suggestion. The case of the Knapps had not then been before the grand jury. The officers of the government did not know what the testimony would be against them. They could not, therefore, have determined what course they should pursue. They intended to arraign all as principals who should appear to have been principals, and all as accessories who should appear to have been accessories. All this could be known only when the evidence should be produced.

But the learned counsel for the defendant take a somewhat loftier flight still. They are more concerned, they assure us, for the law itself, than even for their client. Your decision in this case, they say, will stand as a precedent. Gentlemen, we hope it will. We hope it will be a precedent both of candor and intelligence, of fairness and of firmness; a precedent of good sense and honest purpose pursuing their investigation discretely, rejecting loose generalities, exploring all the circumstances, weighing each, in search of truth, and embracing and declaring the truth when found.

It is said that "laws are made, not for the punishment of the guilty but for the protection of the innocent." This is not quite accurate, perhaps, but, if so, we hope they will be so administered as to give that protection. But who are the innocent whom the law would protect? Gentlemen, Joseph White was innocent. They are innocent who, having lived in the fear of God through the day, wish to sleep in His peace through the night, in their own beds. The law is established that those who live quietly may sleep quietly; that they who do no harm may feel none. The gentlemen can think of none that are innocent except the prisoner at the bar, not yet convicted. Is a proved conspirator to murder innocent? Are the Crown-inshields and the Knapps innocent? What is innocence? How deep stained with blood, how reckless in crime, how deep in depravity may it be, and yet remain innocence? The law is made, if we would speak with entire accuracy, to protect the innocent by punishing the guilty. But there are those innocent out of court, as well as in; innocent citizens not suspected of crime, as well as innocent prisoners at the bar.

The criminal law is not founded in a principle of vengeance. It does not punish that it may inflict suffering. The humanity of the law feels and regrets every pain it causes, every hour of restraint it imposes, and, more deeply still, every life it forfeits. But it uses evil as the means of preventing greater evil. It seeks to deter from crime by the example of punishment. This is its true, main object. It restrains the liberty of the few offenders, that the many who do not offend may enjoy their own liberty. It forfeits the life of the murderer, that other murders may not be committed. The law might open the jails, and at once set free all persons accused of offenses, and it ought to do so if it could be made certain that no other offenses would hereafter be committed; because it punishes, not to satisfy any desire to inflict pain, but simply to prevent the repetition of crimes. When the guilty, therefore, are not punished, the law has so far failed of its purpose; the safety of the innocent is so far endangered. Every unpunished murder takes away something from the security of every man's life. And whenever a jury, through whimsical and ill-founded scruples, suffer the guilty to escape, they make themselves answerable for the augmented danger of the innocent.

We wish nothing to be strained against this defendant. Why, then, all this alarm? Why all this complaint against the manner in which crime is discovered? The prisoner's counsel catch at supposed flaws of evidence, or bad character of witnesses, without meeting the case. Do they mean to deny the conspiracy? Do they mean to deny that the two Crowninshields and the two Knapps were conspirators? Why do they rail against Palmer, while they do not disprove, and hardly dispute, the truth of any one fact sworn to by him? Instead of this, it is made matter of sentimentality that Palmer has been prevailed upon to betray his bosom companions, and to violate the sanctity of friendship. Again I ask, why do they not meet the case? If the fact is out, why not meet it? Do they mean to deny that Captain White is dead? One should have almost supposed even that, from some of the remarks that have been made. Do they mean to deny the conspiracy? Or, admitting a conspiracy, do they mean to deny only that Frank Knapp, the prisoner at the bar, was abetting in the murder, being present, and so deny that he was a principal? If a conspiracy is proved, it bears closely upon every subsequent subject of inquiry. Why don't they come to the fact? Here the defense is wholly indistinct. The counsel neither take ground nor abandon it. They neither fly nor light — they hover. But they must come to a closer mode of contest. They must meet the facts, and either deny or admit them. Had the prisoner at the bar, then, a knowledge of this conspiracy or not? This is the question. Instead of laying out their strength in complaining of the *manner* in which the deed is discovered, of the extraordinary pains taken to bring the prisoner's guilt to light, would it not be better to show there was no guilt? Would it not be better to show that he had committed no crime? They say, and they complain, that the community feel a great desire that he should be punished for his crimes. Would it not be better to convince you that he has committed no crime?

Gentlemen, let us now come to the case. Your first inquiry on the evidence will be, was Captain White murdered in pursuance of a conspiracy, and was the defendant one of this conspiracy? If so, the second inquiry is, was he so connected with the murder itself as that he is liable to be convicted as a *principal?* The defendant is indicted as a *principal.* If not guilty, *as such,* you cannot convict him. The indictment contains three distinct classes of counts. In the *first,* he is charged as having done the deed with his own hand; in the *second,* as an aider and abettor to Richard Crowninshield, Jr., who did the deed; in the *third,* as an aider and abettor to some person unknown. If you believe him guilty on either of these counts, or in in either of these ways, you must convict him.

It may be proper to say, as a preliminary remark, that there are two remarkable circumstances attending this trial. One is that Richard Crowninshield, Jr., the supposed immediate *perpetrator* of the murder, since his arrest, has committed suicide. He has gone to answer before a tribunal of perfect infallibility. The other is that Joseph Knapp, the supposed origin and planner of the murder, having once made a full disclosure of the facts under a promise of indemnity, is, nevertheless, not now a witness. Notwithstanding his disclosure and his promise of indemnity, he now refuses to testify. He chooses his original state, and now stands answerable himself when the time shall come for his trial. These circumstances it is fit you should remember in your investigation of the case.

Your decision may affect more than the life of this defendant. If he be not convicted as principal, no one can be. Nor can anyone be convicted of a participation in the crime as accessory. The Knapps and George Crowninshield will be again on the community. This shows the importance of the duty you have to perform, and to remind you of the care and wisdom necessary to be exercised in its performance. But certainly these considerations do not render the prisoner's guilt any clearer, nor enhance the weight of the evidence against him. No one desires you to regard consequences in that light. No one wishes anything to be strained or too far pressed against the prisoner. Still, it is fit you should see the full importance of the duty devolved upon you.

And now, gentlemen, in examining this evidence, let us begin at the beginning, and see, first, what we know independent of disputed testimony. This is a case of circumstantial evidence; and these circumstances, we think, are full and satisfactory. The case mainly depends upon them, and it is common that offenses of this kind must be proved in this way. Midnight assassins take no witnesses. The evidence of the *facts* relied on has been somewhat sneeringly denominated by the learned counsel *"circumstantial stuff,"* but it is not such *stuff* as dreams are made of. Why does he not rend this *stuff?* Why does he not tear it away with the crush of his hand? He dismisses it a little too summarily. It shall be my business to examine this *stuff*, and try its cohesion.

The letter from Palmer at Belfast, is that no more than flimsy *stuff?*

The fabricated letters from Knapp to the committee and Mr. White, are nothing but *stuff?*

The circumstance that the housekeeper was away at the time the murder was committed, as it was agreed that she would be, is that, too, a useless piece of the same *stuff?*

The facts that the key of the chamber door was taken out and secreted, that the window was unbarred and unbolted, are these to be so slightly and so easily disposed of?

It is necessary, gentlemen, now to settle, at the commencement, the great question of a *conspiracy*. If there was none, or the defendant was not a party, then there is no evidence here to convict him. If there was a conspiracy, and he is proved to have been a party, then these two facts have a strong bearing on others, and all the great points of inquiry. The defendant's counsel take no distinct ground, as I have already said, on this point, neither to admit nor to deny. They choose to confine themselves to a hypothetical mode of speech. They say, supposing there *was* a conspiracy, *non sequitur* that the prisoner is guilty as *principal*. Be it so. But still, if there was a conspiracy, and if he was a conspirator, and helped to plan the murder, this may shed much light on the evidence which goes to charge him with the execution of that plan.

We mean to make out the conspiracy, and that the defendant was a party to it, and then to draw all just inferences from these facts.

Let me ask your attention, then, in the first place, to those appearances, on the morning after the murder, which have a tendency to show that it was done in pursuance of a preconcerted plan of operation. What are they? A man was found murdered in his bed. No stranger had done the deed; no one unacquainted with the house had done it. It was apparent that somebody from within had opened, and somebody from without had entered.[4] There had been there, obviously and certainly, concert and cooperation. The inmates of the house were not alarmed when the murder was perpetrated. The assassin had entered without any riot or any violence. He had found the way prepared before him. The house had been opened. The window was unbarred from within, and its fastening unscrewed. There was a lock on the door of the chamber in which Mr. White slept, but the key was gone. It had been taken away and secreted. The footsteps of the murderer were visible, out doors, tending towards the window. The plank by which he entered the window still remained. The road he pursued had been prepared for him. The victim was slain, and the murderer had escaped. Everything indicated that somebody *within* had cooperated with sombody *without*. Everything proclaimed that some of the inmates, or somebody having access to the house, had had a hand in the murder. On the face of the circumstances, it was apparent, therefore, that this was a premeditated, concerted, conspired murder. Who, then, were the conspirators? If not now found out, we are still groping in the dark, and the whole tragedy is still a mystery.

If the Knapps and the Crowninshields were not the conspirators in this murder, then there is a whole set of conspirators not yet discovered. Because, independent of the testimony of Palmer and Leighton, independent of all disputed evidence, we know from uncontroverted facts, that this murder was, and must have been, the result of concert and cooperation between two or more. We know it was not done without plan and deliberation. We see that whoever entered the house to strike the blow was favored and aided by someone who had been previously in the house, without suspicion, and who had prepared the way. This is concert; this is cooperation; this is conspiracy. If the Knapps and the Crowninshields, then, were not the conspirators, who were? Joseph Knapp had a motive to desire the death of Mr. White, and that motive has been shown.

He was connected by marriage with the family of Mr. White. His wife was the daughter of Mrs. Beckford, who was the only child of a sister of the deceased. The deceased was more than eighty years old, and he had no children. His only heirs were nephews and nieces. He was expected to be possessed of a very large fortune, which would have descended, by law, to his several nephews and

---

[4] It is interesting to compare this matter-of-fact description of the murder with the earlier picture.

nieces in equal shares, or, if there was a will, then according to the will; but as Captain White had but two branches of heirs — the children of his brother, Henry White, and of Mrs. Beckford — according to the common idea each of these branches would have shared one-half of his property.

This popular idea is not legally correct; but it is common, and very probably was entertained by the parties. According to this, Mrs. Beckford, on Mr. White's death without a will, would have been entitled to one-half of Mr. White's ample fortune, and Joseph Knapp had married one of her three children. There was a will, and this will gave the bulk of the property to others; and we learn from Palmer that one part of the design was to destroy the will before the murder was committed. There had been a previous will, and that previous will was known or believed to have been more favorable than the other to the Beckford family; so that, by destroying the last will and destroying the life of the testator at the same time, either the first and more favorabe will would be set up, or the deceased would have no will, which would be, as was supposed, still more favorable. But the conspirators not having succeeded in obtaining and destroying the last will, though they accomplished murder, but the last will being found in existence and safe, and that will bequeathing the mass of the property to others, it seemed at the time impossible for Joseph Knapp, as for anyone else, indeed, but the principal devisee, to have any motive which should lead to the murder. The key which unlocks the whole mystery is the knowledge of the intention of the conspirators to steal the will. This is derived from Palmer, and it explains all. It solves the whole marvel. It shows the motive actuating those against whom there is much evidence, but who, without the knowledge of this intention, were not seen to have had a motive. This intention is proved, as I have said, by Palmer; and it is so congruous with all the rest of the case — it agrees so well with all facts and circumstances — that no man could well withhold his belief, though the facts were stated by a still less credible witness. If one desirous of opening a lock turns over and tries a bunch of keys till he finds one that will open it, he naturally supposes he has found *the* key of *that* lock.[5] So, in explaining circumstances of evidence which are apparently irreconcilable or unaccountable, if a fact be suggested which at once accounts

[5] This homely analogy is commended, along with others in the speech, to the attention of those who think of Webster as constantly indulging in magnificent figures such as that in the conclusion of the Reply to Hayne.

for all and reconciles all, by whomsoever it may be stated, it is still difficult not to believe that such fact is the true fact belonging to the case. In this respect, Palmer's testimony is singularly confirmed. If he were false, then his ingenuity could not furnish us such clear exposition of strange appearing circumstances. Some truth not known before can alone do that.

When we look back, then, to the state of things immediately on the discovery of the murder, we see that suspicion would naturally turn at once, not to the heirs at law, but to those principally bene-fited by the will. They, and they alone, would be supposed or seem to have a direct object for wishing Mr. White's life to be terminated. And, strange as it may seem, we find counsel now insisting that, if no apology, it is yet mitigation of the atrocity of the Knapps' con-duct in attempting to charge this foul murder on Mr. White, the nephew and principal devisee, that public suspicion was already so directed. As if assassination of character were excusable in propor-tion as circumstances may render it easy! Their endeavors, when they knew they were suspected themselves, to fix the charge on others, by foul means and by falsehood, is fair and strong proof of their own guilt. But more of that hereafter.

The counsel say that they might safely admit that Richard Crowninshield, Jr., was the perpetrator of this murder.

But how could they safely admit that? If that were admitted, everything else would follow. For why should Richard Crownin-shield, Jr., kill Mr. White? He was not his heir nor his devisee; nor was he his enemy. What could be his motive? If Richard Crownin-shield, Jr., killed Mr. White, he did it at someone's procurement, who himself had a motive; and who, having any motive, is shown to have had any intercourse with Richard Crowninshield, Jr., but Joseph Knapp, and this principally through the agency of the prisoner at the bar? It is the infirmity, the distressing difficulty, of the prisoner's case, that his counsel cannot and dare not admit what they yet cannot disprove, and what all must believe. He who believes, on this evidence, that Richard Crowninshield, Jr., was the immediate murderer, cannot doubt that both the Knapps were conspirators in that murder. The counsel, therefore, are wrong, I think, in saying they might safely admit this. The admission of so important and so connected a fact would render it impossible to contend further against the proof of the entire conspiracy, as we state it.

What, then, was this conspiracy? J. J. Knapp, Jr., desirous of destroying the will, and of taking the life of the deceased, hired a ruffian, who, with the aid of other ruffians, was to enter the house, and murder him in his own bed.

As far back as January this conspiracy began. Endicott testifies to a conversation with J. J. Knapp at that time, in which Knapp told him that Captain White had made a will, and given the principal part of his property to Stephen White. When asked how he knew, he said, "Black and white don't lie." When asked if the will was not locked up, he said, "There is such a thing as two keys to the same lock." And, speaking of the then late illness of Captain White, he said that Stephen White would not have been sent for if he had been there.

Hence it appears that, as early as January, Knapp had a knowledge of the will, and that he had access to it by means of false keys. The knowledge of the will, and an intent to destroy it, appear also from Palmer's testimony, a fact disclosed to him by the other conspirators. He says that he was informed of this by the Crowninshields on the 2d of April. But then it is said that Palmer is not to be credited; that, by his own confession, he is a felon; that he has been in the state prison in Maine; and, above all, that he was an inmate and associate with these conspirators themselves. Let us admit these facts; let us admit him to be as bad as they would represent him to be; still, in law, he is a competent witness. How else are the secret designs of the wicked to be proved but by their wicked companions, to whom they have disclosed them? The government does not select its witnesses. The conspirators themselves have chosen Palmer. He was the confidant of the prisoners. The fact, however, does not depend on his testimony alone. It is corroborated by other proof, and, taken in connection with the other circumstances, it has strong probability. In regard to the testimony of Palmer, generally, it may be said that it is less contradicted, in all parts of it, either by himself or others, than that of any other material witness, and that everything he has told has been corroborated by other evidence, so far as it was susceptible of confirmation. An attempt has been made to impair his testimony as to his being at the Halfway House on the night of the murder; you have seen with what success. Mr. Babb is called to contradict him. You have seen how little he knows, and even that not certainly; for he himself is proved to have been in an error by supposing him to have been at

the Halfway House on the evening of the 9th of April. At that time
he is proved to have been in Dustin's, in Danvers. If, then, Palmer,
bad as he is, has disclosed the secrets of the conspiracy, and has told
the truth, there is no reason why it should not be believed. Truth
is truth, come whence it may, though it were even from the bottom
of the bottomless pit.

The facts show that this murder had been long in agitation; that
it was not a new proposition on the 2d of April; that it had been
contemplated for five or six weeks before. Richard Crowninshield
was at Wenham in the latter part of March, as testified by Starrett.
Frank Knapp was at Danvers in the latter part of February, as
testified by Allen. Richard Crowninshield inquired whether Captain
Knapp was about home when at Wenham. The probability is that
they would open the case to Palmer as a new project. There are
other circumstances that show it to have been some weeks in agitation. Palmer's testimony as to the transaction on the 2d of April
is corroborated by Allen, and by Osborn's books. He says that
Frank Knapp came there in the afternoon, and again in the evening.
So the book shows. He says that Captain White had gone out to
his farm on that day. So others prove. How could this fact, or
these facts have been known to Palmer, unless Frank Knapp had
brought the knowledge? And was it not the special object of this
visit to give information of this fact, that they might meet him and
execute their purpose on his return from his farm? The letter of
Palmer, written at Belfast, has intrinsic marks of genuineness.[6] It
was mailed at Belfast, May 13th. It states facts that he could not
have known unless his testimony be true. This letter was not an
afterthought; it is a genuine narrative. In fact, it says, "I know
the business your brother Frank was transacting on the 2d of April."
How could he have possibly known this unless he had been there?
The "one thousand dollars that was to be paid" — where could he
have obtained this knowledge? The testimony of Endicott, of Palmer, and these facts are to be taken together; and they most clearly
show that the death of Captain White must have been caused by
somebody interested in putting an end to his life.[7]

---

[6] Dexter had the better of the argument as to the corroborative force of this
letter. Palmer was right about the thousand dollars, as we learn from Joe's
confession, but that confession was not evidence in this trial. There are several
places in Webster's argument where he rests on the assumption that it was
familiar to the jury.

[7] Everett's edition reduces the latter part of this sentence, bad as it is, to
inanity by removing the italics.

As to the testimony of Leighton, as far as manner of testifying goes, he is a bad witness; but it does not follow from this that he is not to be believed. There are some strange things about him. It is strange that he should make up a story against Captain Knapp, the person with whom he lived; that he never voluntarily told anything — all that he said is screwed out of him. But the story could not have been invented by him; his character for truth is unimpeached; and he intimated to another witness, soon after the murder happened, that he knew something he should not tell. There is not the least contradiction in his testimony, though he gives a poor account of withholding it. He says that he was extremely *bothered* by those who questioned him. In the main story that he relates he is universally consistent with himself. Some things are for him, and some against him. Examine the intrinsic probability of what he says. See if some allowance is not to be made for him on account of his ignorance with things of this kind. It is said to be extraordinary that he should have heard just so much of the conversation, and no more; that he should have heard just what was necessary to be proved, nothing else. Admit that this is extraordinary; still, this does not prove it is not true. It is extraordinary that you twelve gentlemen should be called upon, out of all the men in the county to decide this case.[8] No one could have foretold this three weeks since. It is extraordinary that the first clue to this conspiracy should have been derived from information given by the father of the prisoner at the bar. And in every case that comes to trial there are many things extraordinary. The murder itself in this case is a most extraordinary one; but still we do not doubt its reality.

It is argued that this conversation between Joseph and Frank could not have been as Leighton testified, because they had been together for several hours before; this subject must have been uppermost in their minds, whereas this appears to have been the commencement of their conversation upon it. Now this depends altogether upon the tone and manner of the expression; upon the particular word in the sentence which was emphatically spoken. If he had said, "When did you *see* Dick, Frank?" this would not seem to be the beginning of the conversation.[9] With what emphasis it was

[8] It is certainly not remarkable that *some* twelve men should be made jurors. Walter's report on this point is more reasonable than Webster's revision.

[9] In the résumé of the first two hours of the speech printed in the Salem *Gazette*, appears a passage found neither in the *Transcript* version nor in Webster's revision: "With regard to this dialogue, abrupt as it seemed upon repetition, Mr. Webster was not by any means sure that these words were the

uttered it is not possible to learn, and nothing therefore can be made of this argument. If this boy's testimony stood alone, it should be received with caution. And the same may be said of the testimony of Palmer. But they do not stand alone. They furnish a clue to numerous other circumstances, which, when known, react in corroborating what would have been received with caution until thus corroborated. How could Leighton have made up this conversation? "When did you see Dick?" "I saw him this morning." "When is he going to kill the old man?" "I don't know." "Tell him, if he don't do it soon, I won't pay him." Here is a vast amount in a few words. Had he wit enought to invent this? There is nothing so powerful as truth, and often nothing so strange. It is not even suggested that the story was made for him. There is nothing so extraordinary in the whole matter as it would have been for this country boy to invent this story.

The acts of the parties themselves furnish strong presumption of their guilt. What was done on the receipt of the letter from Maine? This letter was signed by Charles Grant, Jr., a person not known to either of the Knapps, nor was it known to them that any other person besides the Crowninshields knew of the·conspiracy. This letter, by the accidental omission of the word "Jr," fell into the hands of the father, when intended for the son. The father carried it to Wenham, where both the sons were. They both read it. Fix your eyes steadily on this part of the *"circumstantial stuff"* which is in the case, and see what can be made of it. This was shown to the two brothers on Saturday, the 15th of May. They, neither one of them, knew Palmer. And, if they had known him, they could not have known him to have been the writer of this letter. It was mysterious to them how anyone at Belfast could have had knowledge of this affair. Their conscious guilt prevented due circumspection.[10] They did not see the bearing of its publication. They advised their father to carry it to the committee of vigilance, and it was so carried. On the Sunday following, Joseph began to think there might be something in it. Perhaps, in the meantime,

commencement. The jury well knew that it was by means of intonation alone that that point could be decided, and the witness was evidently incapable of transmitting that. By emphasizing thus: 'When *is* Dick going to kill the old man?' it is plainly seen that it is but the repetition of an idea before expressed; and so it may be varied in half a dozen ways."

[10] Advising that the Grant letter be turned over to the committee of vigilance does seem folly; yet it is difficult to imagine a wiser course. Webster assumes that Frank had a hand in the letters, and Webster may be right in the assumption, but it is supported by no evidence.

he had seen one of the Crowninshields. He was apprehensive that they might be suspected. He was anxious to turn attention from their family. What course did he adopt to effect this? He addressed one letter, with a false name, to Mr. White, and another to the committee, and, to complete the climax of his folly, he signed the letter addressed to the committee, "Grant," the same name as that signed to the letter they then had from Belfast addressed to Knapp. It was in the knowledge of the committee that no person but the Knapps had seen this letter from Belfast, and that no other person knew its signature. It therefore must have been irresistibly plain to them that one of the Knapps must have been the writer of the letter received by the committee, charging the murder on Mr. White. Add to this the fact of its having been dated at Lynn, and mailed at Salem four days after it was dated, and who could doubt respecting it? Have you ever read or known of folly equal to this? Can you conceive of crime more odious and abominable? Merely to explain the apparent mysteries of the letter from Palmer, they excite the basest suspicions of a man who, if they were innocent, they had no reason to believe guilty, and who if they were guilty, they most certainly knew to be innocent. Could they have adopted a more direct method of exposing their own infamy? The letter to the committee has intrinsic marks of a knowledge of this transaction. It tells the *time* and the *manner* in which the murder was committed. Every line speaks the writer's condemnation. In attempting to divert attention from his family, and to charge the guilt upon another, he indelibly fixes it upon himself.

Joseph Knapp requested Allen to put these letters into the post office, because, said he, "I wish to nip this silly affair in the bud." If this were not the order of an overruling Providence, I should say that it was the silliest piece of folly that was ever practiced. Mark the destiny of crime. It is ever obliged to resort to such subterfuges; it trembles in the broad light; it betrays itself in seeking concealment. He alone walks safely who walks uprightly. Who for a moment can read these letters and doubt of Joseph Knapp's guilt? The constitution of nature is made to inform against him. There is no corner dark enough to conceal him. There is no turnpike broad enough or smooth enough for a man so guilty to walk in without stumbling. Every step proclaims his secret to every passenger. His own acts come out to fix his guilt. In attempting to charge another with his *own crime*, he writes his *own confession*. To do away with the effect of Palmer's letter, signed "Grant," he writes his own letter and affixes to it the name of Grant. He writes in a disguised hand. But how could it happen that the same Grant should be in Salem that was in Belfast? This has brought the whole thing out. Evidently he did it, because he has adopted the same style. Evidently he did it, because he speaks of the price of blood, and and of other circumstances connected with the murder, that no one but a conspirator could have known.[11]

Palmer says he made a visit to the Crowninshields on the 9th of April. George then asked him whether he had heard of the *murder.* Richard inquired whether he had heard the *music at Salem.* They said that *they were suspected,* that a committee had been appointed to search houses, and that they had melted up the dagger the day after the murder, because it would be a suspicious circumstance to have it found in their possession. Now, this committee was not appointed, in fact, until Friday evening. But this proves nothing against Palmer; it does not prove that George *did not tell him so;* it only proves that he gave a false reason for a fact. They had heard that they were suspected. How could they have heard this unless it were from the whisperings of their own consciences? Surely this rumor was not thus public.

About the 27th of April, another attempt is made by the Knapps to give a direction to public suspicion. They reported themselves to have been *robbed,* in passing from Salem to Wenham, near Wenham pond. They came to Salem and stated the particulars of the adventure. They described persons, their dress, size, and appearance, who had been *suspected* of the murder. They would have it understood that the community was infested by a band of ruffians, and that *they* themselves were the particular objects of their vengeance. Now, this turns out to be all fictitious, all false.[12] Can you conceive of anything more enormous — any wickedness greated — than the circulation of such reports than the allegation of crimes, if committed, capital? If no such thing — thus it reacts with double force upon themselves, and goes very far to show their guilt. How did they conduct on this occasion? Did they give information that they had been assaulted that night at Wenham? No such thing. They rested quietly on that night; they waited to be called on for

---

[11] At this point the court adjourned. The *Transcript* was the only paper that reported the remainder of Webster's speech.

[12] No evidence had been presented to support this assertion. Webster is resting again on the excluded confession of Joe.

the particulars of their adventure; they made no attempt to arrest the offenders — this was not their object. They were content to fill the thousand mouths of rumor, to spread abroad false reports, to divert the attention of the public from themselves; for they thought every man suspected them, because they knew they ought to be suspected.

The manner in which the compensation for this murder was paid is a circumstance worthy of consideration. By examining the facts and dates it will satisfactorily appear that Joseph Knapp paid a sum of money to Richard Crowninshield, in five-franc pieces, on the 24th of April.[13] On the 21st of April, Joseph Knapp received five hundred five-franc pieces as the proceeds of an adventure at sea. The remainder of this species of currency that came home in the vessel was deposited in a bank at Salem. On Saturday, the 24th of April, Frank and Richard rode to Wenham. They were there with Joseph an hour or more — appeared to be negotiating private business. Richard continued in the chaise. Joseph came to the chaise and conversed with him. These facts are proved by Hart and Leighton, and by Osborn's books. On Saturday evening, about this time, Richard Crowninshield is proved to have been at Wenham with another person, whose appearance corresponds with Frank, by Lummus. Can anyone doubt this being the same evening? What had Richard Crowninshield to do at Wenham with Joseph, unless it were this business? He was there before the murder; he was there after the murder; he was there clandestinely, unwilling to be seen. If it were not upon this business, let it be told what it was for. Joseph Knapp could explain it. Frank Knapp might explain it. But they do not explain it, and the inference is against them.

Immediately after this, Richard passes five-franc pieces — on the same evening, *one* to Lummus, *five* to Palmer — and, near this time, George passes *three* or *four* in Salem. This is extraordinary. It is an unusual currency. In ordinary business, few men would pass nine such pieces in the course of a year. If they were not received in this way, why not explain how they came by them? Money was not so flush in their pockets that they could not tell whence it came, if it honestly came there. It is extremely important to them to explain whence this money came, and they would do it if they could. If, then, the price of blood was paid at this time, in the

---

[13] It will be seen that this is plain bluff if one scans the evidence. Webster is again making use of the jury's knowledge of Joe's confession.

presence and with the knowledge of this defendant, does not this prove him to have been connected with this conspiracy?

Observe, also, the effect on the mind of Richard of Palmer's being arrested and committed to prison; the various efforts he makes to discover the fact; the lowering, through the crevices of the rock, the pencil and paper for him to write upon; the sending two lines of poetry, with the request that he would return the corresponding lines; the shrill and peculiar whistle; the inimitable exclamations of "Palmer! Palmer! Palmer!" All these things prove how great was his alarm. They corroborate Palmer's story, and tend to establish the conspiracy.[14]

Joseph Knapp had a part to act in this matter. He must have opened the window, and secreted the key. He had free access to every part of the house; he was accustomed to visit there; he went in and out at his pleasure; he could do this without being suspected. He is proved to have been there the Saturday preceding.

If all these things, taken in connection, do not prove that Captain White was murdered in pursuance of a conspiracy, then the case is at an end.[15]

Savary's testimony is wholly unexpected. He was called for a different purpose. When asked who the person was that he saw come out of Captain White's yard between three and four o'clock in the morning, he answered *Frank Knapp*. I am not clear this is not true. There may be many circumstances of importance connected with this, though we believe the murder to have been committed between ten and eleven o'clock. The letter to Dr. Barstow states it to have been done about *eleven o'clock;* it states it to have been done *with a blow on the head,* from a weapon loaded with lead. Here is too great a correspondence with reality not to have some meaning to it. Dr. Peirson was always of the opinion that the two classes of wounds were made with different instruments, and by different hands. It is possible that one class was inflicted at one time, and the other at another. It is possible that, on the last visit, the pulse might not have entirely ceased to beat, and then the finishing stroke was given. It is said, when the body was discovered, some of the wounds weeped, while the others did not. They may

---

[14] It is difficult to see corroboration for Palmer in this story. One suspects Webster put this story into the evidence because he saw a chance to dramatize it. It's good and we do not blame him.

[15] This is a surprising statement. Webster had other strong evidence in Colman's testimony.

have been inflicted from mere wantonness. It was known that Captain White was accustomed to keep specie by him in his chamber. This perhaps may explain the last visit. It is proved that this defendant was in the habit of retiring to bed, and leaving it afterwards, without the knowledge of his family. Perhaps he did so on this occasion. We see no reason to doubt the fact; and it does not shake our belief that the murder was committed early in the night.

What are the probabilities as to the time of the murder? Mr. White was an aged man. He usually retired to bed at about half-past nine. He slept soundest in the early part of the night; usually awoke in the middle and latter parts; and his habits were perfectly well known. When would persons, with a knowledge of these facts, be most likely to approach him? Most certainly in the first hour of his sleep. This would be the safest time. If seen then going to or from the house, the appearance would be least suspicious. The earlier hour would, then, have been most probably selected.

Gentlemen, I shall dwell no longer on the evidence which tends to prove that there was a conspiracy, and that the prisoner was a conspirator. All the circumstances concur to make out this point[16] Not only Palmer swears to it, in effect, and Leighton, but Allen mainly supports Palmer, and Osborn's books lend confirmation, so far as possible from such a source. Palmer is contradicted in nothing, either by any other witness or any proved circumstance or occurrence. Whatever could be expected to support him does support him. All the evidence clearly manifests, I think, that there was a conspiracy; that it originated with Joseph Knapp; that defendant became a party to it, and was one of its conductors, from first to last. One of the most powerful circumstances is Palmer's letter from Belfast. The amount of this was a direct charge on the Knapps of the authorship of this murder. How did they treat this charge — like honest men, or like guilty men? We have seen how it was treated. Joseph Knapp fabricated letters, charging another person, and caused them to be put into the post office.

I shall now proceed on the supposition that it is proved that there was a conspiracy to murder Mr. White, and that the prisoner was party to it.

---

[16] Notice that Webster keeps his listeners clear as to what point he is discussing at a given moment. He announces what he is about to take up, discusses it, and then clinches it with a summary. Summaries are often dull and prosy, but Webster's are not.

The second and the material inquiry is, *was the prisoner present at the murder, aiding and abetting therein?*

This leads to the legal question in the case. What does the law mean when it says, in order to charge him as a principal, "he must be present, aiding and abetting in the murder"?

In the language of the late chief justice: "It is not required that the abettor shall be actually upon the spot when the murder is committed, or even in sight of the more immediate perpetrator of the victim, to make him a principal. If he be at a distance, cooperating in the act, by watching to prevent relief, or to give an alarm, or to assist his confederate in escape, *having knowledge of the purpose and object of the assassin,* this, in the eye of the law, is being present, aiding and abetting, so as to make him a principal in the murder."

"If he be at a *distance*, cooperating." This is not a *distance* to be measured by feet or rods. If the intent to lend aid combine with a knowledge that the murder is to be committed, and the person so intending be so situate that he can by any possibility lend this aid in any manner, then he is *present* in legal contemplation. He need not lend any actual aid, — to be ready to assist is assisting.[17]

There are two sorts of murder. The distinction between them is of essential importance to bear in mind: (1) Murder in an affray, or upon sudden and unexpected provocation; (2) murder secretly, with a deliberate, predetermined intention to commit murder. Under the first class, the question usually is whether the offense be murder or manslaughter in the person who commits the deed. Under the second clsas, it is often a question whether others than he who actually did the deed were present, aiding and assisting thereto. Offenses of this kind ordinarily happen when there is nobody present except those who go on the same design. If a riot should happen in the court house, and one should kill another, this may be murder, or it may not, according to the intention with which it was done, which is always matter of fact, to be collected from the circumstances at the time. But in secret murders, premeditated and determined on, there can be no doubt of the murderous intention. There can be no doubt, if a person be present, knowing a murder

---

[17] Webster quotes the chief justice accurately, but it should be kept in mind that the actual perpetrator must know that his cooperator or abettor is prepared to act if action is required. Justice Putnam stresses this point in his charge to the jury.

is to be done, of his concurring in the act. His being there is a proof of his intent to aid and abet, else why is he there?[18]

It has been contended that proof must be given that the person accused did actually afford aid, — did lend a hand in the murder itself, — and without this proof, although he may be near by, he may be presumed to be there for an innocent purpose; he may have crept silently there to hear the news, or from mere curiosity to see what was going on. Preposterous! Absurd! Such an idea shocks all common sense. A man is found to be a conspirator to do a murder; he has planned it; he has assisted in arranging the time, the place, and the means; and he is found in the place, and at the time, and yet it is suggested that he might have been there, not for cooperation and concurrence, but from curiosity! Such an argument deserves no answer. It would be difficult to give it one in decorous terms. Is it not to be taken for granted that a man seeks to accomplish his own purposes? When he has planned a murder, and is present at its execution, is he there to forward or to thwart his own design? Is he there to assist, or there to prevent? But "curiosity!" He may be there from mere "curiosity!" Curiosity to witness the success of the execution of his own plan of murder! The very walls of a court house ought not to stand, the plowshare should run through the ground it stands on, where such an argument could find toleration.[19]

It is not necessary that the abettor should actually lend a hand, — that he should take a part in the act itself. If he be present ready to assist, that is assisting. Some of the doctrines advanced would acquit the defendant, though he had gone to the bedchamber of

[18] Justice Putnam said in his charge to the second jury: "If, however, the jury should be of opinion that the prisoner was one of the conspirators, and in a situation in which he might have given some aid to the perpetrator at the time of the murder, then it would follow as a legal presumption that he was there to carry into effect the concerted crime, and it would be for the prisoner to rebut that presumption by showing the jury that he was there for another purpose unconcerned with the conspiracy." Note Dexter's argument on this point.

[19] If the reader has followed Dexter's argument, and has tried to imagine what aid Frank could give in Brown Street, this sunburst may be more plausible than convincing. It is not difficult to think that young Frank might have found irresistible the desire to go out and "hear the news." Webster's passage is really magnificent bluff, and is done in his most imperious manner.

There is a well established tradition that before the murder Richard told Frank to go home, and that he did go home, but later slipped back, actuated by the motive Webster ridicules as curiosity. This tradition is incorporated in a statement written by Benjamin Merrill a number of years after the trial. Merrill's statement has been accepted as true by all biographers of Webster.

the deceased, though he had been standing by when the assassin gave the blow. This is the argument we have heard today.

(The court here said they did not so understand the argument of the counsel for defendant. Mr. Dexter said, The intent and power alone must cooperate.)

No doubt the law is that being ready to assist is assisting, if he has the power to assist, in case of need. It is so stated by Foster, who is a high authority. "If A. happeneth to be present at a murder, for instance, and taketh no part in it, nor endeavoreth to prevent it, nor apprehendeth the murderer, nor levyeth hue and cry after him, this strange behavior of his, though highly criminal, will not of itself render him either principal or accessory." "But if a fact amounting to murder should be committed in prosecution of some unlawful purpose, *though it were but a bare trespass,* to which A., in the case last stated, had consented, and he had gone in order to give assistance, if need were, for carrying it into execution, this would have amounted to murder in him, and in every person present and joining with him." "If the fact was committed in prosecution of the original purpose, *which was unlawful,* the whole party will be involved in the guilt of him who gave the blow; for in combinations of this kind, the mortal stroke, though given by one of the party, is considered in the eye of the law, and of sound reason too, as given by every individual present and abetting. The person actually giving the stroke is no more than the hand or instrument by which the others strike." The author, in speaking of being present, means actual presence; not *actual* in opposition ao *constructive,* for the law knows no such distinction. There is but one presence, and this is the situation from which aid, or supposed aid, may be rendered. The law does not say where he is to go, or how near he is to go, but somewhere where he may give assistance, or where the perpetrator may suppose that he may be assisted by him.[20]

---

[20] In his charge to the second jury, Justice Putnam insists on "a position in which he might have given some aid." Almost certainly the charge to the first jury took the same ground; yet Webster stands by his guns, probably confident that his views will appeal to the jury as sound. The argument has a common sense sound; but it really comes to this: It is enough if they thought Brown Street a good place, and we know they thought so because Frank was there. But that begs the whole question, Did Frank intend to be where he could aid? Remember Dexter's keen question: How can you judge that they thought it a fit place, unless you yourselves think it so? 2 *Corpus Juris,* 126, cites this case. It will be noted that Webster, in spite of his contention, does argue very hard, and repeatedly, that Brown Street actually was a place from which aid could be given.

Suppose that he is acquainted with the design of the murderer, and has a knowledge of the time when it is to be carried into effect, and goes out with a view to render assistance, if need be; why, then, even though the murderer does not know of this,[21] the person so going out will be an abettor in the murder.

It is contended that the prisoner at the bar could not be a principal, he being in Brown Street, because he could not there render assistance; and you are called upon to determine this case, according as you may be of opinion whether Brown Street was or was not a suitable, convenient, well-chosen place to aid in this murder. This is not the true question. The inquiry is not whether you would have selected this place in preference to all others, or whether you would have selected it at all. If they chose it, why should we doubt about it? How do we know the use they intended to make of it, or the kind of aid that he was to afford by being there? The question for you to consider is, did the defendant go into Brown Street *in aid of this murder?* Did he go there by agreement, — by appointment with the perpetrator? If so, everything else follows. The main thing — indeed the only thing — is to inquire whether he was in Brown Street by appointment with Richard Crowninshield. It might be to keep general watch; to observe the lights, and advise as to time of access; to meet the prisoner [murderer] on his return, to advise him as to his escape; to examine his clothes, to see if any marks of blood; to furnish exchange of clothes, or new disguise, if necessary; to tell him through what streets he could safely retreat, or whether he could deposit the club in the place designed; or it might be without any distinct object, but merely to afford that encouragement which would be afforded from Richard Crowninshield's consciousness that he was near.[22] It is of no consequence whether, in your opinion, the place was well chosen, or not, to afford aid. If it was so chosen — if it was by appointment that he was there — it is enough. Suppose Richard Crowninshield, when applied to to commit the murder, had said, "I won't do it unless there can be someone near by to

[21] This, too, is contrary to the charge, which insists upon prearrangement. But see below.
[22] Webster will return again and again to this question of what could be done in Brown Street. Logical order placed his main argument on this point after the argument that Frank was in Brown Street. While he uses the argument that Brown Street was a good place for the abettor's purpose to support the probability that they chose it, he no doubt realized that it was difficult to establish Brown Street as a place where aid could be given, and for that reason wished to accustom the minds of the jury to his suppositions by repetition.

favor my escape. I won't go unless you will stay in Brown Street.[23] Upon the gentleman's argument, he would not be an aider and abettor in the murder, because the place was not well chosen, though it is apparent that the being in the place chosen was a condition without which the murder would never have happened.

You are to consider the defendant as one in the league, in the combination, to commit the murder. If he was there by appointment with the perpetrator, he is an abettor. The concurrence of the perpetrator in his being there is proved by the previous evidence of the conspiracy. If Richard Crowninshield, for any purpose whatsoever, made it a condition of the agreement that Frank Knapp should stand as *backer,* then Frank Knapp was an aider and abettor, no matter what the aid was, or what sort it was or degree, be it ever so little, even if it were to judge of the hour when it was best to go, or to see when the lights were extinguished, or to give an alarm if anyone approached. Who better calculated to judge of these things than the murderer himself? And, if he so determined them, that is sufficient.

Now as to the facts. Frank Knapp knew that the murder was that night to be committed. He was one of the conspirators; he knew the object; he knew the time. He had that day been to Wenham to see Joseph, and probably to Danvers to see Richard Crowninshield, for he kept his motions secret. He had that day hired a horse and chaise of Osborn and attempted to conceal the purpose for which it was used. He had intentionally left the *place* and the *price* blank on Osborn's books. He went to Wenham by the way of Danvers.[24] He had been told the week before to hasten Dick. He had seen the Crowninshields several times within a few days. He had a saddle horse the Saturday night before. He had seen Mrs. Beckford at Wenham, and knew she would not return that night. She had not been away before for six weeks, and probably would not soon be again. He had just come from there. Every day, for the week previous, he had visited one or other of these conspirators, save Sunday, and then probably he saw them in town. When he saw Joseph on the 6th, Joseph had prepared the house, and would naturally tell him of it. There were constant communications between them; daily and nightly visitations; too

---

[23] This hypothetical mode of argument is legitimate provided the arguer does not later assume that his supposition is a fact, as Webster comes near doing at the end of the next paragraph.

[24] Notice that Webster now discards the word "probably."

much knowledge of these parties and this transaction to leave a
particle of doubt on the mind of anyone that Frank knew that
the murder was to be committed this night. The hour was come,
and he knew it. If so, and he was in Brown Street without explaining why he was there, can the jury for a moment doubt whether
he was there to countenance, aid, or support, or for curiosity alone,
or to learn how the wages of sin and death were earned by the perpetrator?

(Here Mr. Webster read the law from Hawkins, — 1 Hawk. 204,
lib. 1, c. 32, sec. 7.)

The perpetrator would derive courage and strength and confidence from the knowledge of the fact that one of his associates was
near by. If he was in Brown Street, he could have been there for no
other purpose. If there for this purpose, then he was, in the language
of the law, *present*, aiding and abetting in the murder.

His interest lay in being somewhere else. If he had nothing to
do with the murder, no part to act, why not stay at home? Why
should he jeopard his own life if it was not agreed that he should
be there? He would not voluntarily go where the very place would
probably cause him to swing if detected. We would not voluntarily
assume the place of danger. His taking this place proves that he
went to give aid. His staying away would have made an alibi. If he
had nothing to do with the murder, he would be at home, where
he could prove his alibi. He knew he was in danger, because he
was guilty of the conspiracy, and, if he had nothing to do, would
not expose himself to suspicion or detection.

Did the prisoner at the bar countenance this murder? Did he concur, or did he nonconcur, in what the perpetrator was about to do?
Would he have tried to shield him? Would he have furnished his
cloak for protection? Would he have pointed out a safe way of
retreat? As you would answer these questions, so you should answer the general question whether he was there *consenting to the
murder*, or whether he was there *a spectator only*.

One word more on this *presence*, called *constructive presence*.
What aid is to be rendered? Where is the line to be drawn between
acting and omitting to act? Suppose he had been in the house, suppose he had followed the perpetrator to the chamber, what could
he have done? This was to be a murder by stealth. It was to be a
secret assassination. It was not their purpose to have an open com-
bat; they were to approach their victim unawares, and silently
give the fatal blow. But if he had been in the chamber, no one **can**

doubt that he would have been an abettor, because of his presence and ability to render services, if needed. What service could he have rendered if there? Could he have helped him fly? Could he have facilitated his retreat on the first alarm? Surely this was a case where there was more safety in going alone than with another; where company would truly embarrass. Richard Crowninshield would prefer to go alone. He knew his errand too well. His nerves needed no collateral support. He was not the man to take with him a trembling companion. He would prefer to have his aid at a distance. He would not wish to be embarrassed by his presence. He would prefer to have him out of the house. He would prefer that he should be in Brown Street. But whether in the chamber, in the house, in the garden, or in the street, whatsoever is aiding in *immediate presence* is aiding in *constructive presence;* anything that is aid in one case is aid in the other.

(Here Mr. Webster read the law from Hawkins, — 4 Hawk. 201, lib. 4, c. 29, sec. 8.)

If, then, the aid be anywhere, that emboldens the perpetrator, that affords him hope or confidence in his enterprise, it is the same as though the person stood at his elbow with his sword drawn. His being there ready to act, with the power to act — that is what makes him an abettor.

(Here Mr. Webster referred to the cases of Kelly, of Hyde, and others, cited by the counsel for the defendant, and showed that they did not militate with the doctrine for which he contended. The difference is, in those cases there was open violence. This was a case of secret assassination. The aid must meet the occasion. Here no *acting* was necessary, but watching, concealment of escape, management.)

What are the facts in relation to his presence? Frank Knapp is proved a conspirator; proved to have known that the deed was now to be done. Is it not probable that he was in Brown Street to concur in the murder? There were four conspirators. It was natural that some one of them would go with the perpetrator. Richard Crowninshield was to be the perpetrator; he was to give the blow. No evidence of any casting of the parts for the others. The defendant would probably be the man to take the second part. He was fond of exploits; he was accustomed to the use of sword canes and dirks. If any aid was required, he was the man to give it. At least there is no evidence to the contrary of this.

Aid could not have been received from Joseph Knapp or from George Crowninshield. Joseph Knapp was at Wenham, and took good care to prove that he was there. George Crowninshield has proved satisfactorily where he was, — that he was in other company, such as it was, until eleven o'clock. This narrows the inquiry. This demands of the prisoner to show that if he was not in this place, where he was. It calls on him loudly to show this, and to show it truly. If he could show it, he would do it. If he don't tell, and that truly, it is against him. The defense of an alibi is a double-edged sword. He knew that he was in a situation that[25] he might be called upon to account for himself. If he had had no particular appointment or business to attend to, he would have taken care to have been able so to account. He would have been out of town, or in some good company. Has he accounted for himself on that night to your satisfaction?[26]

The prisoner has attempted to prove an alibi in two ways: In the first place, by four young men with whom he says he was in company, on the evening of the murder, from seven o'clock till near ten o'clock. This depends upon the *certainty of the night*. In the second place, by his family, from ten o'clock afterwards. This depends upon the *certainty of the time of the night*. These two classes of proof have no connection with each other. One may be true, and the other false; or they may both be true, or both be false. I shall examine this testimony with some attention, because, on a former trial, it made more impression on the minds of the court than on my own mind. I think, when carefully sifted and compared, it will be found to have in it more *plausibility* than *reality*.

Mr. Page testifies that, on the evening of the 6th of April, he was in company with Burchmore, Balch, and Forrester, and that he met the defendant about seven o'clock, near the Salem Hotel; that he afterwards met him at Remond's, about nine o'clock, and that he was in company with him a considerable part of the evening. This young gentleman is a member of college, and says that he came in town the Saturday evening previous; that he is now able to say

---

25 "That" is changed to "where" in the Everett edition. This is noted to indicate how slight most of the changes were.

26 Having labored to convince the jury of the probability that Frank was the man in Brown Street, Webster chooses, before proceeding to his positive evidence, to attack the alibi. He thinks that if he can discredit the alibi witnesses, the jury will more readily accept the rather shaky evidence that Frank was in Brown Street.

that it was the night of the murder when he walked with Frank
Knapp, from the recollection of the fact that he called himself to an
account, on the morning after the murder, as was natural for men
to do when an extraordinary occurrence happens. Gentlemen, this
kind of evidence is not satisfactory; general impressions as to time
are not to be relied on. If I were called upon to state the particular
day on which any witness testified in this cause, I could not do it.
Every man will notice the same thing in his own mind.[27] There is
no one of these young men that could give an account of himself
for any *other* day in the month of April. They are made to remember the fact, and then they think they remember the time.
He has no means of knowing it was Tuesday, more than any other
time. He did not know it at first; he could not know it afterwards.
He says he called himself to an account. This has no more to do
with the murder than with the man in the moon. Such testimony
is not worthy to be relied on in any forty-shilling case. What occasion had he to call himself to an account? Did he suppose that he
should be suspected? Had he any intimation of this conspiracy?

Suppose, gentlemen, you were either of you asked where you were,
or what you were doing, on the fifteenth day of June. You could not
answer that question without calling to mind some event to make it
certain. Just as well may you remember on what you dined on
each day of the year past. Time is identical. Its subdivisions are
all alike. No man knows one day from another, or one hour from
another, but by some fact connected with it. Days and hours are
not visible to the senses, nor to be apprehended and distinguished
by the understanding. The flow of time known only by something
which marks it; and he who speaks of the date of occurrences with
nothing to guide his recollection speaks at random, and is not to
be relied on. This young gentleman remembers the facts and occurrences; he knows nothing why they should not have happened on
the evening of the 6th; but he knows no more. All the rest is
evidently conjecture or impression.

Mr. White informs you that he told him he could not tell what
night it was. The first thoughts are all that are valuable in such
case. They miss the mark by taking second aim.

Mr. Balch believes, but is not sure, that he was with Frank
Knapp on the evening of the murder. He has given different ac-

---

[27] Webster's analogies lack the element of an extraordinary occurrence to fix
the time in memory. Note, too, that he omits mention of the weather.

counts of the time. He has no means of making it certain. All he knows is that it was some evening before Fast [Day] but whether Monday, Tuesday, or Saturday, he cannot tell.

Mr. Burchmore says, to the best of his belief, it was the evening of the murder. Afterwards he attempts to speak positively, from recollecting that he mentioned the circumstances to William Peirce as he went to the Mineral Spring on Fast Day. Last Monday morning he told Colonel Putnam he could not fix the time. This witness stands in a much worse plight than either of the others. It is difficult to reconcile all he has said with any belief in the accuracy of his recollections.

Mr. Forrester does not speak with any certainty as to the night, and it is very certain that he told Mr. Loring and others that he did not know what night it was.

Now, what does the testimony of these four young men amount to? The only circumstance by which they approximate to an identifying of the night is that three of them say it was cloudy. They think their walk was either on Monday or Tuesday evening, and it is admitted that Monday evening was clear, whence they draw the inference that it must have been Tuesday.

But, fortunately, there is one *fact* disclosed in their testimony that settles the question. Balch says that on the evening, whenever it was that he saw the prisoner, the prisoner told him he was going out of town on horesback for a distance of about twenty minutes' ride, and that he was going to get a horse at Osborn's. This was about seven o'clock. At about nine, Balch says he saw the prisoner again, and was then told by him that he had had his ride, and had returned. Now, it appears by Osborn's books that the prisoner had a saddle horse from his stable, not on Tuesday evening, the night of the murder, but on the Saturday evening previous. This fixes the time about which these young men testify, and is a complete answer and refutation of the attempted alibi on Tuesday evening.[28]

[28] One may be somewhat puzzled by the so-called completeness of this answer. Having a horse on Saturday night does not preclude having one on Tuesday night. It is true that Osborn's records do not show that Frank had a horse on Tuesday night, but it is obvious that Osborn's books were carelessly kept. Frank might have borrowed a horse, or he might have paid for it in cash, or, as Dexter suggested, he might have lied, not wishing to tell these nice young men he had been to see a girl in South Salem, the less respectable part of the town. It will be recalled that the one thing young Page was sure about was that he was not out on either Saturday or Sunday night. It can be seen from the charge to the jury, however, that Webster's argument about the horse impressed Justice Putnam.

I come now to speak of the testimony adduced by the defendant to explain where he was after ten o'clock on the night of the murder. This comes chiefly from members of the family —from his father and brothers.

It is agreed that the affidavit of the prisoner should be received as evidence of what his brother, Samuel H. Knapp, would testify if present. Samuel H. Knapp says that, about ten minutes past ten o'clock, his brother, Frank Knapp, on his way to bed, opened his chamber door, made some remarks, closed the door, and went to his chamber, and that he did not hear him leave it afterwards. How is this witness able to fix the time at ten minutes past ten? There is no circumstance mentioned by which he fixes it. He had been in bed, probably asleep, and was aroused from his sleep by the opening of the door. Was he in a situation to speak of time with precision? Could he know, under such circumstances, whether it was ten minutes past ten or ten minutes before eleven when his brother spoke to him? What would be the natural result in such a case? But we are not left to conjecture this result. We have positive testimony on this point. Mr. Webb tells you that Samuel told him, on the 8th of June, "that he did not know what time his brother Frank came home, and that he was not at home when *he* went to bed." You will consider the testimony of Mr. Webb as indorsed upon this affidavit, and, with this indorsement upon it, you will give it its due weight. This statement was made to him after Frank was arrested.

I come to the testimony of the father.[29] I find myself incapable of speaking of him or his testimony with severity. Unfortunate old man! Another Lear, in the conduct of his children; another Lear, I fear, in the effect of his distress upon his mind and understanding. He is brought here to testify, under circumstances that disarm severity, and call loudly for sympathy. Though it is impossible not to see that his story cannot be credited, yet I am not able to speak of him otherwise than in sorrow and grief. Unhappy father! he

---

[29] In both his cross-examination and in his summation, Webster deals gently with Frank's father. Plainly he wishes to avoid the appearance of severity with this unfortunate man (although Walter's report of Webster's speech in the Boston *Transcript* does suggest perjury more plainly). Probably Webster was genuinely sorry for a man ruined in business and with two sons in the shadow of the gallows, and he probably realized that a ruthless attack might turn sympathy the wrong way. Webster prefers to say in elegant language that Mr. Knapp is soft in the head. Knapp, whose age Webster stresses, was fifty-seven years old—eight years older than Webster. It is difficult to find any evidence of mental degeneration in his testimony.

strives to remember, perhaps persuades himself that he does remember, that on the evening of the murder he was himself at home at ten o'clock. He thinks, or seems to think, that his son came in at about five minutes past ten. He fancies that he remembers his conversation; he thinks he spoke of bolting the door; he thinks he asked the time of night; he seems to remember his then going to his bed. Alas! these are but the swimming fancies of an agitated and distressed mind. Alas! they are but the dreams of hope, its uncertain lights, flickering on the thick darkness of parental distress. Alas! the miserable father knows nothing, in reality, of all these things.

Mr. Shepard says that the first conversation he had with Mr. Knapp was soon after the murder, and *before* the arrest of his sons. Mr. Knapp says it was *after* the arrest of his sons. His own fears led him to say to Mr. Shepard that his "son Frank was at home that night, and so Phippen told him," or "as Phippen told him." Mr. Shepard says that he was struck with the remark at the time; that it made an unfavorable impression on his mind. He does not tell you what that impression was, but when you connect it with the previous inquiry he had made, whether Frank had continued to associate with the Crowninshileds, and recollect that the Crowninshields were then known to be suspected of this crime, can you doubt what this impression was? Can you doubt as to the fears he then had?

This poor old man tells you that he was greatly perplexed at the time; that he found himself in embarrassed circumstances; that on this very night he was engaged in making an assignment of his property to his friend, Mr. Shepard. If ever charity should furnish a mantle for error, it should be here. Imagination cannot picture a more deplorable, distressed condition.

The same general remarks may be applied to his conversation with Mr. Treadwell as have been made upon that with Mr. Shepard. He told him that he believed Frank was at home about the usual time. In his conversations with either of these persons, he did not pretend to know, of his own knowledge, the time that he came home. He now tells you positively that he recollects the time, and that he so told Mr. Shepard. He is directly contradicted by both these witnesses, as respectable men as Salem affords.

This idea of an alibi is of recent origin. Would Samuel Knapp have gone to sea if it were then thought of? His testimony, if true, was too important to be lost. If there be any truth in this part of the alibi, it is so near in point of time that it cannot be relied on. The mere variation of half an hour would avoid it. The mere variations of different timepieces would explain it.

Has the defendant proved where he was on that night? If you doubt about it, there is an end of it. The burden is upon him to satisfy you beyond all reasonable doubt.[30] Osborn's books, in connection with what the young men state, are conclusive, I think, on this point. He has not, then, accounted for himself. He has attempted it, and has failed. I pray you to remember, gentlemen, that this is a case in which the prisoner would, more than any other, be rationally able to account for himself on the night of the murder if he could do so. He was in the conspiracy, he knew the murder was then to be committed, and, if he himself was to have no hand in its actual execution, he would of course, as a matter of safety and precaution, be somewhere else, and be able to prove afterwards that he had been somewhere else. Having this motive to prove himself elsewhere, and the power to do it if he were elsewhere, his failing in such proof must necessarily leave a very strong inference against him.

But, gentlemen, let us now consider what is the evidence produced on the part of the government to prove that John Francis Knapp, the prisoner at the bar, was in Brown Street on the night of the murder. This is a point of vital importance in this cause. Unless this be made out, beyond reasonable doubt, the law of *presence* does not apply to the case. The government undertakes to prove that he was present, aiding in the murder, by proving that he was in Brown Street for this purpose. Now, what are the undoubted facts? They are that two persons were seen in that street, at several times during that evening, under suspicious circumstances, —under such circumstances as induced those who saw them to watch their movements. Of this there can be no doubt. Mirick saw a man standing at the post opposite his store from fifteen minutes before nine until twenty minutes after, dressed in a full

---

[30] The burden is never on the prisoner to prove anything beyond all reasonable doubt. *Commonwealth* v. *York,* 9 Met. (Mass.) 95, 116-117. The burden is upon the prosecution to prove beyond a reasonable doubt every "constituent element of the crime," and in this case presence is a constituent element. In *Massachusetts Trial Evidence,* Norman and Houghton, section 959, we read: "In the case of an alibi, if the evidence of the defendant is such that, taken with the other evidence, the jury have reasonable doubt that the defendant was present, they must acquit him."

frock coat, glazed cap, and so forth, in size and general appearance answering to the prisoner at the bar. This person was waiting there, and, whenever any one approached him, he moved to and from the corner, as though he would avoid being suspected or recognized. Afterwards, two persons were seen by Webster walking in Howard Street with a slow, deliberate movement that attracted his attention. This was about half-past nine. One of these he took to be the prisoner at the bar; the other he did not know.

About half-past ten a person is seen sitting on the ropewalk steps, wrapped in a cloak. He drops his head when passed, to avoid being known. Shortly after, two persons are seen to meet in this street, without ceremony or salutation, and in a hurried manner to converse for a short time, then to separate, and run off with great speed. Now, on this same night, a gentleman is slain — murdered in his bed — his house being entered by stealth from without, and his house situated within three hundred feet of this street. The windows of his chamber were in plain sight from this street. A weapon of death is afterwards found in a place where these persons were seen to pass, in a retired place, around which they had been seen lingering. It is now known that this murder was committed by a conspiracy of four persons, conspiring together for this purpose. No account is given who these suspicious persons thus seen in Brown Street and its neighborhood were. Now I ask you gentlemen, whether you or any man can doubt that this murder was committed by the persons who were thus in and about Brown Street. Can any person doubt that they were there for purposes connected with this murder? If not for this purpose, what were they there for? When there is a cause so near at hand, why wander into conjecture for an explanation? Common sense requires you to take the nearest adequate cause for a known effect. Who were these suspicious persons in Brown Street? There was something extraordinary about them; something noticeable, and noticed at the time; something in their appearance that aroused suspicion. And a man is found the next morning murdered in the near vicinity.[31]

Now, so long as no other account shall be given of those suspicious persons, so long the inference must remain irresistible that

[31] Webster is again using his favorite argument of probability to bolster weak evidence. In this passage, as in many others in his works, we may note Webster's ability to give crispness and movement to narration.

they were the murderers.[32] Let it be remembered that it is already shown that this murder was the result of conspiracy and of concert; let it be remembered that the house, having been opened from within, was entered by stealth from without; let it be remembered that Brown Street, where these persons were repeatedly seen under such suspicious circumstances, was a place from which every occupied room in Mr. White's house is clearly seen; let it be remembered that the place, though thus very near to Mr. White's house, was a retired and lonely place; and let it be remembered that the instrument of death was afterwards found concealed very near the same spot. Must not every man come to the conclusion that these persons thus seen in Brown Street were the murderers? Every man's own judgment, I think, must satisfy him that this must be so. It is a plain deduction of common sense. It is a point on which each one of you may reason like a Hale or a Mansfield. The two occurrences explain each other. The murder shows why these persons were thus lurking, at that hour, in Brown Street, and their lurking in Brown Street shows who committed the murder.[33]

If, then, the persons in and about Brown Street were the plotters and executers of the murder of Captain White, we know who they were, and you know that *there* is one of them.[34]

This fearful concatenation of circumstances puts him to an account. He was a conspirator. He had entered into this plan of murder. The murder is committed, and he is known to have been within three minutes' walk of the place. He must account for himself. He has attempted this, and failed. Then, with all these general reasons to show he was actually in Brown Street, and his failures in

---

[32] Beyond a reasonable doubt? No one saw the second man go from White's house to Brown Street. Bray was uncertain even as to the direction from which the man came, and neither Bray nor Southwick professed to have recognized him. Is it an irresistible inference that of the thirteen thousand people in Salem none but the murderers were about, and perhaps engaged in nefarious schemes? Nevertheless, the paragraph is an effective summary.

[33] In commenting on a similar argument of Webster's regarding the time of the murder, Dexter said in his first summation, "Two men were seen in Brown Street at half-past ten, and the murder thus proved to have been committed at that time, the men seen in Brown Street must be the murderers. This is reasoning in a circle." Webster is more convincing when he points out that one of these men is, as he claims, a proved conspirator, and therefore almost certainly one of the murderers.

[34] Almost fifty years after the trial, William Ward, who had been a close friend of Frank Knapp, wrote, "When at times he [Webster] turned toward the prisoner at the bar, with his finger pointed at him and gave vent to one of those almost superhuman bursts of eloquence and overpowering invective everyone present seemed to hold his breath—but the prisoner met the eye of Mr. Webster as calmly and stoically as though he was a statue."

his alibi, let us see what is the direct proof of his being there. But first let me ask, is it not very remarkable that there is no attempt to show where Richard Crowninshield, Jr., was on that night? We hear nothing of him. He was seen in none of his usual haunts about the town. Yet, if he was the actual perpetrator of the murder, which nobody doubts, he was in the town somewhere. Can you therefore entertain a doubt that he was one of the prisoners seen in Brown Street? And as to the prisoner, you will recollect that, since the testimony of the young men has failed to show where he was that evening, the last we hear or know of him on the day preceding the murder is that at four o'clock P.M. he was at his brother's in Wenham. He had left home, after dinner, in a manner doubtless designed to avoid observation, and had gone to Wenham, probably by way of Danvers. As we hear nothing of him after four o'clock P.M. for the remainder of the day and evening; as he was one of the conspirators; as Richard Crowninshield, Jr., was another; as Richard Crowninshield, Jr., was in town in the evening, and yet seen in no usual place of resort — the inference is very fair that Richard Crowninshield, Jr., and the prisoner were together, acting in execution of their conspiracy. Of the four conspirators, J. J. Knapp, Jr., was at Wenham, and George Crowninshield has been accounted for, so that, if the persons seen in Brown Street were the murderers, one of them must have been Richard Crowninshield, Jr., and the other must have been the prisoner at the bar.

Now as to the proof of his identity with one of the persons seen in Brown Street.

Mr. Mirick, a cautious witness, examined the person he saw closely, in a light night, and says that he thinks the prisoner at the bar is the person, and that he should not hesitate at all if he were seen in the same dress. His opinion is formed partly from his own observation, and partly from the description of others; but this description turns out to be only in regard to the dress. It is said that he is now more confident than on the former trial. If he has varied in his testimony, make such allowance as you may think proper. I do not perceive any material variance. He thought him the same person when he was first brought to court, and as he saw him get out of the chaise. This is one of the cases in which a witness is permitted to give an opinion. This witness is as honest as yourselves — neither willing nor swift; but he says he believes it was the man — "this is my opinion," and this it is proper for him to give. If partly founded on what he has *heard*, then his opinion is not to be taken; but *if* on what he *saw*, then you can have no better evidence. I lay no stress on similarity of dress. No man will ever be hanged by my voice on such evidence. But then it is proper to notice that no inferences drawn from any *dissimilarity* of dress can be given in the prisoner's favor, because, in fact, the person seen by Mirick was dressed like the prisoner.

The description of the person seen by Mirick answers to that of the prisoner at the bar. In regard to the supposed discrepancy of statements, before and now, there would be no end to such minute inquiries. It would not be strange if witnesses should vary. I do not think much of slight shades of variation. If I believe the witness is honest, that is enough. If he has expressed himself more strongly now than then, this does not prove him false.

Peter E. Webster saw the prisoner at the bar, as he then thought, and still thinks, walking in Howard Street at half-past nine o'clock. He then thought it was Frank Knapp, and has not altered his opinion since. He knew him well; he had long known him. If he then thought it was he, this goes far to prove it. He observed him the more, as it was unusual to see gentlemen walk there at that hour. It was a very retired, lonely street. Now, is there reasonable doubt that Mr. Webster did see him there that night? How can you have more proof than this? He judged by his walk, by his general appearance, by his deportment. We all judge in this manner. If you believe he is right, it goes a great way in this case. But then this person, it is said, had a cloak on, and that he could not, therefore, be the same person that Mirick saw. If we were treating of men that had no occasion to disguise themselves or their conduct, there might be something in this argument. But as it is, there is little in it. It may be presumed that they would change their dress. This would help their disguise. What is easier than to throw off a cloak, and again put it on? Perhaps he was less fearful of being known when alone than when with the perpetrator.

Mr. Southwick swears all that a man can swear.[35] He has the best means of judging that could be had at the time. He tells you that he left his father's house at half-past ten o'clock, and, as he passed to his own house in Brown Street, he saw a man sitting on the steps of the ropewalk; that he passed him three times, and each

---

[35] A surprisingly infelicitous phrase, reminding us all too strongly that Southwick had been a most accomodating witness.

time he held down his head, so that he did not see his face; that the man had on a cloak, which was not wrapped around him, and a glazed cap; that he took the man to be Frank Knapp at the time; that, when he went into his house, he told his wife that he thought it was Frank Knapp; that he knew him well, having known him from a boy. And his wife swears that he did so tell her at the time. What could mislead this witness at the time? He was not then suspecting Frank Knapp of anything. He could not then be influenced by any prejudice. If you believe that the witness saw Frank Knapp in this position at this time, it proves the case.[36] Whether you believe it or not depends upon the credit of the witness. He swears it. If true, it is solid evidence. Mrs. Southwick supports her husband. Are they true? Are they worthy of belief? If he deserves the epithets applied to him, then he ought not to be believed. In this fact they cannot be mistaken; they are right, or they are perjured. As to his not speaking to Frank Knapp, that depends upon their intimacy. But a very good reason is, Frank chose to disguise himself. This makes nothing against his credit. But it is said that he should not be believed. And why? Because, it is said, he himself now tells you that, when he testified before the grand jury at Ipswich, he did not then say that he thought the person he saw in Brown Street was Frank Knapp, but that "the person was about the size of Selman." The means of attacking him, therefore, come from himself. If he is a false man, why should he tell truths against himself? They rely on his veracity to prove that he is a liar.[37] Before you can come to this conclusion, you will consider whether all the circumstances are now known that should have a bearing on this point. Suppose that, when he was before the grand jury, he was asked by the attorney this question, "Was the person you saw in Brown Street about the size of Selman?" and he answered, "Yes." This was all true. Suppose, also, that he expected to be inquired of further, and no further questions were

---

[36] Webster finds it inconvenient to answer Dexter's keen argument which was based on the fact that Southwick was unable to identify the man on the ropewalk steps with the man he and Bray saw later at Shepard's post and in front of Bray's house. This serious gap in the government's proof was never satisfactorily filled, although Bray did his best, after refusing to identify Frank in the first trial, by swearing in the second that he had no doubt Frank was the person he saw in Brown Street.

[37] This information was not voluntarily given, as Webster's words might imply, but was secured by cross-examination. Furthermore, Southwick's statements before the grand jury were probably widely known, and it would have been futile for him to deny having made them. Webster is making the best of a bad job.

put to him. Would it not be extremely hard to impute to him perjury for this? It is not uncommon for witnesses to think that they have done all their duty when they have answered the questions put to them. But suppose that we admit that he did not then tell all he knew, this does not alter the *fact* at all, because he did tell, at the time, in the hearing of others, that the person he saw was Frank Knapp. There is not the slightest suggestion against the veracity or accuracy of Mrs. Southwick. Now, she swears positively that her husband came into the house and told her that he had seen a person on the ropewalk steps, and believed it was Frank Knapp.

It is said that Mr. Southwick is contradicted, also, by Mr. Shillaber. I do not so understand Mr. Shillaber's testimony. I think what they both testify is reconcilable and consistent. My learned brother said, on a similar occasion, that there is more probability, in such cases, that the persons hearing should misunderstand, than that the person speaking should contradict himself. I think the same remark applicable here.

You have all witnessed the uncertainty of testimony when witnesses are called to testify what other witnesses said. Several respectable counselors have been called on, on this occasion, to give testimony of that sort. They have, every one of them, given different versions. They all took minutes at the time, and without doubt intended to state the truth. But still they differ. Mr. Shillaber's version is different from everything that Southwick has stated elsewhere. But little reliance is to be placed on slight variations in testimony, unless they are manifestly intentional. I think that Mr. Shillaber must be satisfied that he did not rightly understand Mr. Southwick. I confess I misunderstood Mr. Shillaber on the former trial, if I now rightly understand him. I therefore did not then recall Mr. Southwick to the stand. Mr. Southwick, as I read it, understood Mr. Shillaber as asking him about a person coming out of Newbury Street, and whether, for aught he knew, it might not be Richard Crowninshield, Jr. He answered that he could not tell. He did not understand Mr. Shillaber as questioning him as to the person whom he saw sitting on the steps of the ropewalk. Southwick, on this trial, having heard Mr. Shillaber, has been recalled to the stand, and states that Mr. Shillaber entirely misunderstood him. This is certainly most probable, because the controlling fact in the case is not controverted, — that is, that Southwick did tell his wife, at the very moment he entered his house, that he had seen a person on the ropewalk steps, whom he believed to be Frank Knapp. Nothing can prove with more certainty than this: that Southwick, at the time, *thought* the person whom he thus saw to be the prisoner at the bar.[38]

Mr. Bray is an acknowledged accurate and intelligent witness. He was highly complimented by my brother on the former trial, although he now charges him with varying his testimony. What could be his motive? You will be slow in imputing to him any design of this kind. I deny altogether that there is any contradiction. There may be differences, but no contradiction. These arise from the difference in the questions put; the difference between *believing* and *knowing*. On the first trial, he said he did not *know* the person, and now says the same. Then, we did not do all we had a right to do. We did not ask him who he *thought* it was. Now, when so asked, he says he *believes* it was the prisoner at the bar. If he had then been asked this question, he would have given the same answer. That he has expressed himself stronger I admit; but he has not contradicted himself. He is more confident now, and that is all. A man may not assert a thing, and still not have any doubt upon it. Cannot every man see this distinction to be consistent? I leave him in that attitude; that only is the difference. On questions of identity, opinion is evidence. We may ask the witness, either if he *knew* who the person seen was, or who he *thinks* he was. And he may well answer, as Captain Bray has answered, that he does not *know* who it was, but that he *thinks* it was the prisoner.[39]

We have offered to produce witnesses to prove that, as soon as Bray saw the prisoner, he pronounced him the same person. We are not at liberty to call them to corroborate our own witness. How, then, could this fact of the prisoner's being in Brown Street be better proved? If ten witnesses had testified to it, it would be no better. Two men, who knew him well, took it to be Frank Knapp, and one of them so said, when there was nothing to mislead them. Two others that examined him closely, now swear to their opinion that he is the man.

Miss Jaqueth saw three persons pass by the ropewalk several evenings before the murder. She saw one of them pointing towards

[38] Southwick told his wife that he saw Frank on the ropewalk steps. Shillaber asked about the two men who later met near Bray's house.
[39] Bray swore "I have no doubt."

Mr. White's house. She noticed that another had something which appeared to be like an instrument of music; that he put it behind him, and attempted to conceal it. Who were these persons? This was but a few steps from the place where this apparent instrument of music (of *music* such as Richard Crowninshield, Jr., spoke of to Palmer) was afterwards found. These facts prove this a point of rendezvous for these parties.[40] They show Brown Street to have been the place for consultation and observation, and to this purpose it was well suited.

Mr. Burn's testimony is also important. What was the defendant's object in his private conversation with Burns? He knew that Burns was out that night; that he lived near Brown Street, and that he had probably seen him, and he wished him to say nothing. He said to Burns, "If you saw any of your friends out that night, say nothing about it; my brother Joe and I are your friends." This is plain proof that he wished to say to him, if you saw me in Brown Street that night, say nothing about it.

But it is said that Burns ought not to be believed because he mistook the color of the dagger, and because he has varied in his description of it. These are slight circumstances, if his general character be good. To my mind they are of no importance. It is for you to make what deduction you may think proper, on this account, from the weight of his evidence. His conversation with Burns, if Burns is believed, shows two things: First, that he desired Burns not to mention it, if he had seen him on the night of the murder; second, that he wished to fix the charge of murder on Mr. Stephen White. Both of these prove his own guilt.[41]

I think you will be of opinion that Brown Street was a *probable place* for the conspirators to assemble, and for an aid to be. If we knew their whole plan, and if we were skilled to judge in such a case, then we could perhaps determine on this point better. But it is a retired place, and still commands a full view of the house; a lonely place, but still a place of observation; not so lonely that a person would excite suspicion to be seen walking there in an ordinary manner; not so public as to be noticed by many. It is near enough to the scene of action in point of law. It was their point of *centrality*. The club was found near the spot, in a place provided for it, in a place that had been previously hunted out, in a concerted

---

[40] Webster's bland assertion is impressive.
[41] In many places Webster uses the word "prove" very loosely.

place of concealment. *Here was their point of rendezvous;* here might the lights be seen; here might an aid be secreted; here was he within call; here might he be aroused by the sound of the *whistle;* here might he carry the weapon; here might he receive the murderer after the murder.

Then, gentlemen, the general question occurs, is it satisfactorily proved, by all these facts and circumstances, that the defendant was in and about Brown Street on the night of the murder? Considering that the murder was effected by a conspiracy; considering that he was one of the four conspirators; considering that two of the conspirators have accounted for themselves on the night of the murder, and were not in Brown Street; considering that the prisoner does not account for himself, nor show where he was; considering that Richard Crowninshield, the other conspirator and the perpetrator, is not accounted for, nor shown to be elsewhere; considering that it is now past all doubt that two persons were seen in and about Brown Street at different times, lurking, avoiding observation, and exciting so much suspicion that the neighbors actually watched them; considering that, if these persons thus lurking in Brown Street at that hour were not the murderers, it remains to this day wholly unknown who they were or what their business was; considering the testimony of Miss Jaqueth, and that the club was afterwards found near this place; considering, finally, that Webster and Southwick saw these persons, and then took one of them for the defendant, and that Southwick then told his wife so, and that Bray and Mirick examined them closely, and now swear to their belief that the prisoner was one of them — it is for you to say, putting these considerations together, whether you believe the prisoner was actually in Brown Street at the time of the murder.[42]

By the counsel for the defendant, much stress has been laid upon the question whether Brown Street was a place in which aid could be given — a place in which actual assistance could be rendered in this transaction. This must be mainly decided by their own opinion

[42] Webster ties his points together with great effect by means of frequent summaries and with many parallel constructions. Less skillful pleaders sometimes leave to the jurors an impossible task. Webster treats his jury with respect; but he knows that no body of men, however intelligent, can be expected to hold in mind such a mass of evidence and appreciate the bearing of each part. He, therefore, gives the jury all the help he can by repetition and summaries. F. N. Scott in his *First Bunker Hill Oration and Other Addresses* says, "Excess in parallelism, the common vice of oratorical compositions is of rare occurrence." However parallelism may affect nice literary taste, it is an effective means of giving coherence to spoken discourse.

who selected the place; by what they thought at the time, according to their plan of operation.

If it was agreed that the prisoner should be there to assist, it is enough. If they thought the place proper for their purpose, according to their plan, it is sufficient.

Suppose we could prove expressly that they agreed that Frank should be there, and he was there, and you should think it not a well-chosen place for aiding and abetting, must he be acquitted? No! It is not what *I* think or *you* think of the appropriateness of the place; it is what *they* thought *at the time*.

If the prisoner was in Brown Street by appointment and agreement with the perpetrator, for the purpose of giving assistance if assistance should be needed, it may safely be presumed that the place was suited to such assistance as it was supposed by the parties might chance to become requisite.

If, in Brown Street, was he there by appointment? Was he there to aid, if aid were necessary? Was he there for or against the murderer? to concur, or to oppose? to favor, or to thwart? Did the perpetrator know he was there — waiting? If so, then it follows, he was there by appointment. He was at the post half an hour. He was waiting for somebody. This proves *appointment, arrangement, previous agreement;* then it follows he was there to aid, to encourage, to embolden the perpetrator, and that is enough. If he were in such a situation as to afford aid, or that he was relied upon for aid, then he was aiding and abetting. It is enough that the conspirator desired to have him there. Besides, it may be well said that he could afford just as much aid there as if he had been in Essex Street — as if he had been standing even at the gate or at the window. It was not an act of power against power that was to be done; it was a secret act, to be done by stealth. The aid was to be placed in a position secure from observation. It was important to the security of both that he should be in a lonely place. Now, it is obvious that there are many purposes for which he might be in Brown Street.

1. Richard Crowninshield might have been secreted in the garden, and waiting for a signal;

2. Or he might be in Brown Street to advise him as to the time of making his entry into the house;

3. Or to favor his escape;

4. Or to see if the street was clear when he came out;

5. Or to conceal the weapon or the clothes;

6. To be ready for any other unforeseen contingency.

Richard Crowninshield lived in Danvers. He would retire by the most secret way. Brown Street is that way. If you find him there, can you doubt why he was there!

If, gentlemen, the prisoner went into Brown Street, by appointment with the perpetrator, to render aid or encouragement in any of these ways, he was *present,* in legal contemplation, aiding and abetting in this murder. It is not necessary that he should have done anything; it is enough that he was ready to act, and in a place to act. If his being in Brown Street, by appointment, at the time of the murder, emboldened the purpose and encouraged the heart of the murderer by the hope of instant aid if aid should become necessary, then, without doubt, he was present, aiding and abetting, and was a principal in the murder.

I now proceed, gentlemen, to the consideration of the testimony of Mr. Colman. Although this evidence bears on every material part of the cause, I have purposely avoided every comment on it till the present moment, when I have done with the other evidence in the case.[43] As to the admission of this evidence, there has been a great struggle, and its importance demanded it. The general rule of law is that confessions are to be received as evidence. They are entitled to great or to little consideration, according to the circumstances under which they are made. Voluntary, deliberate confessions are the most important and satisfactory evidence; but confessions hastily made, or improperly obtained, are entitled to little or no consideration. It is always to be inquired whether they were purely voluntary, or were made under any undue influence of *hope* or *fear;* for, in general, if any influence were exerted on the mind of the person confessing, such confessions are not to be submitted to a jury.

Who is Mr. Colman? He is an intelligent, accurate, and cautious

---

[43] Webster had wished to convince the jury that the prisoner was guilty without reference to Colman's testimony, knowing that the most important part of it had been admitted only provisionally and that the court would charge the jury to ignore that part if they believed that Frank, before making any disclosures, had consented that Joe might confess. He knew that while no man could forget that testimony, still there might be one or more hardheaded jurymen who would decide that Frank had consented, and that that part of the testimony was out of consideration. Moreover, when Webster planned his speech and up until the last moments of the defense summation, he must have expected that Dexter would, as in his first summation, make a strong argument that the jury should disregard the evidence in question.

witness; a gentleman of high and well known character, and of un-
questionable veracity; as a clergyman, highly respectable; as a man,
of fair name and fame.

Why was Mr. Colman with the prisoner? Joseph J. Knapp was
his parishioner; he was the head of a family, and had been married
by Mr. Colman. The interests of his family were dear to him. He
felt for their afflictions, and was anxious to alleviate their sufferings.
He went from the purest and best of motives to visit Joseph
Knapp.[44] He came to save, not to destroy; to rescue, not to take
away life. In this family he thought there might be a chance to save
one. It is a misconstruction of Mr. Colman's motives, at once the
most strange and the most uncharitable — a perversion of all just
views of his conduct and intentions the most unaccountable — to
represent him as acting, on this occasion, in hostility to anyone, or as
desirous of injuring or endangering anyone. He has stated his own
motives and his own conduct in a manner to command universal
belief and universal respect. For intelligence, for consistency, for
accuracy, for caution, for candor, never did witness acquit himself
better, or stand fairer. In all that he did as a man, and all he has
said as a witness, he has shown himself worthy of entire regard.

Now, gentlemen, very important confessions made by the prisoner are sworn to by Mr. Colman. They were made in the prisoner's
cell, where Mr. Colman had gone with the prisoner's brother, N.
Phippen Knapp. Whatever conversation took place was in the
presence of N. P. Knapp. Now, on the part of the prisoner, two
things are asserted: First, that such inducements were suggested
to the prisoner, in this interview, that any confessions made by him
ought not to be received; second, that, in point of fact, he made
no such confession as Mr. Colman testifies to, nor, indeed, any

---

[44] It is evident that Webster feels that Colman's conduct requires defense.
Even with Joe, Mr. Colman was acting a double part as clergyman-friend and
as agent of the committee of vigilance. (It is quite possible that Colman did
not fully understand the situation, but it seems clear now that if all the conspirators had kept their mouths shut there could have been no convictions.)
It was not, of course, Colman's business, either as a clergyman or as a citizen,
to save the murderers, though he made it very much his business to save the
meanest of the group. But to imply, as Webster does, that Colman was acting
from kindness to the Knapps is "a bit too thick." It is difficult not to believe
that he worked upon the inexperienced Phippen to gain entrance to Frank's
cell, and for the purpose of drawing out admissions.
One is tempted to apply harsh terms to Mr. Colman; but probably he was
one of those who, whatever they do, always have the comfortable assurance
that their motives are pure. Detective work is necessary; but one cannot always
admire the detective, and especially when he covers the wolf with a clergyman's
robe. There will be a note at the end of the book on Colman's later career.

confessions at all. These two propositions are attempted to be
supported by the testimony of N. P. Knapp. These two witnesses,
Mr. Colman and N. P. Knapp, differ entirely. There is no possibility of reconciling them. No charity can cover both. One or the
other has sworn falsely. If N. P. Knapp be believed, Mr. Colman's
testimony must be wholly disregarded. It is, then, a question of
credit — a question of belief between the two witnesses. As you
decide between these, so you will decide on all this part of the case.

Mr. Colman has given you a plain narrative, a consistent account,
and has uniformly stated the same things. He is not contradicted by
anything in the case except Phippen Knapp. He is influenced, as
far as we can see, by no bias or prejudice, any more than other men,
except so far as his character is now at stake. He has feelings on
this point doubtless, and ought to have. If what he has stated be
not true, I cannot see any ground for his escape. If he be a true
man, he must have heard what he testifies. No treachery of memory
brings to memory things that never took place. There is no reconciling his evidence with good intentions if the facts are not as he
states them. He is on trial as to his veracity.

The relation in which the other witness stands deserves your
careful consideration. He is a member of the family. He has the
lives of two brothers depending, as he may think, on the effect of
his evidence; depending on every word he speaks. I hope he has
not another responsibility resting upon him. By the advise of a
friend, and that friend Mr. Colman, J. Knapp made a full and free
confession, and obtained a promise of pardon. He has since, as
you know, probably by the advice of other friends, retracted that
confession, and rejected the offered pardon. Events will show who
of these friends and advisers advised him best and befriended him
most. In the meantime, if this brother, the witness, be one of these
advisers, and advised the retraction, he has, most emphatically, the
lives of his brothers resting upon his evidence and upon his conduct.
Compare the situation of these two witnesses. Do you not see
mighty motive enough on the one side, and want of all motive on the
other? I would gladly find an apology for that witness in his
agonized feelings, in his distressed situation; in the agitation of
that hour, or of this. I would glady impute it to error, or to want
of recollection, to confusion of mind, or disturbance of feeling.
I would gladly impute to any pardonable source which cannot
be reconciled to facts and to truth; but, even in a case calling for

so much sympathy, justice must yet prevail, and we must come to the conclusion, however reluctantly, which that demands from us.[45]

It is said Phippen Knapp was probably correct, because he knew he should be called as a witness. Witness to what? When he says there was no confession, what could he expect to bear witness of? But I do not put it on the ground that he did not hear. I am compelled to put it on the other ground, that he did hear, and does not now truly tell what he heard.

If Mr. Colman were out of the case, there are other reasons why the story of Phippen Knapp should not be believed. It has in it inherent improbabilities. It is unnatural, and inconsistent with the accompanying circumstances. He tells you that they went "to the cell of Frank, to see if he had any objection to taking a trial, and suffering his brother to accept the offer of pardon," — in other words, to obtain Frank's consent to Joseph's making a confession, — and, in case this consent was not obtained, that the pardon would be offered to Frank. Did they bandy about the chance of life, between these two, in this way? Did Mr. Colman, after having given this pledge to Joseph, after having received a disclosure from Joseph, go to the cell of Frank for such a purpose as this? It is impossible; it cannot be so.

Again, we know that Mr. Colman found the club the next day; that he went directly to the place of deposit, and found it at the first attempt, exactly where he says he had been informed it was. Now, Phippen Knapp says that Frank stated nothing respecting the club; that it was not mentioned in that conversation. He says, also, that he was present in the cell of Joseph all the time that Mr. Colman was there; that he believes he heard all that was said in Joseph's cell; and that he did not himself know where the club was, and never had known where it was, until he heard it stated in court. Now, it is certain that Mr. Colman says he did not learn the particular place of deposit of the club from Joseph; that he only learned from him that it was deposited under the steps of the Howard Street meeting house, without defining the particular steps.

[45] A less skillful pleader might have called Phippen a liar and perjurer in outright terms. Webster probably felt pity for a young man who had taken the stand with the lives of two brothers possibly depending upon his testimony. There is no very pleasant way of calling a man a perjurer, but Webster showed considerable restraint. Harsher terms might have antagonized many who pitied Phippen. But Webster's treatment of him is noticeably sterner than that accorded to his father, though whether it is kinder to call a man insane than to call him a liar might be debated.

It is certain, also, that he had more knowledge of the position of the club than this; else how could he have placed his hand on it so readily? and where else could he have obtained this knowledge, except from Frank?

Here Mr. Dexter said that Mr. Colman had had other interviews with Joseph, and might have derived the information from him at previous visits. Mr. Webster replied, that Mr. Colman had testified that he learned nothing in relation to the club until this visit. Mr. Dexter denied there being any such testimony. Mr. Colman's evidence was read, from the notes of the judges, and several other persons, and Mr. Webster then proceeded.

My point is to show that Phippen Knapp's story is not true — is not consistent with itself; that, taking it for granted, as he says, that he heard all that was said to Mr. Colman in both cells, by Joseph and by Frank, and that Joseph did not state particularly where the club was deposited, and that he knew as much about the place of deposit of the club as Mr. Colman knew, why, then, Mr. Colman must either have been miraculously informed respecting the club, or Phippen Knapp has not told you the whole truth. There is no reconciling this without supposing that Mr. Colman has misrepresented what took place in Joseph's cell, as well as what took place in Frank's cell.

Again, Phippen Knapp is directly contradicted by Mr. Wheatland. Mr. Wheatland tells the same story as coming from Phippen Knapp, as Colman now tells. Here there are two against one. Phippen Knapp says that Frank made no confessions, and that he said he had none to make. In this he is contradicted by Wheatland. He, Phippen Knapp, told Wheatland that Mr. Colman did ask Frank some questions, and that Frank answered them. He told him also what these answers were. Wheatland does not recollect the questions or answers, but recollects his reply, which was: "Is not this *premature*? I think this answer is sufficient to make Frank a principal." Here Phippen Knapp opposes himself to Wheatland, as well as to Mr. Colman.

Do you believe Phippen Knapp against these two respectable witnesses, or them against him?

Is not Mr. Colman's testimony credible, natural, and proper? To judge of this, you must go back to that scene.

The murder had been committed. The two Knapps were now arrested. Four persons were already in jail supposed to be concerned in it — the Crowninshields, and Selman, and Chase. Another person at the eastward was supposed to be in the plot. It was important to learn the facts. To do this, some one of those suspected must be admitted to turn state's witness. The contest was, *who should have this privilege?* It was understood that it was about to be offered to Palmer, then in Maine. There was no good reason why he should have the preference. Mr. Colman felt interested for the family of the Knapps, and particularly for Joseph. He was a young man who had hitherto sustained a fair standing in society. He was a husband. Mr. Colman was particularly intimate with his family. With these views he went to the prison. He believed that he might safely converse with the prisoner, because he thought confessions made to a clergyman were sacred, and that he could not be called upon to disclose them. He went, the first time, in the morning, and was requested to come again. He went again at three o'clock, and was requested to call again at five o'clock. In the meantime he saw the father and Phippen, and they wished he would not go again, because it would be said the prisoners were making confession. He said he had engaged to go again at five o'clock, but would not, if Phippen would excuse him to Joseph. Phippen engaged to do this, and to meet him at his office at five o'clock. Mr. Colman went to the office at the time, and waited; but, as Phippen was not there he walked down street, and saw him coming from the jail. He met him, and while in conversation near the church, he saw Mrs. Beckford and Mrs. Knapp going in a chaise towards the jail. He hastened to meet them, as he thought it not proper for them to go in at that time. While conversing with them near the jail, he received two distinct messages from Joseph that he wished to see him. He thought it proper to go; he then went to Joseph's cell, and while there it was that the disclosures were made. Before Joseph had finished his statement, Phippen came to the door. He was soon after admitted. A short interval ensued, and they went together to the cell of Frank. Mr. Colman went in by invitation of Phippen. He had come directly from the cell of Joseph, where he had for the first time learned the incidents of the tragedy. He was incredulous as to some of the facts which he had learned, they were so different from his previous impressions. He was desirous of knowing whether he could place confidence in what Joseph had told him. He therefore put the questions to Frank as he has testified before you, in answer to which Frank Knapp informed him:

1. That the murder took place between ten and eleven o'clock.

2. That Richard Crowninshield was alone in the house.

3. That he, Frank Knapp, went home afterwards.

4. That the club was deposited under the steps of the Howard Street meeting house, and under the part nearest the burying ground, in a rathole.

5. That the dagger or daggers had been worked up at the factory.

It is said that these five answers just fit the case; that they are just what was wanted, and neither more or less. True, they are; but the reason is because truth always fits. Truth is always congruous, and agrees with itself. Every truth in the universe agrees with every other truth in the universe; whereas falsehoods not only disagree with truths, but usually quarrel among themselves. Surely Mr. Colman influenced by no bias, no prejudice. He has no feelings to warp him, except now, he is contradicted, he may feel an interest to be believed.

If you believe Mr. Colman, then the evidence is fairly in the case.

I shall now proceed on the ground that you do believe Mr. Colman.

When told that Joseph had determined to confess, the defendant said: "It is hard or unfair that Joseph should have the benefit of confessing, since the thing was done for his benefit." What thing was done for his benefit? Does not this carry an implication of the guilt of the defendant? Does it not show that he had a knowledge of the object and history of the murder?

The defendant said: "I told Joseph, when he proposed it, that it was a silly business, and would get us into trouble." He knew, then, what this business was. He knew that Joseph proposed it, and that he agreed to it, else it could not get us into trouble. He understood its bearings and its consequences. Thus much was said, under cirmumstances that make it clearly evidence against him, before there is any pretense of an inducement held out.[46] And does not this prove him to have had a knowledge of the conspiracy?

He knew the daggers had been destroyed, and he knew who committed the murder. How could he have innocently known these facts? Why, if by Richard's story, this shows him guilty of a knowledge of the murder and of the conspiracy. More than all, he

---

[46] Webster's statement is correct. The testimony referred to, however, does not connect Frank with Richard in the conspiracy. In the next paragraph, where he passes without notice to testimony that came after the alleged inducement, his conclusion "that the prisoner was in Brown Street for the purposes ascribed to him" is not justified.

knew *when* the deed was done, and that he went home *afterwards*. This shows his participation in that deed. "Went home afterwards!" Home *from what scene?* home *from what fact?* home *from what transaction?* home *from what place?* This confirms the supposition that the prisoner was in Brown Street for the purposes ascribed to him. These questions were directly put, and directly answered. He does not intimate that he received the information from another. Now, if he knows the time, and went home afterwards, and does not excuse himself, is not this an admission that he had a hand in this murder? Already proved to be a conspirator in the murder, he now confesses that he knew who did it, at what time it was done, that he was himself out of his own house at the time, and went home afterwards. Is not this conclusive, if not explained? Then comes the club. He told where it was. This is like possession of stolen goods. He is charged with the guilty knowledge of this concealment. He must *show*, not *say*, how he came by this knowledge. If a man be found with stolen goods, he must *prove* how he came by them. The place of deposit of the club was premeditated and selected, and he knew where it was.[47]

Joseph Knapp was an accessory, and an accessory only; he knew only what was told him. But the prisoner knew the particular spot in which the club might be found. This shows his knowledge something more than that of an accessory.

This presumption must be rebutted by evidence, or it stands strong against him. He has too much knowledge of this transaction to have come innocently by it. It must stand against him until he explains it.

The testimony of Mr. Colman is represented as new matter, and therefore an attempt has been made to excite a prejudice against it. It is not so. How little is there in it, after all, that did not appear from other sources. It is mainly confirmatory. Compare what you learn from this confession with what you before knew;

As to its being proposed by Joseph, was not that true?

---

[47] This paragraph is not up to Webster's standard of coherence, for it does not separate clearly the evidence bearing upon the conspiracy from that bearing upon presence. The dagger and the club have nothing to do with presence; for, like Joe, Frank had no direct knowledge that "the dagger or daggers" had been melted, or that the club had been put into the rathole. Nor can we follow Webster's statement in the next paragraph: "This shows his knowledge something more than that of an accessory." The prosecution's own evidence shows that Frank did not deposit the club; and even if he had been present when the dagger was melted, the fact could have no bearing on his presence at the murder.

As to Richard's being alone in the house, was not that true?

As to the daggers, was that not true?

As to the time of the murder, was not that true?

As to his being out that night, was not that true?

As to his returning afterwards, was not that true?

As to the club, was not that true?

So this information confirms what was known before, and fully confirms it.[48]

One word as to the interview between Mr. Colman and Phippen Knapp on the turnpike. It is said that Mr. Colman's conduct in this matter is inconsistent with his testimony. There does not appear to me to be any inconsistency. He tells you that his object was to save Joseph, and to hurt no one, and least of all the prisoner at the bar. He had probably told Mr. White the substance of what he heard at the prison. He had probobly told him that Frank *confirmed* what Joseph had *confessed*. He was unwilling to be the instrument of harm to Frank. He therefore, at the request of Phippen Knapp, wrote a note to Mr. White, requesting him to consider Joseph as authority for the information he had received. He tells you that this is the only thing he has to regret, as it may seem to be an evasion, as he doubts whether it was entirely correct. If it was an evasion, if it was a deviation, if it was an error, it was an error of mercy, an error of kindness — an error that proves he had no hostility to the prisoner at the bar. It does not in the least vary his testimony or affect its correctness. Gentlemen, I look on

---

[48] These questions and answers that follow "must be scanned." "As to its being proposed by Joseph," it is true that Palmer and Leighton made Joe the paymaster. "As to Richard's being alone in the house," the answer is distinctly no. No witness recognized Richard in Salem on the night of the murder. Webster has only the argument that Richard must have been the assassin since the other three conspirators were otherwise accounted for. The probability arising from such an argument does not, however, put the answer to this vitally important question beyond a reasonable doubt, especially since the probability rested on some shaky evidence. "As to the daggers," there is only the evidence of the dubious Palmer. "As to the time of the murder," the evidence is conflicting, and does not put the matter beyond reasonable doubt. "As to his being out that night," both sides agree, but with a difference. "As to his returning afterwards," we have the testimony of Southwick and Bray. "As to the club," if Webster means that a club was found in a certain rathole, the fact was proved with Colman's testimony; what else was known about it?

The conclusion must be that Colman's testimony was not merely or mainly confirmatory; but that without it, conviction would have been extremely doubtful. There might have been a conviction without any evidence about the club and the daggers; but something more than speculation about the time and the perpetrator was demanded, and only Colman furnished it. The fact that Webster contended that Colman's evidence was mainly confirmatory indicates that he still feared the jury might reject it.

the evidence of Mr. Colman as highly important, not as bringing into the cause new facts, but as confirming, in a very satisfactory manner, other evidence. It is incredible that he can be false, and that he is seeking the prisoner's life through false swearing. If he is true, it is incredible that the prisoner can be innocent.

Gentlemen, I have gone through with the evidence in this case, and have endeavored to state it plainly and fairly before you. I think there are conclusions to be drawn from it, which you cannot doubt. I think you cannot doubt that there was a conspiracy formed for the purpose of committing this murder, and who the conspirators were.

That you cannot doubt that the Crowninshields and the Knapps were parties in this conspiracy.

That you cannot doubt that the prisoner at the bar knew that the murder was to be done on the night of the 6th of April.

That you cannot doubt that the murderers of Captain White were the suspicious persons seen in and about Brown Street on that night.

That you cannot doubt that Richard Crowninshield was the perpetrator of that crime.

That you cannot doubt that the prisoner at the bar was in Brown Street on that night.

It there, then it must be by agreement, to countenance, to aid, the perpetrator, and, if so, then he is guilty as *principal*.[49]

Gentlemen, your whole concern should be to do your duty, and leave consequences to take care of themselves. You will receive the law from the court. Your verdict, it is true, may endanger the prisoner's life, but then it is to save other lives. If the prisoner's guilt has been shown and proved beyond all reasonable doubt, you will convict him. If such reasonable doubt of guilt still remain, you will acquit him. You are the judges of the whole case. You owe a duty to the public, as well as to the prisoner at the bar. You cannot presume to be wiser than the law. Your duty is a plain, straightforward one. Doubtless we would all judge him in mercy. Towards him, as an individual, the law inculcates no hostility; but towards him, if proved to be a murderer, the law, and the

---

[49] This admirable summary lacks one element essential to conviction: that Brown Street was a place where aid might be given. Webster has belittled the importance of this element, though he has repeatedly argued it. He may have thought it good strategy to omit it from his final summary since he had hardly been able to meet Dexter on the point.

oaths you have taken, and public justice demand that you do your duty.

With consciences satisfied with the discharge of duty, no consequences can harm you. There is no evil that we cannot either face or fly from but the consciousness of duty disregarded.

A sense of duty pursues us ever. It is omnipresent, like the Deity. If we take to ourselves the wings of the morning, and dwell in the uttermost parts of the sea, duty performed or duty violated is still with us, for our happiness or our misery. If we say the darkness shall cover us, in the darkness, as in the light, our obligations are yet with us. We cannot escape their power, nor fly from their presence. They are with us in this life, will be with us at its close; and in that scene of inconceivable solemnity, which lies yet farther onward, we shall still find ourselves surrounded by the consciousness of duty, to pain us wherever it has been violated, and to console us so far as God may have given us grace to perform it.

CHAPTER 10

COMMENTS ON
WEBSTER'S ORATORY

IN OUR NOTES we have made some adverse criticisms of Webster's speech, without stopping often to praise the portions that all must admire. The speech "speaks for itself," and its tremendous power is obvious; and Rufus Choate's praise of the "clearness with which a multitude of minute facts is arranged, and the ingenuity with which a long chain of circumstantial evidence is drawn out," must be accepted by any one who studies the speech.

By comparison with some pleaders at the bar Webster appears fair and restrained. His occasional misstatements of the law were due, in part, to the fact that the law was not clearly settled prior to this case. It became a "leading case" and is still cited as authority.

Certain passages have been much quoted, sometimes to be praised and sometimes to be sneered at as "mere eloquence." But if one knows the part these passages played in the argument, he sees that they were not mere words.

Perhaps the best discussion of Webster's oratory is found in Edwin P. Whipple's essay, "Daniel Webster as a Master of English Style." Speaking of the "Defense of the Kennistons," he says: "Webster . . . addressed the jury, not as an advocate bearing down upon them, but rather as a thirteenth juryman, who had cosily introduced himself into their company, and was arguing the case with them after they had retired for consultation among themselves." There are places in the Webster arguments against Frank Knapp where he was the thirteenth juror; but of course it would be foolish to say that either in the Kenniston or the Knapp cases he maintains that attitude. The point is that he could easily come close to the jury. He would have no difficulty in speaking in the simpler style of today.

We have heard two notable statesmen declare in lectures at Dartmouth College that Webster would be laughed at today in the courts or in Congress. We suspect that these men had read only his more elevated passages, out of their settings, or only such speeches as his addresses at Bunker Hill and the "First Settlement of New England." And they seem to forget that eloquence, and attempts at eloquence, are common enough in the speech-making of today. How could they forget the sessions of Congress in which dead members are eulogized? And they have overlooked the speeches in political conventions, as the nominations of Franklin D. Roosevelt, which were highly praised, but certainly were as "highflung" as any passages that can be found in the speeches of Webster. They forget, too, wild orgies in the courts of today.

Oratory may be great, or it may be "oratory." Much depends upon the theme and the situation, and very much depends upon the man and his delivery. Webster was a magnificent human being. It is said that when he stepped out from his office to the street in Boston, the word went around, "Webster is out," and every window was filled with heads. When he landed in Liverpool, a navvy exclaimed, "There goes a king!" Carlyle wrote to Emerson, "No man was ever so great as Daniel Webster looks."

Justices Story and Marshall are said to have been deeply affected at the end of Webster's plea in the Dartmouth College cases. (The speech is hard reading as a whole and it did not end with that touching passage beginning, "It is a little college, but there are those who love it.") Those judges had heard too many pleas to be affected easily. Samuel Hopkins Adams says in his book on Webster, "They were 'easybleeders' in those days." Even if there is something in that, one can hardly believe Story and Marshall were sentimentalists. One has to remember Daniel Webster. He had all that goes to make a real orator. His power had much to do with the verdict in the Knapp cases.

We quote here the comments of able critics, all of whom save Choate, who heard both summations, base their opinions on the speech Webster "re-built."

Rufus Choate: "It was a more difficult and higher effort of the mind than the more famous "Oration on the Crown."

Samuel McCall, a notable lawyer and statesman: "The greatest ever delivered to an American jury."

John Nichol, English critic: "The terrible power of the speech and its main interest lie in the winding chain of evidence link by link, coil by coil, round the murderer and his accomplices. One seems to hear the bones of the victim crack under the grasp of a boa-constrictor."

But Harriet Martineau did not hear the cracking bones. "I read it before I knew anything of the circumstances which I have related; and I was made acquainted with them in consequence of my inquiry how a man could be hanged on evidence so apparently insufficient as that adduced by the prosecution. . . . Mr. Webster has made all that could be made of it."

That able and cool English critic, Goldwin Smith, said in an article in the *Nineteenth Century* in 1888: "There can be no doubt that Webster was a magnificent speaker, or that his speeches, like those of Bright and unlike those of Clay, have a literary value of the highest and most lasting kind. In political oratory it would be hard to find anything superior to the Reply to Hayne; in forensic oratory it would be hard to find anything superior to the speech on the murder of White. . . . The comparison of Webster to Demosthenes is not inappropriate. Simplicity is the characteristic of both."[1]

From Henry Cabot Lodge's not too friendly life of Webster we take these bits: "The opening of the speech comprising the account of the murder and the analysis of the workings of a mind seared with the remembrance of a horrid crime, must be placed among the very finest masterpieces of modern oratory. . . . The whole exhibits the highest imaginative excellence, and displays the possession of an extraordinary dramatic force such as Mr. Webster rarely exercised. . . . I have studied this famous exordium with great care, and I have sought diligently in the works of all the great modern orators, and of some of the ancients as well, for similar passages of higher merit. My quest has been in vain. . . . [It] has never been surpassed in dramatic force by any speaker, whether in debate or before a jury. . . . Before a jury Webster fell behind Erskine as he did behind Choate, although neither of them ever produced anything at all comparable to the speech on the White murder. . . . Take him for all in all, he was not only the greatest orator this country has ever known, but in the history of eloquence his name will stand with those of Demosthenes and Cicero, of Chatham and Burke."

[1] We must humbly bow before Goldwin Smith and Henry Cabot Lodge, men of great ability; but as I go through the laborious process of proof-reading, I hesitate a bit. They are thinking only of the standard edition of Webster's speech, with little or no knowledge of the story or the evidence. Perhaps I have worked over the speech so long that I cannot now make a proper respense and proof-reading does not put one in a state of mind that yields to eloquence; but, knowing the eloquence is in the speech, the words that come to me now are *power, skill, shrewdness, cleverness.*—Winans.

CHAPTER 11

THE TRIAL OF
JOSEPH JENKINS KNAPP

November 9 to November 15

THE *Salem Gazette* tells us that Joseph "appears miserable and broken down in body and spirit, . . . and with difficulty utters articulate words."

He was put on trial as accessory before the fact to the murder of Joseph White.

The three judges who had presided in Frank Knapp's trials sat on the bench in this case, and the same lawyers appeared for the government and for the defense.

The defense made a strong fight. Several days after the trial started the *Boston Courier* said "it would be vain to predict the termination," and there is reason to believe that Webster did not feel sure of the outcome.

When the attorney general moved that Webster be permitted to appear for the government, Gardiner objected. The defense understood that Webster now appeared for a private prosecutor. No case could be cited where a private prosecutor had been allowed to employ counsel to assist in the conviction of a prisoner.

Justice Putnam said: "Mr. Webster avows that he is induced to aid the attorney general merely at his request and without any other consideration. . . . [He has only] a disinterested regard for the public good. We think the application should be granted."

The next day Webster wrote to Justice Story saying that he had stated to the justices "that I appeared at the request of the attorney general, and had not received, and should not receive, any fee in this case; which, of course, was and is true." (*Private Correspondence*, L, 506.)

Webster has been attacked for his denial of payment by a private prosecutor. There might be a slim defense in the words "in this case," but what shall we do with this receipt kept in the records of the Massachusetts Historical Society?

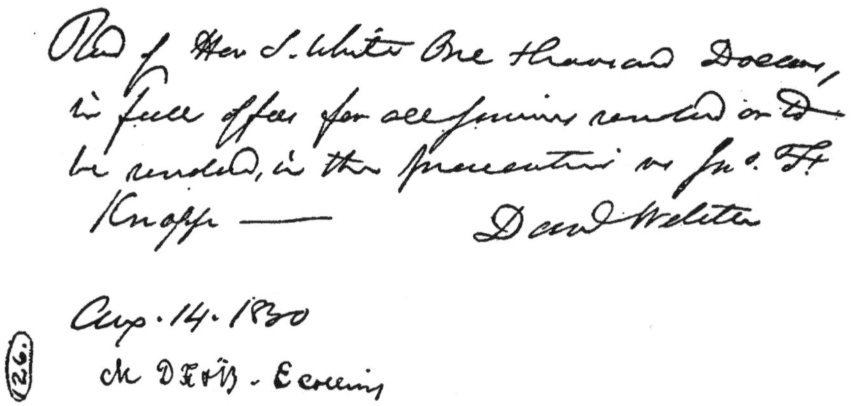

(handwritten note at top of page)

(Rec'd of Hon. S. White One Thousand Dollars, in full of fees for all services rendered or to be rendered, in the prosecution vs. Jo and F. Knapp.)

Dexter protested the admissibility of any confessions made by the prisoner. They were obtained by menaces and the hope of reward. After a long battle the court ruled that Joe's confessions should be admitted in evidence.[1]

One reading the confessions will see that Joe's case was hopeless. The attorney general read Joe's first confession to the jury.[2]

JOSEPH'S CONFESSION

Salem Gaol, 29th May, 1830.

I mentioned to my brother, John Francis Knapp, in February last, that I would not begrudge one thousand dollars that the old gentleman, meaning Capt. Joseph White, of Salem, was dead. He asked me why. I mentioned to him that the old gentleman had a Will, which if destroyed, half of the property would come on this side; that is, to my mother in law Mrs. Beckford; that with the present Will, the bulk of the property would go to Stephen White; that he had injured me in the opinion of the old gentleman, and I had no doubt had also prejudiced him against all the family, and that I thought it right to get the property if I could. I mentioned to him also in a joking way, that the old gentleman had often said he wished he could go off like a flash. We then contrived how it could be done. One way was to meet him on the road, but the old gentleman was never out at night. — Another was to attack him in the house, but Frank said he had not the pluck to do it, but he knew who would. I asked him who, and he said he would see George and Dick Crowninshield. I told him, well, I did not think they would, but he could go and see. He got a chaise with Wm. H. Allen and went to their house, as he said, and proposed it to

[1] The decision of the court is found in 10 Pick. 489.
[2] The original confessions may be seen at the office of the Clerk of Courts in Salem.

both of them. . . . Dick appointed a night to meet Frank. They met two or three different times. . . . There was another meeting appointed at the Salem Common for the 2nd of April. I went on the Common that same evening, and met Richard Crowninshield at eight o'clock in the very center of the Common. I told Richard Crowninshield how matters stood, and that I had taken the Will of Captain White either that day or the day before. . . . Richard Crowninshield then showed me the tools he would do it with, which were a club and a dirk. The club was about two feet long, turned of hard wood, loaded at the end, and very heavy. . . . The dirk was about five inches long on the blade, having a white handle, as I think — it was flat, sharp at both edges, and tapering to a point. . . . My brother came to the farm at Wenham, on the next Tuesday afternoon; I told him my Mother Beckford was at the farm and was to pass the night; she had come up because Mrs. Davis wanted her assistance. I mentioned this to my brother, and told him he had better tell this to Richard Crowninshield. On the Friday preceding, I unbarred and unscrewed the window of Capt. White's house, closing the shutter again. My brother said he would inform Richard Crowninshield; my brother left the farm about tea time, with the chaise in which he came up; my brother made this remark as he went off, I guess he will go tonight. . . .

Wednesday, 7th of April, my brother came to the farm about noon — he asked if we had heard the news; we told him yes, and how we heard it. After dinner he told me aside how it occurred. He said Richard Crowninshield met him, I think, in Brown Street, in Salem, about ten o'clock in the evening, and that he, Richard, left him and came round through the front yard, passed through the garden gate, pushed up the back window and got in by it; and passed through the entry, by the front stairs into Capt. White's chamber; that he struck Capt. White with the club above named, while asleep, and after striking him he used the dirk, and hit him several times with the dirk, and covered him up, and came off, and met my brother again in Brown Street, or by the Common, I think about eleven o'clock. . . . They separated and went home. . . . This is all I know of the affair until I saw my brother again after he had seen Richard Crowninshield again. I came down to Salem on the afternoon of the 7th of April, and staid in Salem a fortnight; my brother informed me . . . that Richard Crowninshield having seen the accounts of the number of stabs in the Newspapers said he had stabbed him but four times, and Richard Crowninshield remarked that   really believed there had been another person in the chamber.

A fortnight or three weeks after the murder Richard Crowninshield rode up with my brother Frank to the farm in Wenham; he staid there a little while, and I gave him one hundred five franc pieces, which a few days before I had received from Guadaloupe by Capt. Josiah Dewing. While Richard was at the farm, he told me the same story which my brother had done. . . . Richard Crowninshield informed me that same evening, that he had put the club with which he killed Capt. White, under the Branch Meeting House steps; my brother went to look for it since, but could not find it. . . .

I wrote a letter, dated I think, the 12th of May, addressed to the Hon. Stephen White, at the house in Wenham, on Sunday Morning, the 16th of May, signed either Grant or Claxton, and another addressed to the Hon. Gideon Barstow, signed either Grant or Claxton, . . . which letters I brought to Salem, and gave them to Wm. H. Allen, who said he would put them in the Post Office, that evening. . . .

(Signed)   Joseph J. Knapp, Jr.

Attest.   (Signed)   Henry Colman.

Salem Gaol, Saturday, 29th May, 1830, 7 o'clock P.M.

We pass over a supplementary confession made two days later in answer to questions by Dr. Barstow and Mr. Phillips of the committee of vigilance, as it adds little.

The defense then took the ground that the fact that Frank Knapp was a principal in the murder must be proved by evidence other than the court sentence in his case; but after brilliant arguments the court ruled that the verdict in John Francis Knapp's trial was to be taken as prima facie evidence of guilt, but it might be rebutted.[3]

Many witnesses testified, but most of the evidence is known to one who has followed through Frank's trials.

Very strong speeches in summation were delivered by Dexter and Webster. We quote only Webster's conclusion:

To the catalogue of his crimes, already enormous, he has added perfid to the state and to the government which would have savedyhim.[4] There is not the slightest extenuating circumstance in his guilt; its blackness is not illuminated by a single spark of contrition; not a ray of penitence falls upon it; it is all black as ink. From first to last, from conception to execution, from detection to punishment, it is all dreadful! dreadful! dreadful![5]

The jury quickly found Joseph Knapp guilty and he was executed on December 31st.

---

[3] Justice R. S. Wilkins of the Supreme Judicial Court of Massachusetts adds this note to our manuscript: This holding was overruled by the Supreme Judicial Court in 1915 in Commonwealth v. Tilley, 327 Mass. 540, 546-549.

[4] This "perfidy" is the only honorable thing we know about Joe.

[5] One who has the greatest admiration for the oratory of Daniel Webster and who may agree that the deeds of Joe Knapp were diabolically dreadful, may feel while reading that paragraph that it is the most "dreadful" thing the godlike Daniel ever said. But one who heard him utter the words says in the *Transcript* of November 12th that Webster closed his argument "in a peroration of surpassing pathos." What greater tribute could be paid to Webster's eloquence? Still it may be a relief for us smaller folk to think that he was not always sublime.

CHAPTER 12

THE TWO TRIALS OF
GEORGE CROWNINSHIELD

WHILE THE JURY was deliberating in the case of Joseph Knapp, on the afternoon of Friday, November 12, the trial of George Crowninshield was begun before the same justices.

Webster had an urgent engagement in the courts of Rhode Island and could not assist in this trial. The government was represented by the attorney general and the solicitor general; the prisoner was defended by Samuel Hoar and Ebenezer Shillaber.

The chief witness for the government was *Palmer*, who repeated the testimony he had given against Frank Knapp.

Benjamin Leighton and *Ezra Lummus* testified much as in Frank's trial. George's expenditure of five-franc pieces was proved. *Mary Weller* did her bit; *Benjamin Newhall* testified to seeing George on Williams Street about ten o'clock on the evening of the murder; *T. W. Taylor* testified that he saw George on Newbury Street. Palmer's letter from Belfast was read to the jury.

When the government rested, Hoar moved that the court direct a verdict for the defendant. He said it would be absurd to defend a case made out like this; "there was not a tittle of evidence to criminate the prisoner except that given by Palmer, which was altogether unworthy of credit. It was not a case weakly made out; it was one not made out at all."

The court denied the motion.

Shillaber's opening speech for the defense was extremely brief. He introduced evidence of Palmer's conviction in Maine, and called *Mr. Babb* to testify concerning the duebill to which Palmer had signed the name of George Crowninshield. The defense then rested.

At the opening of court on Monday, November 15, Hoar began his summation.

He said that George Crowninshield was not charged with influencing Richard to the commission of the crime; the question was, Did the prisoner persuade Frank Knapp to commit the crime?

Gentlemen, this case is an important one, and demands our

deliberate consideration; but I can hardly speak with the gravity on the evidence that has been introduced, that the occasion requires.

The government say George was in Salem on the night of the murder, but they take care not to call the witnesses who could describe his actions that night.

But take Palmer's[1] evidence in the strongest light, it does not make out the offense with which the prisoner is charged. To make out the charge it must be shown that he influenced Frank Knapp to commit murder, that he contenanced and encouraged him. But, according to Palmer, Frank came already prepared for the murder. Nothing has appeared to show that he is guilty of this crime, that he took any part or lot in the matter.

Taking for truth what Leighton says—is that anything against George Crowninshield? "When did you see Dick?" Not George. Would not something have been said of George had he been in the plot?

Taking both Leighton and Palmer's testimony to be entirely true, my client is safe.

I have taken too much time on this worthless man, Palmer. An insect, the smallest fly is not worthy of much regard; but if it forces itself into your eye, you must attend to it. I should have no confidence in our boasted trial by jury, if I thought it possible for a jury to convict a man on such evidence.

The attorney general closed with a brief argument. He rested chiefly on the testimony of Palmer. "Palmer stands uncontradicted in every particular, and you cannot but believe him. The government does not wish a multiplicity of victims, but every man concerned in such a horrid transaction ought to be brought to punishment."

The jury took the case at twelve forty-five on November 15, and were able to partake of their midday meal and complete their deliberations by three, when they returned a verdict of not guilty.

It is said that when the verdict was pronounced there was a great shout on the part of a few spectators, some hisses, and a great deal of applause. William Ward, Frank Knapp's friend, said, "Little effort was made to add another victim to the gallows. No one in the community really desired George Crowninshield convicted, as all knew he had been led astray by Richard who had acquired absolute control over him from his youth."

---

[1] In his summation Hoar delivered an excoriation of Palmer that outdid Dexter's best efforts.

But the last scene of this tragedy had not yet been enacted. The attorney general moved that George be arraigned on an indictment charging him with misprison of felony, in that "having had knowledge of a conspiracy to murder Captain White, he had kept it secret."

The case came up for trial on November 27 and ended the same day, before the justices who sat in the earlier trials.

Solicitor General Davis and County Attorney Huntington appeared for the government, and Ebenezer Shillaber and John Walsh for the defendant.

Thirteen witnesses were called, and after the evidence was completed on both sides, Shillaber addressed the jury for three hours, the solicitor general for one hour.

The jury was charged at half-past seven in the evening, and in half an hour they brought in a verdict of not guilty.

It is said that George seemed to enjoy his trials very much.

CHAPTER 13

"A FEW LAST WORDS IN CONCLUSION"

INTEREST IN the White murder continued strong both in and out of Salem. Innumerable sermons were preached on the subject, poems were written about the Knapps and the Crowninshields, and makers of wax figures thrived on the interest. Robert Rantoul describes life-sized figures on the common of Beverly which showed Mary Knapp bidding farewell to Joe on his way to the gallows; and Edmond Pearson tells of an exhibition on Boston Common in which one saw "the ghastly form of Captain White lying in his bed and weltering in his gore. Over him, with knife raised, . . . leaned the sinister figure of 'Crowninshield, the hired assassin.' "

As late as 1845 a new edition of the *Life of the Celebrated Murderer* was published with a preface stating that "everything connected with this horrid transaction is read with avidity." And in 1848 Henry Wright, a political enemy of Zachary Taylor, compared Taylor with the best known murderer of the time in a pamphlet entitled *Dick Crowninshield, the Assassin and Zachary Taylor, the Soldier.*

It may be said that our lamented interest in murders today does not show any backsliding from the standards of the early nineteenth century.

But some people in Salem preferred to suppress all reference to the case. It is said (we do not know on what authority) that attempts have been made to collect and burn all the pamphlets that deal with the crime; and it is reported that at one time no volume of Webster's speeches was permitted in the schools of Salem if it contained his argument in the Knapp-White case. When the reminiscences of Caroline Howard King (whose father was one of the attorneys employed by Stephen White in the case) was published not long ago, under the title, *When I Lived in Salem,* it was found that shortly before her death in 1909 she had destroyed the chapter dealing with the murder of Captain White because she felt its publication would be "indiscreet."

Even today there are a few people in Salem who look upon a stranger with alarm if he inquires concerning the town's most celebrated crime. As stated in our introduction, the rich sources of information in the Essex Institute were shielded from us at first. But there are many who like to talk about the case, though their information is usually inaccurate, like that of the fine old lady who had written a paper on the case for her club. She greeted us by saying, "So you wish to learn about Webster's speech ending 'There is no refuge from confession but in suicide, and suicide is confession.'"

Hawthorne wrote to his friend, John Dikes, in September of 1831, "George Crowninshield still lives at his father's and seems not at all cast down by what has taken place. I saw him walk by our house, arm-in-arm with a girl." In the *Transcript* of July 26, 1888 is found his obit:

Mr. George C. Crowninshield, for years a well known resident of Roxbury and a member of the old and noted Crowninshield family of Salem, died yesterday at the age of eighty-five. He was always greatly interested in scientific matters and had several times made voyages around the world. He leaves no family other than a granddaughter.

Other *Transcript* notes show that he lived under the shadow of the crime and that he quarreled with his granddaughter, who set up a candy store near his home to spite him. He lived in a humble cottage, but he left her $80,000.

Mrs. Beckford lived on her farm in Wenham until her death at the age of seventy-nine. She and her daughter suffered from much gossip. Mary White Knapp lived with her mother; but after four years she married a Boston lawyer. We hope she "lived happy ever after" and that her dreams were troubled by no guilty memories.

Robert Rantoul felt so keenly the hostility of many of Salem's citizens that he moved to Boston. In his lecture entitled "Idols," Wendell Phillips said of him —

Boston had a lawyer once, . . . one whose untiring energy held up the right hand of Horace Mann, and made this age and all coming ones his debtors; one whose clarion voice . . . waked the faltering pulpit to its duty in the cause of temperance, . . . one whose humane and incessant efforts to make the penal code worthy of our faith, and our age ranked his name with McIntosh and Romilly, with Bentham, Becarria, and Livingston. Best of all, one who had some claim to say, with Selden, "Above all things, Liberty," for in the slave's battle his voice was the bravest.

Joseph Knapp, Senior, whom Webster saw as another Lear, tottering on the brink of the grave, carried on a small business as a maker of cigars and in 1839 he took himself a second wife.

Phippen Knapp left the law and became an Episcopal clergyman. He was very successful in the South and at his death high tributes were paid to him.

But the most interesting story arises from the later career of the Reverend Henry Colman. In 1831 he left the ministry and devoted himself to the study of agriculture. He wrote voluminously on the subject and came to be considered an outstanding authority. In 1845 he went to England carrying letters of introduction to wealthy men. His two volume report on European agriculture went through six editions.

While in London he became acquainted with an American, John Lord, author of *Beacon Lights of History*. Mr. Lord says of Colman:

Without money or fame he contrived to see more distinguished people, and to be on friendly terms with them than any American, I apprehend, that had not a high official position who ever visited England. The Duke of Richmond was his bosom friend. . . . The secret of his queer fascination to English noblemen was his wit, his knowledge, and plain manners as if he were a mere farmer.

In a letter to Emerson, Carlyle speaks of Colman as "a kind of Agricultural Missionary, much in vogue here at present." Colman had no difficulty in getting Lord a ticket of admission to the opening of Parliament, "an unusual favor," says Lord.

Colman returned to America in 1848 and published *European Life and Manners*, a gossipy book on the great people he had known. The London *Times* speaks of "the glee with which Mr. Colman relates his intimacy with English dukes and earls . . . and the continual attempts he makes to impress upon his friends an adequate notion of his own importance by minutely describing the more than affectionate attentions of the great." "We promise him," wrote a reviewer in *Frazer's Magazine*, "that should he return to this country, he will never be asked to their houses again." Lord says that when Colman returned to England the next year "he was neglected, which broke his heart, and he died soon after."

So in London, as in Salem, Mr. Colman was strong for the bigwigs.

BOOKS OF REFERENCE

A report of the evidence and points of law, arising in the trial of *John Francis Knapp, for the murder* of *Joseph White, esquire.* (Includes the charge of His Honor Chief Justice Parker to the grand jury.) Salem. W. & S. B. Ives. 1830.

Appendix to the report of the trial of John Francis Knapp . . . Containing the new evidence, the arguments of counsel, and the charge of His Honor Judge Putnam to the jury, on the second trial. Salem 1830.

Trial of George Crowninshield, J. J. Knapp, Jun. and John Francis Knapp for the murder of Capt. Joseph White. . . . Reported by John W. Whitman. 1830.

Second trial by a new jury . . . *for the murder* of *Captain Joseph White* . . . Dutton and Wentworth, 1830.

American State Trials. Vol. VII. pp. 395-593, pp. 594-639, pp. 640-670.

Reports of cases in the Supreme Judicial Court of Massachusetts. Vols. IX and X.

Principles of Judicial Proof. John H. Wigmore. Sections 225, 266.

Daniel Webster as a Master of English Style, as essay found in *Great Speeches and Orations of Daniel Webster.*

Retrospect of Western Travels. Harriet Martineau.

Most libraries have several lives of Webster and most of them dwell upon the Knapp-White case. A few libraries will have the pamphlets printed in 1830.

THE WITNESSES

INDEX